The Man Who Shot Jesse James

• • •

Carl W. Breihan

South Brunswick and New York: A. S. Barnes and Company
London: Thomas Yoseloff Ltd

© 1979 by A. S. Barnes and Company, Inc.

A. S. Barnes and Co., Inc.
Cranbury, New Jersey 08512

Thomas Yoseloff Ltd
Magdalen House
136–148 Tooley Street
London SE1 2TT, England

Library of Congress Cataloging in Publication Data

Breihan, Carl W., 1915–
    The man who shot Jesse James.

    Includes index.
    1. Ford, Robert Newton, 1862–1892. 2. Ford, Charles Wilson, 1857–
1884. 3. James, Jesse Woodson, 1847–1882. 4. Outlaw—The West—
Biography. 5. Frontier and pioneer life—The West. 6. The West—
History—1848–1950. I. Title.
F594.B806   364.1′55′0924   [B]   77-84562
ISBN 0-498-02068-1

To

Fred Ford, Amanda Ford,
Dr. Frank O'Kelley, *and*
Norval Jennings,
without whose notes and assistance
this book could never have
been written

Contents

Foreword

By many scholarly and at the same time fascinating books, Carl W. Breihan, once a deputy sheriff himself (!) has established himself as the greatest authority on the colorful bad men of the West. His books, such as *The Day Jesse James Was Killed, Quantrill and His Civil War Guerrillas, Younger Brothers, Great Gunfights of the West*, and *Date with Destiny: Billy the Kid* have all won the praise not only of historians but of the general readers.

In this work, he gives a truly fascinating account of Robert Ford, the slayer of Jesse James.

His table of acknowledgments indicates how tireless he has been in obtaining information about this figure hitherto so little known in detail, including Amanda Ford Segal, the sister of Robert; Barrett S. Heddens, Jr., the grandson of Coroner Heddens; Dr. Frank O'Kelley, brother of Ed O'Kelley, the slayer of Robert; Norval Jennings, eyewitness to Robert's death; and even Stella James, daughter-in-law of Jesse. Indeed, it is almost unbelievable how the author has actually contacted such almost legendary folk!

This is a book that would have greatly interested my kinsman Samuel Langhorne Clemens, who would indeed have reveled in all the daring, if misguided, exploits so vividly detailed by author Breihan. We all remember how fascinated Clemens was by the notorious outlaw Slade described in *Roughing It* and recall how Clemens thought his last hour had come, because he took the last cup of coffee from the pot that Slade had been eying at the stagecoach station breakfast. I was much interested in Breihan's mention of Deputy Marshal Maurice Langhorne, a former Confederate soldier under General Jo Shelby. Who knows but that Clemens received his middle name from this Langhorne family! Although, I do remember that Nancy Langhorne, later Lady Astor, once told me that Clemens obtained his middle name

9

from her grandfather Langhorne of Virginia, where the Clemens and Langhorne families originally dwelled.

This book is full of fascinating details, such as when Governor Crittenden, the great *bête noire* of all the outlaws ravaging Missouri, learning that an officer in Lafayette County was unable to procure riding horses at the town of Lexington, so savagely "sent eight horses via special train from Kansas City to a given point in Lafayette County."

Breihan breaks fresh ground, as he does so often, when he tells us that Jesse's cruel torture of Bob's fourteen-year-old cousin, Albert Ford, to elicit information, was one reason (perhaps the post important one) that Bob Ford turned against James. This newly presented motivation for Ford's shooting of his former friend and leader is one of many facts that will make this book invaluable for all future historians, both legitimate and fictional.

I was surprised at the enormous sum (for those days) that the newly elected Governor Thomas T. Crittenden offered at a meeting of the railroad executives at the Southern Hotel in St. Louis:

The result of this conference was the Governor's proclamation that fifty-five thousand dollars would be awarded anyone capturing the entire robber band, or five thousand dollars for the arrest and conviction of any single member. In the case of Frank and Jesse James, an extra five thousand dollars apiece was offered for conviction. A very definite proof of how anxious Crittenden and the people of Missouri were to restore peace and order.

Every fact presented by Breihan rings true, as when Bob Ford tells Commissioner Craig in Kansas City, while arranging what may be described as "the legal murder," that there was no chance whatsoever of Jesse being captured alive. Such was even the contemporary reputation of this great outlaw, who even before his death had become a legend.

As all the world knows, Bob shot Jesse while the latter was dusting a picture. But Breihan is the first to tell us that Jesse was only *pretending* to do so, because Mrs. James was a superb housekeep (Isn't that an interesting little incident to know!) and never in the world would have allowed any dust to settle in her spotless home. The fact was that Jesse, who had reason to conclude that Bob had become a traitor, was doing everything possible to put Bob at his ease, so that he could kill him when they went riding that very night.

Another fascinating incident is that Jesse's mother, Mrs. Samuel (she had remarried after Jesse's father's death), after the funeral service became convinced that someone had cut off her dead son's arm to obtain a gruesome souvenir. She could only be satisfied after the coffin was reopened to prove that her suspicions were unfounded. Incidentally, when the contents of Jesse's house were auctioned off, the nondescript furniture obtained enormous prices. Thus early had everything connected with America's most famous outlaw become collectors' items. I envy author Breihan's possession of a Jesse James letter. I digress a moment to say that when I was arranging a symposium for Henry James, the famous novelist, I asked my late friend, the genial Kentucky humorist Irvin Cobb, to send a tribute, and he responded, "I can't help you on Henry. My favorites in the family are Jesse and Frank"!

I have intentionally not said too much about the details of Bob and his brother Charlie Ford's careers because they are all ahead of the reader in this magnificent book. And I promise the reader a wonderful reading treat—a book all true and based on discerning, tireless, and *original* research. My very considered conclusion is that no one can hope to understand Jesse James's character, activities, and place in American bandit history without first having read this Carl Breihan book on his killer, Bob Ford. Would that all our historical biographies were half so deftly done. Carl Breihan, you have put all lovers of American history in your debt forever!

Cyril Clemens
Kinsman and Chronicler of Mark Twain
Editor *Mark Twain Journal* since 1936

Acknowledgments

I extend my humble and grateful appreciation to those many fine and dedicated people who went out of their way to assist me in the Herculean task of compiling this work. Their continued assistance, encouragement, and footwork enabled me to locate data that otherwise might have remained hidden years longer.

My warm thanks to O. C. Shelley, Independence, Missouri, now deceased; Kerry Ross Boren, meticulous historian of Salt Lake City, Utah; Jack DeMattos, a friend and dedicated researcher, North Attleboro, Massachusetts; Fred A. Ford, who helped in many ways, Blue Springs, Missouri; Ed Fink, Garnett, Kansas; B. James George, Sr., son of Quantrillian Hiram George, Kansas City, Missouri; Amanda Ford Segal, sister of Robert Ford, who left important notes; Wilbur Zink, historian, Appleton City, Missouri; Barrett S. Heddens, Jr., grandson of Coroner Heddens, Kansas City, Missouri; Wayne Montgomery, pioneer of Western trails, Leavenworth, Kansas; Rex Bundy, able historian, Victor, Montana; Dr. Frank O'Kelley, deceased, brother of Ed O'Kelley, slayer of Robert Ford, Patton, Missouri; Norval Jennings, deceased, eyewitness to the death of Bob Ford and other related incidents, New York City; Bill Kelly, able historian; Stella James, daughter-in-law of Jesse James, Los Angeles, California; Mae James, deceased, daughter-in-law of Frank James, Kearney, Missouri; Robert Franklin James, son of Frank James, now deceased, Kearney, Missouri; Harry Younger Hall, deceased, nephew of Cole Younger, Lee's Summit, Missouri; Charles Kemper, Jackson County Historical Society and friend of the James family, Independence, Missouri; Mary Morrow, daughter of Ben Morrow, ex-Quantrillian, Independence, Missouri; Lulu May Courtright, daughter of Big Jim Courtright, lawman-scout, Capitola, California; J. Winston-Coleman, Jr., historian-author, Lexington, Kentucky; Ray County Historical Society; files of the Kansas

13

City Police Department; John K. Gott, Arlington, Virginia; Duane Smith, Durango, Colorado; and the Missouri State Historical Society, Columbia, Missouri; the State Historical Society of the Library of Colorado, Denver; Virginia State Historical Society, Richmond; Oklahoma State Historical Society, Oklahoma City; Kansas State Historical Society, Topeka; and the numerous newspaper files, libraries, and museums I visited as well as the helpful folks at the National Archives in Washington and the Census Files.

No doubt there are many I have missed; if so, please forgive me, since it is most difficult to list the hundreds of fine people who were so helpful to me in this matter.

Warm thanks to all.

The Man Who Shot Jesse James

● ● ●

1 • • •

The Ford Family in Virginia and Missouri

In the days of our youth many of us heard or read about Rob Roy, the brave Highlander who fought to remove tyrannical oppression from the shoulders of his people, or about Claude Duval and Jack Shepherd, and their daring exploits in old England; some might even recall hearing about John A. Murrell, who obtained great distinction as an outlaw in the Southern states. It was he who planned a reign of terror unparalleled in the history of any nation. He had planned a gigantic Negro insurrection, a complete overthrow of the white power, and named himself director of the bastard nation to be created through his bizarre plot. It was to begin on Christmas Day, 1835. Murrell's plot was overthrown by a brave young man named Virgil Stewart, with the master plotter being sent to prison.

The two Harpe brothers of East Tennessee were sadistic and bestial as they killed and plundered along the Wilderness Road during the 1790s, Wiley Harpe later to be captured at Greenville, Mississippi, and hanged on February 8, 1804. Micajah "Big" Harpe was shot and wounded by Samuel Leiper. Moses Steigel then cut off Harpe's head and rode down the trace to Red Bank, to a crossing at Robertson's Lick, where he nailed the head to a tree. Even today this spot is referred to as "Harpe's Head." The murder of Steigel's family by the Harpes had been avenged.

The brigands I speak of in this book, however, are not like the aforesaid, or like Agatone, the terror of the Rio Grande border, or like William de la Marck, the outlawed nobleman of the low countries, and known in history as the "The Wild Boar of Ardennes."

The Ford brothers were latecomers upon the crime scene in Missouri, known then as "The Robber State." Even prior to joining up with the James brothers they had proceeded along the outlaw trail on their own initiative. They robbed for profit and for the sensation it created. Many returning Quantrillians turned to robbery as a necessity, at least during the early years following the close of the Civil War. In their case old wounds had not healed along the border. There were malignant stars in the zenith of the ex-guerrillas. These men sought their childhood homes where they had dwelled with their loved ones before they had become slayers of men. Yet the bright gleam of hope faded; the clouds of anguish overspread their sky. The lurid lightning of the old bitterness flashed, and the ex-guerrillas were pushed and hunted, like felons, beyond the pale of hope or pardon.

It has been common belief all these years that Charley and Bob Ford were born in Fauquier County, Virginia, and even though they did spend some years of their early youth there, they were not born in Virginia but in Clark County, Missouri. Apparently this early residence in Virginia led most writers to believe they had been born there. According to Bob's sister, Amanda Ford Seigel (or Segal), who lived until 1945, her father, James Thomas Ford, rented the downstairs rooms and acreage of the home of George Washington at Mt. Vernon, Fairfax County, Virginia, when Bob was just a toddler, sometime in 1862. Later the family moved to Fauquier County, Virginia, where her father had been born, and where Bob attended school near Salem, now Marshall, Virginia. This also was reported by Mrs. Mary Jeffries Moore, who went to school with the Ford brothers.

In later years the Ford children used to tell how they had sailed toy boats on the Potomac River and had played in what once was Martha Washington's small summerhouse, with its fine iron lacework. At that time there was much of General Washington's furniture still stored in the attic, the portion not rented to J. T. Ford. The children used to play with Nellie Custis's little piano stored there and handle the huge Bastille key that had been presented to Washington by General Lafayette. To this day these items remain on display at Mt. Vernon. The last member of the Washington family to use the farm was John A. Washington and his wife, Ellina L., who had three children, as listed in the 1850 Census Records: Louisa F., Jane G., and Elizabeth L. Washington.

The question of the correct birthplace of the Ford brothers triggered an all-out attempt to clarify the matter, and it is believed the following information will do just that.

The Missouri Census report for 1880, Ray County, Richmond, Missouri, #36600 pt. 1176, indicated James Thomas Ford and his wife were residing there, with children. All listed children shown as being born in Missouri, with Mr. and Mrs. Ford listed as being born in Virginia.

Austin Ford, grandfather of Charley and Bob, was born about 1790 in Fauquier County, Virginia. His parents are unknown, except that his father was reportedly a close personal friend of George Washington, and for many years Austin Ford resided on the estate of Washington at Mt. Vernon in Fairfax County, Virginia. His occupation was that of a stonemason, and it can be surmised that some of the buildings at Mt. Vernon were the result of his caretaking.

Austin Ford was a soldier in the War of 1812. It is stated that he was a participant in some of the worst battles of that conflict, including the Battle of New Orleans. He was also active in the campaigns against the Indians in Florida, and while there he became acquainted with the Allison family. He returned to Florida after spending several years at his home in Fauquier County, Virginia, after the war. In Florida he married Jane Allison in about 1817–18. Jane Allison was born in 1794 (by some accounts in Fauquier County, while another states she was born in Florida) and was the daughter of French parentage and of the leading society of Florida and Virginia.

Following his marriage, Austin Ford resided in Fauquier County, where he pursued his trade of stonemason, and there reared a family of six boys and four girls. Only one child, the eldest being a girl, is unknown, the others being James Thomas, John W., Lucella, Charles, Elizabeth, Mary Jane, William H., Arthur F. (who died at Excelsior Springs, Missouri, in 1885), and Robert A. Ford, all of whom were born in Fauquier County, Virginia, near the town of Marshall. The eldest daughter probably died young, since the records of 1893 show that two children had died previous to that time.

In 1840, Austin Ford brought his family to Clark County, Missouri, where he assumed the management of a large tract of land and was overseer of forty slaves owned by a fellow Virginian named Lee.

In July 1841, Lee came to Missouri and, in an altercation with Austin Ford, struck him over the head with a club, Ford dying from the effects of the blow two days later.

John Wesley Ford, the eldest son, then became the head of the family. He went to work at ten dollars to twelve dollars a month and cared for the large family until he was twenty-eight years old. The 1850 Clark County, Missouri, Census Records, 977.834 555/555, indicate Mrs. Jane Ford, born in Virginia, as head of the family, and the oldest child as John W., age twenty-eight.

In 1849 or 1850 John went to California, where he later worked on the Feather River Ranch for $130 a month. He bought a mule team of six and later went into business for himself, eventually returning to Missouri, where he bought Seybold's Tavern in 1870. He married Anna Maria Storey (or Story), by whom he had the following children: William Ezra, Mary Jane, Georginia, John H., Edwin, and Luther. In September 1887, Georginia was taken ill with pneumonia and passed away on October 7th. Another daughter, Florida, born in 1865, also had died, previous to 1880.

During the Civil War John W. Ford joined the State Militia under Captain Garth, but saw no other activity except that he lost most of his property during the conflict.

The widow, Jane Allison Ford, resided with her family in Clark County, Missouri, until 1851, at which time they went to Clay County, where she died in 1857, leaving many young children to fare for themselves with the aid of their older brothers. Following are brief biographical sketches of some of the family other than John W. Ford, which preceded.

Charles Ford was born in Fauquier County, Virginia, in 1828 and came with his family to Clark County, Missouri, in 1840, where he remained until 1851, going to Clay County and finally to Richmond, Ray County, Missouri, where he resided on a farm with his wife, Martha, of Tennessee and children as neighbors to his brother, James Thomas Ford.

Robert Austin Ford was born in Fauquier County, Virginia, March 13, 1840. He was an infant when his parents removed to Clark County, Missouri, and was about one year of age when his father was killed by Mr. Lee, and only eleven when his mother died. He entered the Confederate Army in 1861, serving under General Sterling Price in the State Guard. After serving six months, he returned to Clay County, Missouri, and in 1863 went to Colorado, where he remained until 1866, at which time he returned to Clay County, residing in Washington Township near the town of Lawson.

On October 6, 1867, Robert Austin Ford married Mary E. Story, daughter of Thomas and Luck A. (Baldwin) Story of Clay County, she having been born in Clay County in 1850. They had ten children: Oscar A., John T., Jesse James, Ella T., Walter N., Maggie L., and Robert A., who all lived beyond 1885, while three others, Flora Belle, James T., and Arthur F., all died when young. Oscar Ford, even at the age of fourteen, was known as an unusually accomplished penman and was often called upon to write cards, letters, and do professional penmanship, and in some quarters, was considered a genius.

James Thomas Ford (J. T., as he was usually called), father of the outlaws Charley and Bob Ford, was born in Fauquier County, Virginia, in 1820 and came with his father to Clark County, Missouri, shortly after his marriage to Mary Ann Bruin, daughter of Elias and Ann Bruin, on August 10, 1840.

Soon after the death of his father in 1841, J. T. Ford returned to Virginia, where he became a tenant farmer for John A. Washington at Mt. Vernon, Fairfax County, Virginia. In 1843 J. T. Ford and his wife returned to Missouri, where the following children were born to them, all in Clark County: Georgia, 1844; John T., 1846; Elias Capline; Martha and Amanda, twins, 1855; Charles Wilson, July 9, 1857; Wilber, 1860; and Robert Newton, January 31, 1862.

It was shortly after Bob's birth that the family went back to Mt. Vernon, Virginia, for a short time, as stated by Bob's sister Amanda. Later the family returned to the area of Fauquier County, Virginia, where Bob and his brothers and sisters attended school for a short time.

When Bob Ford was seven years old the family moved to a farm in what was then Ray County and now is Clay County, Missouri. They settled a mile and a half from the area that was to become Excelsior Springs, Missouri, a famous spa resort region in later years. Near their home was a church that had no pastor at the time. Mr. J. T. Ford, a well-known Bible student, consented to act as temporary pastor, seeing to it also that his entire family attended all regular services.

Even as a child Bob Ford became obsessed with the thought of capturing the notorious Jesse James. Much discussion was carried on at the supper table with regard to the daring exploits of the young Missouri outlaw, all this adding fuel to a young man's mind in his quest to slay the dragon. The Ford children attended the Moore School, located near the Crescent Lake area, often visiting their uncle William Ford, who lived near Kearney, Missouri, with his wife and two children, Fanny and Albert. William H. Ford had married Artella Cummins on September 21, 1862, Lafayette Munkirs, M.G., officiating. The records indicate that on February 27, 1866, William H. Ford married one Amana Goode, G. L. Moad, M.G., officiating, recorded March 9, 1866.

Near the Ford home was a place called Seybold's Tavern, operated by an uncle of Bob and Charley, John Wesley Ford, where the J. T. Ford boys spent much time in conversation, games, and target shooting. This place had been built by Louis and Nellie Seybold, who came to Missouri from Virginia in 1821, buying their 110 acres for $2.50 an acre from the government. They built their home on the new land after the fashion of the one they had left in Virginia. It was a twelve-room affair, built of great walnut logs, chinked with a plaster composition. The floors were of split logs, and the house was built with an ell extending from the main building. There was a huge stone fireplace. In 1870 the log walls of the house were covered with walnut weatherboarding, and the interior finished. It was also during that year when the homestead became the property of John Wesley Ford, also a native Virginian, who married Ann Maria Storey on February 24, 1858, William H. Price, M.G., officiating. John Wesley Ford had come to Missouri as a small boy, later joining the caravan of covered wagons over the Santa Fe Trail to California with six teams of oxen. Instead of panning for gold when he reached Sacramento, after a journey of six months, Ford found employment and hired his oxen teams out for twenty dollars a day. After a few years he returned to Missouri, a wealthy man. He made the trip back from California on horseback, and used saddle bags to transport thousands of dollars in money and gold nuggets. As late as 1936 these same saddlebags were in the possession of his son, John H. Ford.

Seybold's Tavern was dubbed the "Half-Way Tavern" because it was halfway between Liberty and Richmond, Missouri, and John Wesley Ford paid three thousand dollars for it and its acreage. The tavern was used as a lodging place for travelers, with two large sleeping rooms, no connecting doors, and a flight of stairs with four-inch-wide treads, leading upstairs. One stair led to the men's sleeping quarters; the other to the women's. It is a shame this building no longer exists.

These Ford children also attended the Moore School and had their clothing made at the Watkins' Mill, still standing near Excelsior Springs, Missouri. Their grain was ground at the mill at Missouri City, Missouri.

2 • • •

Childhood Incidents

Charley and Bob Ford at an early age yearned for firearms and knives. It was the way of life in primitive Missouri at that time. The young boys of the families were expected to learn the art of firearms in order to supply the family table with meats and fowl of the forest.

The boys were provided shotguns by their father, much to their delight. They became expert shots, and Bob, while nearly five years younger than his brother Charley, seemed to be the more accurate of the two. It was said that Bob had a mean disposition, and a determination to have revenge for any wrong that might have been done to him. Little is known of their very early years inasmuch as no records were kept other than what the family wrote in their Bible. However, it appears that Bob's father was a domineering man, wanting his every command carried out to the letter; this perhaps rankled the high-strung and independent Bob. It is known that Mrs. Ford was a kind, sweet woman, always taking care to raise her children as she saw fit.

Charley Ford, on the other hand, was more the silent type, not too ambitious and not worrying what tomorrow would bring. In the case of Jesse and Frank James, however, the parental guidance was just the opposite. Dr. Reuben Samuel, their stepfather, was kind, easygoing, seldom correcting the boys. Mrs. Zerelda James Samuel was tough and took nothing from anyone, always on the alert for the safety of her boys, cursing out those who would make the wrong remarks about them. She ruled the household with an iron hand indeed.

One time, while doing his daily chores, which included the milking the five cows on the farm, young Bob remarked to his brother

Charley, "If that damned Jersey kicks me again, I will certainly kill her."

Charlie laughed, and the boys went about their business of starting for the barn lot with their milk pails. The evening was warm and the buzzing flies made the work more distasteful to Bob than before. The big Jersey swished her tail back and forth in an effort to dislodge the big black flies pestering her. Muttering cuss words, Bob sat down on the stool and began to milk the cow.

The pail was nearly filled with milk when the cow decided to let out a kick in protest to both the milking and the flies. Unfortunately the cow's hind foot struck Bob forcibly in the thigh.

With a loud oath of pain and rage, Bob and his milk pail went rolling across the lot, while the cow darted for another part of the lot.

Charley laughed and chided his younger brother. "What a fancy summersault that was, you should have seen yourself."

"Never mind, it was her last kick, you can bet your boots on that. Her next will be to kick the bucket."

Charley paid no further attention to his brother, and continued to milk the quiet animal he had chosen.

Bob went to the house, and Charley did not notice what he was up to. Suddenly the loud crack of a small handgun rent the air.

"Damn, he went and done it!" cried Charley, leaping off his stool. There stood Bob in the middle of the barnyard, a small pistol grasped in his hand.

The Jersey cow lay upon her side, kicking her last, while the other animals dashed around the lot, half frightened to death.

"What the hell did you do that for?" asked Charley.

"I swore I'd kill her if she kicked, and she kicked."

The cow was dead and Bob got the tanning of his life from his irate father, J. T. Ford.

If the Ford boys were subjected to much actual parental restraint, it never manifested itself. They took special delight in punishing small animals by cutting off their tails and ears, sometimes burying the cats and dogs alive, ever anxious to inflict some pain or misfortune on someone or something.

Bob Ford was remembered by his schoolmates as a bully who stole the lunches of his smaller classmates, who, it is reported, retaliated by hanging him with a grapevine near a spring in a deserted part of the woods. The smaller boys ganged up on him and hung him thusly, and had he not been rescued by some larger boys coming that way, Bob Ford would have left this earth that very day.

The Ford boys had few friends in the neighborhood, but those who professed to be their friends were followers and not leaders. They were disagreeable boys, forcing their leadership upon the other young-sters, and inflicting hardship upon those who disagreed with their will.

One day Bob Ford and a companion named Charles Coburn were walking in the woods near the river. Many long and strong tree branches extended over the bank of the river above the water. Bob Ford pointed to one of the sturdiest branches and suddenly exclaimed, "I'd like to hang a bunch of those kids on that limb. I bet it would hold up to ten or more!"

Charles gave a startled look at Bob; then darted home as fast as he could. He explained in an excited manner what Ford had told him. After that his parents forbade him to ever have anything more to do with the morbid Bob Ford.

One day Bob Ford took a heavy stick and beat a young dog named Prince. Ron Graves, about Bob's age, resented the fact that his favorite dog had been beaten, and, unlike many of the other lads in the valley, Ron refused to be intimidated by the cruel actions of young Bob. The Graves boy learned that the Fords were planning to move, so he made up his mind to speak to Bob about the injuring of his dog.

Ron walked several miles to the Ford home; on reaching the house he called Bob outside.

"What the hell you want?" rasped the Ford boy.

"What right you got to beat my dog?"

"I'll do it again if I get the chance," promised Bob.

That did it.

Ron Graves, about the same build as Bob Ford, waded in, fists flying. Bob's bravado broke, but he fought back with a determination unusual for him. But Ron, with a cause he wanted to avenge, beat Ford in a fair fist fight.

Charley Ford was apprised of what had happened. He promised his brother they would get even. Some time passed. Heavy rains had swelled the creeks and streams, and they were full and deep.

"It's about time we paid a visit to Ron Graves," suggested Bob.

"You sure pick a hell of a time, Bob," lamented Charley, "this weather is awful to mess around in."

"Better for us, he'll not be expecting us."

The two Ford boys walked to the Graves home, stopping out of sight in a nearby woods. There they decided to await their opportunity to administer "justice" to their enemy.

Several hours later Ron Graves left his home and walked toward the woods, apparently to get a bucket of water from the nearby spring. There the Ford brothers attacked him, and succeeded in administering to him a severe thrashing. They then procured thongs of strong bark, bound their victim securely, and threw him into the shallow spring. Fortunately, a neighbor, out hunting game, chanced by the spring and went to Ron's assistance. But the boy had spent several hours in the cold water, the exposure causing him to contract a fever from which he did not recover for a month.

Nothing is shown in any record to indicate that there was any legal prosecution in the matter of Ron Graves.

Two other brothers who came to Missouri from Rixeyville, Culpepper County, Virginia, also became members of the notorious Jesse James gang later on. They were Tom and William "Bud" McDaniels. Bud McDaniel was involved in the robbery of the Kansas Pacific train at Muncie, Kansas, in December of 1874, when over twenty-five thousand dollars in currency and gold dust was stolen. Bud was later arrested, escaped jail, but was shot and killed near Lawrence, Kansas, by a German farmer named Bierman.

Tom McDaniels met his fate shortly after the robbery of the bank at Huntington, West Virginia, September 6, 1875. On September 14th, the outlaws were afoot near the home of the Dillon family. Two Dillon boys were in the field nearby, armed with old muskets, when they saw the four men walking in the woods. Ordering the outlaws to halt, the Dillon boys threw their muskets into firing position. The reply was a number of pistol shots in their direction. The Dillon boys fired and killed Tom McDaniels.

Mrs. J. T. Ford, Mother of Bob and Charley.

Bob and Charley Ford at the time of Jesse's death.

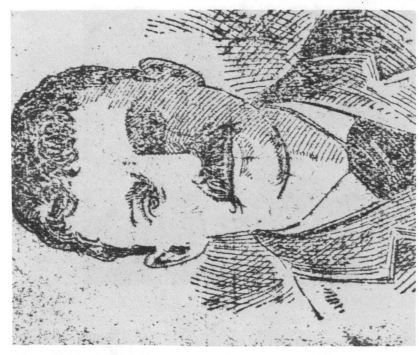

Bob Ford, as he looked at time of death.

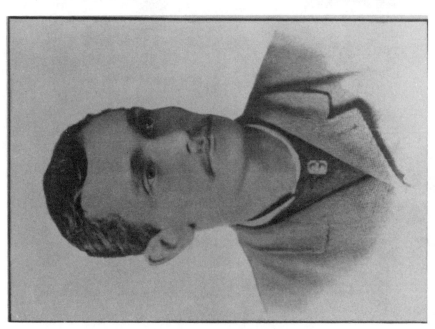

Charley Ford, brother of Bob, 1882.

Bob Ford, 1880.

Bob Ford, 1882.

Bob Ford's .44 Smith & Wesson, used to kill Jesse James.

Smith & Wesson Model #3, which Bob Ford preferred.

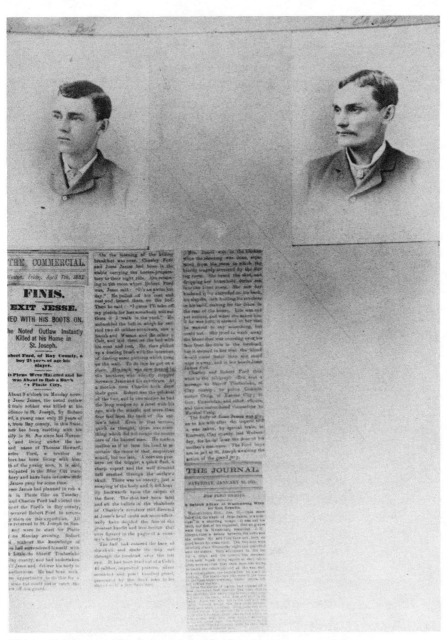

Newspaper items with photos of the Fords.

Early Baxter Springs, Kansas.

Baxter Springs, Kansas, bank building.

Baxter Springs bank building today.

Winston, Missouri, depot, scene of train robbery.

Site of train robbery, Winston, Missouri.

Conductor William Westfall, killed during Winston robbery.

Grave and marker of Frank McMillen, killed in Winston robbery.

3 • • •

Involved in Several
Robberies

Bob was superior to Charley in courage and in intelligence, and also was a crack shot with either pistol or rifle. He had demonstrated this at various times while living near Seybold's Tavern, close to the now Excelsior Springs, Missouri. Still in his teens, he took no kidding or smart remarks from fellows older than he. Most of the local farmers, aware of Bob's temper and his prowess with firearms, seldom bothered him.

One day two farmers were discussing the Fords.

"Why do you keep Bob Ford on as a hand?" one asked the other.

"Why? He seems a good hand and is not lazy. Gives me a fair day's work."

"He's a bad egg and people do not like him."

"Why?"

"They think that he steals from anyone every chance he gets," was the reply

"Oh, I don't know. He's got a bad temper, that's for certain, He'd probably kill before he'd steal."

One of the farmers, John Forbes, continued the conversation with James Black, the second farmer.

"He's a great lover of good horses, isn't he?" inquired Forbes.

"Yes, that is right."

"And doesn't the family always have an abundance of fine horse-flesh around and then they disappear in a day or so?" asked Forbes.

"What I am getting at is that they are a bunch of horse thieves as well."

"You talk too much, Forbes," said Black.

"Well, Silas Lyons lost several more good animals on the day the Ford brothers were off work."

"You don't say?"

"I do say, and everyone suspects the thieves were Bob, Charley, and Capline (Cap) Ford."

"All right, John, I'll watch myself and my stock as well."

A week or two later, as Bob and Charley Ford were riding home from Richmond, they discovered that they were being pursued. Being well mounted, the boys thought they could outride their pursuers.

"Bob, are you armed?" asked Charley.

"Yes. You?"

"Dammit, no, I wish I were, we could shoot it out with them."

"Come on then, let's ride!" cried Bob, starting his mount off at a swift pace.

Near the bottom of the hill skirting the dense woods a half dozen dark forms sprang upon them, and their horses were seized.

"Damn you, take that!" cried Bob, pulling the trigger of his pistol.

As he fired, Bob was struck in the stomach by one of their assailants, sending the bullet flying harmlessly into the air. The Ford boys did not know who the men were, since they all wore masks.

The furious sound of flying hoofs could be plainly heard to their rear, and the next moment another half dozen masked men dashed upon the scene. Bob and Charley Ford were fighting like demons, to no avail.

"What is this all about?" cried the infuriated Bob.

"Shut up! Another word and we'll blast you right here."

"I'll shut up when I'm told why we are being molested in this manner, and not before!" yelled Bob, unafraid.

"You'll know in good time," one of the men told them.

It was useless to struggle. The Ford brothers thought their time had come as the masked men took them several hundred yards down the road, where their horses were tied, and they were taken to a desolate spot in the woods. There one of the men produced two ropes with nooses at one end.

"What the hell's the matter with you men? You going to lynch us?" cried Bob, struggling and cursing oaths that would have done credit to an old salt.

"Yep, that's about it."

"What have we done?"

"As if you did not know."

"Well, there are several hundred counts against you for horse-stealing to start off with," said one of the men, apparently the leader.

"That's a damned lie!" screamed Bob.

Charley was morose and sullen, but Bob was defiant and cursed the vigilantes to their faces, again and again.

The ropes were thrown over a stout branch of a huge oak tree, the men then adjusting the nooses around the necks of Charley and Bob Ford. Just as the men were getting ready to hoist the luckless lads into the air a volley of shots filled the night air. Taken by complete surprise, the masked men dashed for their horses, anxious to depart the scene. At the same time three men, unrecognizable in the dark, raced up to the Fords, cut their bonds, and told them to run as fast as they could. They did not have to be told a second time.

The Ford brothers located their horses, and were soon racing toward home.

"Charley, this is mighty strange," said Bob.

"It is, but I think right now we'd better get the hell out of here."

Possibly the vigilantes had been right. Perhaps the Fords had been tied in with horse-stealing and the like. As a matter of fact, it was known in some quarters that they did carry on such a business with the famous horse thief "Dutch Henry" Born of Kansas.

When they reached home they found their sister, Widow Bolton, also present. They quickly gave a graphic account of their adventure and of their rescue.

"Yes, I was expecting this," said Mrs. Bolton. "The public sentiment right now is against you boys, and you should get out of this vicinity."

After an all-night discussion, the boys finally agreed it was the best thing to do. Of course, their farming activities were only a front for their other methods of operation, stage-robbing and horse-stealing. It was agreed they should hide out for a while at the Harbison place near Richmond, Missouri, a farm that Mrs. Bolton was to rent in the near future.

Evidently the Fords had been involved in various crimes prior to becoming members of the James gang. They did very little farming, but took long trips, usually returning with plenty of money. In most instances they were accompanied by their brother Elias "Cap" Ford.

One day in 1876 three young riders rode into Baxter Springs,

Kansas. By that time the town had its own bank, the Bank of Baxter, organized by H. R. Crowell and situated on the corner of Eleventh Street and Military Avenue, in what now is the Douthit Building. Murphy's Restaurant occupied the corner where the outlaws invaded the bank in broad daylight.

The three strangers were well mounted and armed to the teeth. One was a short, slender man, one taller and somewhat heavier; the third appeared to be just a teenager (probably Bob Ford). Posing as cattlemen, they visited the bank several times during their stay, stating they had a herd of cattle just across the line, and wanted to make financial arrangements to handle the transaction with the buyers when they arrived in Baxter Springs.

On Wednesday, about 11:00 A.M., the three men rode up to the bank building, leaving the younger man to remain with the horses at the hitch rack. The other two men entered the bank and commenced a conversation with H. R. Crowell, the cashier, who was alone in the bank. The pair approached Crowell, asking him to change a five dollar bill. The fact that the men wore six-guns did not bother the cashier, since in those days most men went armed.

When Crowell turned to comply with the request, the older man suddenly pulled a revolver and placed it at the man's head.

"Here's a sack, put all the money in it!" he commanded.

Some reports stated that the one robber held Crowell at gunpoint, while the other bandit calmly and coolly placed the money into the grain sack. In any event, the bandits netted themselves a cool two thousand, nine hundred dollars, a handsome sum in those days. They then forced Mr. Crowell to accompany them to the rear of the bank building, where the bandits mounted their horses. They told him to raise the alarm as soon as he pleased, and the three then rode off, in the direction of the Indian Nation.

The bold robbery was a parallel with the most daring jobs of the James and Younger brothers, and many felt the job was pulled off by three other experienced men in that particular field. Many stated openly they thought Jesse James, his brother, Frank, and Cole Younger had been responsible for the daring robbery. However, Jesse and Cole never were on good terms; it is doubtful if those two would have been together on such a caper without others of the Younger clan being present. Besides, one of the robbers had been a young fellow, not old enough to be Jesse, Frank, or Cole.

A posse was quickly formed and went in pursuit of the outlaws, to no avail. At a blacksmith shop several miles from Baxter Springs, the posse came upon the three nervy bandits, who had stopped to have their horses shod.

The posse of citizens rode up to the blacksmith shop to face the bandit guns, fearing a well-planned ambush. Feeling that they were riding to certain death, the riders stopped their horses. Laughing, the three robbers stepped from the blacksmith shop, guns in hand. They disarmed the possemen and broke their guns on a large, nearby rock.

The disarmed possemen gulped and sputtered.

"Well, now that we're all together," said one of the bandits, "we might as well have a little coffee and lunch."

The outlaws then "invited" the members of the posse to eat with them. The men walked from the blacksmith shop to a nearby small restaurant that the little hamlet boasted, telling the posse members to be seated.

"All right, now, you men," said the apparent leader of the outlaw trio, "line up against the wall."

The sheriff from Baxter Springs wondered what was going on. The leader of the robbers told them it was unmanly to chase after honorable men just because their bank had been robbed.

The teenager of the robber trio then said, "You fellows look too sick to eat, maybe we just best leave you here and get."

After the robbers had left, the sheriff and his men lost no time in getting out of the little restaurant to return to Baxter Springs with a story no one seemed to believe.

The robbers made off in the direction of Texas, only to backtrack and return to Clay County, Missouri. Several days after, they appeared at the home of Mrs. Bolton, their sister, with a bag of loot. Yes, the bandits were Cap, Bob, and Charley Ford.

Many people of Ray and Clay Counties firmly believed that the Fords were also connected with various bands of horse thieves. Even before the Fords went on their bank- and train-robbing sprees, the neighbors in their area were mysteriously losing their best horses. They suspected Ford and his sons, but nothing ever came of it, other than the near-lynching of Charley and Bob.

One winter horse thieves ran rampant over Kansas. They raided the Round Topped A, a ranch located on the old cattle trail leading from Dodge City to Ogallala, Nebraska, and which was operated by E. T. Webber & Company. Quickly organizing a posse, Webber and his men followed the trail toward Dodge City. A running fight followed, and Ike Cramer, a notorious horse thief, was wounded, but the remaining rustlers managed to escape.

"I'd swear that Dutch Henry was among those thieves," some of the possemen said. However, no real proof was forthcoming, so Henry was allowed to continue his shady business. It was also noted that fifteen fine-looking horses suddenly appeared in the barnyard of the Bolton farm in Ray County, Missouri.

Whether or not the Fords continued their association with the horse thieves, Dutch Henry did establish a methodical routine of disposing of stolen animals. His previous activities enabled him to contact nearly all other operators in the business. As time passed, even the most noted of the fraternity came under Henry's banner; it no longer was a "hit-and-run" business of stealing small bands of horses here and there and disposing of them miles distant. Dutch Henry's organized crime ring now simply turned their stolen animals over to one of their agents and then, afterwards, collected their share of the sale.

Henry's organization was comprised of both active and associate members, the latter taking no actual part in stealing horses, but acting as underground agents. Many of these were small ranchers, settlers, and farmers, who, for a share of the profit, would shelter bands of horses brought in by the rustlers. They sometimes acted as decoys by throwing pursuing posses off the trail of the rustlers.

Cap, Charley, and Bob Ford often acted in the capacity of holding stolen horses for Dutch Henry. However, their actions became so obvious that they were forced to abandon their efforts in that direction. In any event, the Dutch Henry ring was smashed in 1878 when he was arrested in Trinidad, Colorado, and returned to Ford County, Kansas, by Sheriff Bat Masterson. The Fords had gotten out of the horse-stealing business just in time.

4 • • •

Robbing a Store at Westpoint

Cass County, Missouri, was all set for Christmas; the snow had transformed the bleak countryside into a sparkling arena of white, beautiful and awe-inspiring. It was December 1878 when word reached Zeke Edwards at Harrisonville, home of the Younger brothers, that another robbery had occurred in his county. It was not a sensational bank or train holdup; it was the robbery of a small country store and dry-goods outlet located south of Grand River and a few miles from the little town of Westpoint, Missouri. It was a nice little store, serving the farmers of the area, and was located at the crossroads about a half mile east of the Kansas state line.

It had just begun to snow as the shades of evening fell, casting grotesque and varied shapes across the countryside, when two strangers rode up to the store hitchrack. They were young men, apparently between eighteen and twenty-five years old. One was a fair complexioned man wearing light whiskers that seemed adamant about growing; the other, younger, had dark eyes and a small mustache, his face spotted with skin blemishes. Both men appeared to be about five feet eight or nine inches tall.

The store was operated by Messrs. Bryant and Chandler, but only Mr. Bryant was in the store when the strangers trudged in. He later said it was hard to remember just what they really looked like. The oldest wore a brown chinchilla overcoat; the younger man wore a

41

soldier's overcoat, and both had their black felt hats pulled down over their foreheads.

Mr. Bryant was alone in the store at the time, and due to the sudden snow and cold, with the closest house four or five hundred yards away, he did not expect any local callers at that time. The young men walked up to the pot-bellied stove to warm themselves. They entered into a pleasant conversation with Mr. Bryant and appeared to be well acquainted with that part of the country. Mr. Bryant later said that the younger man appeared mean and vicious, but controlled himself. They asked to see some woolen scarfs and finally selected one, paid for it, and turned to the stove.

The proprietor proceeded with his various duties in the store, all the time keeping up a careless and jovial conversation with the two good-looking young men. Mr. Bryant turned from his shelves, where he had been busily engaged in straightening up the merchandise, when he found himself staring into the muzzles of two large revolvers, while the smiling faces of his two visitors assumed a very businesslike aspect.

"Mr. Bryant, we want all your available cash. We must have it or take something you value more dearly. So shell out without noise or delay."

"No, I will not give in to you two young whippersnappers."

"Yes, you will," replied the robbers, and in another second the newly purchased scarf was over the man's mouth, and his arms soon tied to his sides. Bryant's eyes were then covered with another scarf and the two robbers proceeded to rifle the store. The first secured the cash, amounting to about one thousand dollars; then they proceeded to select such articles of merchandise as suited their fancy, selecting the best quality of materials.

While the two robbers were carrying on their act of robbery in a gay and festive mood, doing their Christmas shopping, so to speak, an old farmer dropped in to pass away the long evening, and to talk over current news as he sat comfortably around the stove in the little store at the crossroads. The young men received him courteously, and took care of him speedily by gagging and blindfolding him, and emptying his pockets of his wallet, his knife, several pieces of twine, a buckle, and a few nails and some papers. Indeed, the farmer had come in to talk about the news, never realizing that he was making it. The prisoner was then escorted to a seat beside Bryant, there to silently study and wonder what next might befall him.

That business was scarcely concluded when two other farmers walked into the store, knocking the snow off their heavy boots. They were welcomed by the bandits and quickly seized. One of the men expressed a desire to return home. He ran a short distance down the road when he was stopped by a pistol shot in his hip. One of the bandits escorted the wounded man back into the store. There he and his companion were seated upon the counter with the other two men, and their pockets rifled. Two more men straggled in, one of them an Irishman. They also were quickly seized and bound; then seated beside the others. It was an odd sight, no doubt, seeing the six men ranged in a row, helpless and uncertain as to their fate.

The robbers, having secured the silence and security of their prisoners, pressed into service a little boy who was employed around the store, and who had just dropped in. With his assistance they proceeded to ransack the store, manifesting good taste and discretion in their selection of goods and trinkets. They took an abundant supply of cigars, tobacco, and whiskey, fitted themselves out with new gloves, handkerchiefs, shirts, and other items of clothing.

During their operations the bandits discovered one of their prisoners was a schoolmaster. The younger robber took occasion to lecture him on the immorality of being out late at night, and its tendency to promote bad habits, and advised him never to go out late again. The Irishman was upbraided for having only forty cents in his pockets.

"That's not enough to pay for the rope we bound you with," laughed the older outlaw.

The wounded man was examined, and found to sustain only a slight flesh wound, and he was made to stand up with the others. After a few drinks from one of the bottles of whiskey, the two bandits proceeded to make their departure. Before leaving, however, they lifted a whiskey bottle to the lips of each man, asking him to take a drink.

"Merry Christmas, gentlemen!"

The prisoners were then escorted outside the store, and ranged in a line facing the road; the boy was tied and blindfolded like the others and placed with them. The robbers then led their horses and a third mount that had been ridden there by one of the captured farmers. The oldest outlaw then addressed the prisoners.

"I want you gentlemen to stand perfectly still until my partner is out of sight, I will remain here with you for a spell. The first man that raises a noise or attempts to get away. I will shoot his head off.

You must stand here perfectly still for two hours, if you don't, I'll make mincemeat of you. The cold will not bother you, since you are all well bundled up."

One of the bandits left the scene with the lead horse. The second robber walked stealthily away some distance, and soon afterwards was heard galloping away in the direction of the state line. The boy managed to free himself from his bonds, and soon had the rest of the prisoners free. But the bold highwaymen were far out of sight and sound.

As soon as daylight came, a number of indignant citizens were out trailing the outlaws. The snow, which had stopped falling, made it possible for the posse to trail the two men into Indian territory, but they were never sighted.

Mr. Bryant was very emphatic when he said later on, "It is time these scandalous deeds of outlawry were put to a stop in western Missouri. Too long have the people in the western counties been annoyed by these desperate men. A little more hemp, with more vigorous pursuit of them, would have a wonderful effect in putting a stop to these outrages."

Zeke and his friends over in Harrisonville felt differently about the matter. Many of them felt that such outlaws were justified in doing what they did, particularly if it were the Jameses or their bunch. Due to the description of the two bandits, it was believed by the people of Ray County that Charley and Bob Ford had pulled off the caper at Westpoint.

Neighbors of the Fords were not surprised to see them, as well as Cap's wife and children, and Jim Cummins, Bob's relation through marriage, since their Uncle Bill Ford had married Jim's sister, all decked out in the fineries obtained at the little store at the crossroads in Cass County.

5 • • •

The Brave and Resolute
Sheriff Timberlake

James R. Timberlake, one of the most efficient sheriffs Clay County, Missouri, had ever seen, and the relentless pursuer of outlaw Jesse James and his men, was born in Platte County, Missouri, March 22, 1846. His father, John Timberlake, a native Kentuckian, was born in 1809 and later married Patsy Noland in Kentucky. In 1830 the family came to Missouri, locating in the Platte Purchase in what is now Platte County, where he bought land and improved a farm.

The Timberlake family remained there until 1864, when, owing to the unsettled condition of affairs because of the Civil War, they moved to Illinois for a short time. Later, John Timberlake returned to Platte County, but soon purchased a farm in Clay County, Missouri, where he resided from 1866 to 1880. Some reports claim that young James Timberlake accompanied his family to Illinois. If this is the case, he returned in a short while, because he entered the Confederate Army in 1864, in Colonel Slayback's cavalry regiment. He became a second lieutenant of Co. B, General Jo Shelby's Iron Brigade, and thereby participated in a number of fierce engagements.

At last the war was over. The terms of surrender were published, and the Confederate troops from all quarters who had remained organized to the end marched toward Shreveport for the final dissolution. But not so General Shelby. He thought that thousands of men would rally to his side, eager to keep up the hostilities; that Texas would rally to a man and send thousands of men to his support. But the weary men knew the situation was hopeless, and many of them yearned for home, to see their families and their sweethearts. Thus, it was that these brave men who never questioned a command of General Jo Shelby now felt the strong ties of other loves drawing them ever homeward.

General Shelby felt that an arrangement could be made with either Emperor Maximilian or President Juarez that would at least grant his men homes and asylum. Yet, it was not to be. Some followed Shelby into Mexico; most did not. The separation of his command took place on June 2, 1865, and was a sorrowful sight. Among those brave men who went into Mexico with Shelby was James Timberlake. Since no report of this great lawman tells anything of his Mexican journey, it is felt that his trip should be followed as a matter of interest and of record.

After the sorrowful separation at Corsicana, Texas, Shelby, surrounded by five hundred officers and men, determined to follow his fortunes to the end, halted for several days for the purpose of formulating plans necessary to make. General Herron was at Shreveport with nearly a thousand Federal troops, and Shelby was determined to attack that body. However, the plan was abandoned, since most of his aides declared that the war was over; to do something like that would only bring outraged clamor upon those other thousands upon thousands of faithful Confederate soldiers who had surrendered in good faith.

Although young Timberlake was just a lieutenant in Shelby's force he was often asked for his suggestions and opinions. The trust was well placed, since the young officer had often shown good judgment on the field of battle in Missouri.

It was Shelby's intention to follow General Preston, who had gone to Mexico City some weeks prior, and from Corsicana he marched to Waco, Texas. His supplies were good, and they included four rifled cannon, several thousand Enfield rifles, six hundred rounds of artillery ammunition, and about fifty thousand rounds of small-arms ammunition. There also was a large wagon train of food supplies. Each man was armed with a Sharps carbine, several revolvers, and plenty of ammunition.

At Waco the Mexican firm of Gonzales & Gonzales was threatened by mobs of unruly lawless outlaws and renegade soldiers.

"Timberlake," said Shelby to the lad from Missouri, "take a

guard and escort the Gonzales caravan southward. Ten men will do; you can return to the main body as soon as it is assigned."

Straight as an arrow in his saddle, Timberlake saluted and without a reply rode off toward the troops. Shelby's men were all mounted on the best obtainable horseflesh. They presented a picture of awe, men drilled to explicit discipline; a marching body looked upon as something from another world. The people of Waco just stood, open-mouthed, and gazed silently as the magnificent scene passed from view.

From Waco the troops went on to Austin, where a group of outlaws and deserters under the command of Captain Jack Rabb were taking advantage of the presence of Shelby's men by looting and robbing, feeling that the blame would fall upon the Confederates. At one point Rabb and some of his men made a daring raid on the state treasury by using chisels and sledgehammers on the heavy vaults. The citizens, on learning of the raid, made an onslaught against the treasury building. One of Rabb's men was killed, another escaping with about fifteen thousand dollars, which was recovered shortly after by the mob of citizens who followed the robber. After that no further raids were made by Rabb and his men. General Shelby ably took care of the money, seeing to it that it returned to the rightful owners.

At San Antonio Shelby and his men ran across Captain A. B. Miller, a former Confederate officer who had supplied their army with supplies, food, and ammunition. Now he requested Shelby to assist him in raiding the town of San Antonio for the purpose of loot. Shelby refused to provide Miller with the requested number of men. Too late did he fully realize his mistake. Miller gathered around him a horde of money-hungry Texans who invaded the town and swarmed over it like a cloud of locusts, devouring everything in their path. During the raid General Shelby lost most of his supplies, as well as the city losing all its money.

Finally, after the arrival of all of Shelby's men in San Antonio, things settled down, and those few Confederate officers who had been in hiding came forth to be greeted cordially by the general and his staff. A number of Confederate exiles were waiting for Shelby in San Antonio, brave men who had fought long and hard for their beliefs. Among those of high rank were Generals Cadmus M. Wilcox, John B. Magruder, Thomas C. Hindman, Gustavas W. Smith, Hyland B. Lyon, and Daniel Leadbetter, the last being one who had made a mark for himself as being a brilliant engineer during the war. Civilians of note included Governor Murrah, of Texas; Governor Morehead, of Kentucky; Governor Allen, of Louisiana; and Governor Polk, of Missouri, and some men of lesser grade.

After remaining at San Antonio for nearly a week, Shelby gathered sufficient supplies and then headed toward the Rio Grande. Rigid discipline prevailed, the men always showing respect and obedience to the orders issued by General Shelby. One of his strict orders was not to pillage or bother anyone living in the areas through which they passed. Necessary provisions were either purchased with gold coin or foraged from the open prairies or the wooded slopes. The group's next stop was New Braunfels, where the German element treated them to all the lager beer they could manage.

General Smith requested and received an escort from General Shelby in order that his group might pass safely from the area. Among those in this escort across the Rio Grande were James Timberlake, later Sheriff of Clay County, Missouri, Captain Maurice M. Langhorne, and several other Missourians, all later prominent in that state's political arena. It was Timberlake and Langhorne who became the nemesis of the James bunch, along with W. G. Keshlaer, the latter two named becoming deputy marshals under Marshal James Liggett of Kansas City, Missouri. Langhorne had also ridden with Jesse and Frank James prior to joining the regular Confederate cavalry, as had Cole Younger when he tired of the seesaw struggle in Missouri.

At the trial of one James gang member, Whiskey-Head Ryan, at Independence on November 6, 1880, it was thought that Jesse James would attempt to rescue his ally. However, when he discovered that Deputy Marshal Langhorne was the man guarding the prisoner, he dropped his plans, and Ryan was sentenced to prison.

In Eagle Pass, across the Rio Grande from Piedras Negras, Shelby camped his troops after setting up pickets and training his rifled cannons toward the Mexican side of the river. Apparently fearing that the alignment of troops and guns meant an attack upon Piedras Negras, that very evening two Mexicans, under a white flag, rowed across the river in a skiff, asking to see the officer in command. They asked that the town be allowed to remove all women and children before the bombardment commenced. Shelby laughed. He assured the two men that no harm was intended, that the measure was one of self-protection only.

The next day, Shelby, along with some of his staff, including Timberlake, crossed the Rio Grande to discuss negotiations for the sale of his heavy supplies of war. Prominent landowners arrived to participate, along with the governors of the states of New Leon and Coahuila, and for two days the talks continued. Finally, it was agreed that eighteen thousand dollars should be paid for the war materials Shelby wished to dispose of, excluding the cannon and its ammunition. For those he was paid sixteen thousand dollars in silver and a like amount of Juarez script, which turned out to be worthless.

The money was equally divided among Shelby's men, small as the amount to each might have been. After all activities had been attended to, Shelby gave the order for his men to begin their thousand-mile journey into a strange land—a land where they were ignorant as to the language and the habits and the customs of the Mexican people.

The night before the departure of the Confederates from Piedras Negras Timberlake and Langhorne had gone to visit a saloon and gambling house in town. Of course, this was much against the rules, but they decided to have a little fun before taking their departure from that wicked Mexican town. Several hours of drinking and idle conversation passed between these two young soldiers when they noticed a rough-looking man enter the place. One native, in pitiful English, muttered that the man was a no-good *gringo*, a Texan named "The Dutchman." This man sat down at a table occupied by four or five men as rough-looking as himself. Their heads huddled together, it was easy for Timberlake and Langhorne to see that they were discussing something private and important.

About an hour later, the two Americans stood up and started to walk toward the entrance of the cantina. For some reason or another the Dutchman fellow leaped to his feet and yelled, "Get 'em; they know what we are up to!"

Timberlake and Langhorne made for the door, but their way was blocked by several of the Liberal soldiers of Mexico. One man stabbed at Timberlake, but Langhorne shot him dead with a bullet through the heart. Other Mexicans went for their knives and daggers. The bedlam was such that the two young men were able to clear the doorway and make for their horses. Along the way Timberlake smashed in the head of one of his pursuers as the man attempted to drag him from his saddle. They were pursued only a short distance, for the two soldiers were too close to the Shelby camp.

Timberlake and Langhorne thought nothing much of the affair until the next day, when the man called the Dutchman, riding at the head of some thirty or more Liberals, boldly marched into the plaza and claimed all of Shelby's mounts that were Mexican branded. Of course, Shelby had no such papers for his horses, but he decided to end the matter then and there. Six bugle notes and the six hundred Confederate veterans were mounted and in line, eagerly awaiting the signal to attack. Even the local authorities had by that time turned against the Americans; by then, six or seven hundred men of all descriptions—Mexicans, renegade whites, Dutch, Negroes, and Indians—were ready to fight Shelby and his Iron Brigade. Piedras Negras was in a state of fear; Shelby's men were clamoring for a fight, and the general was taxed to the utmost in restraining them. Then Shelby gave the orders: half his group was to attack the opposing forces; the other half was to retrieve all the supplies sold to the Mexicans. The Dutchman, the man who had started all the ruckus, disappeared at the first sound of the bugle. Shortly thereafter Governor Biesca arrived upon the scene, had the Mexicans arrested, as well as the Dutchman, who was quickly run down, and he then offered signs of peace and goodwill to Shelby and his command.

"Well, I'll be damned!" said Timberlake to Langhorne. "So that was why they tried to kill us at the casino. They figured we had learned of this fiasco." Both young men laughed out loud.

Following the near-battle, General Shelby was offered complete command of the states of New Leon and Coahuila by the respective governors. However, Shelby and his officers were more favorable to the Imperialists under Emperor Maximilian rather than the cause of the Liberals, so the offer was declined. The offer from Juarez, of course, would have put Shelby at the head of a great army of mounted soldliers, but the war at hand did not especially appeal to their honor or their beliefs.

Now, as Shelby marched southward from Piedras Negras toward the Rio Grande, there occurred a sad scene to behold. The old, tattered battle flag of Shelby's division was brought for the last time from its place of security. Ironically, it was the Fourth of July, 1865, when Colonels Elliott, Williams, Gordon, and Slayback held the Stars and Bars up for a few brief moments above the rushing tide of the river. It was early morning, yet the outline of the El Paso del Aquilar Mountains was plain to see. The solemn grandeur weighed heavily upon those battle-ridden five hundred Confederate soldiers as the magnificent explqits of Shelby's Missouri Cavalry flashed before their eyes. There was not a dry eye among those stalwart soldiers of the South, their eyes turned heavenward in silent prayer. Sadly and slowly the battle flag of Shelby's division was lowered beneath the water.

The sale of his supplies to the Liberals did not set too well with the Imperialists, even though Shelby had expressed his sympathy to that cause. Even so, he boldly marched his men toward Monterey, then into the hands of General Jeanningros, a French army officer with six hundred or more French soldiers at his command. Jeanningros sent word to Shelby that he would shoot him and all his officers and hang his men. The Frenchman was bitter because Shelby had been friendly with the Juaristas group. When within four miles of Monterey, Shelby was forced to sell his guns and ammunition in order to buy bread for his men. There was but one thing to do: have a parley with the French commander.

Raney McKinney, a beardless, youthful veteran of many Missouri skirmishes, was selected to carry the message under a flag of truce. He was selected because he had previously been to Monterey and was aware of the conditions there. With him went Major John Thrailkill, formerly a captain in the command of William Clarke Quantrill, the famous Missouri guerrilla. John Thrailkill was a Missourian turned fiend. Before the outbreak of the Civil War, he was a painter engaged to marry a beautiful girl. One night twenty Federal militiamen walked into her home and murdered her invalid father right before her. She lost her reason and soon afterward died. Thrailkill swore death to the militiamen as he reverently kissed the stilled lips of his betrothed. His closest friend was Jesse James, with whom he rode throughout the war years. At that time he joined Quantrill and was personally responsible for the death of eighteen of the twenty soldiers he had vowed to exterminate.

If the French general refused to listen to him, Shelby vowed to return to Piedras Negras, organize a strong force, and attack him in his quarters. The truce flag caused much comment in the French camp, but as soon as Jeanningros learned the nature of Shelby's communication, he expressed delight and remarked a number of times that Shelby was the only soldier who had broken through his lines.

General Jeanningros gave his permission for Shelby and his men to enter the city, where they were fed, while the general personally invited Shelby to a splendid supper in his own quarters. It was easy to see that Jeanningros was a splendid soldier, but one without mercy or pity; one who would give his all for his career, allowing nothing whatsoever to stand in his path in so doing. Shelby was told one story of the grim discipline of the French army. One night a young officer, under the influence of liquor or drugs, walked away from the camp. Hours later he regained his senses and, although half crazed by the lack of freedom, he nevertheless returned to his command. He was immediately arrested and sentenced to be shot as a deserter. He was a rich young man and supposedly related to the Empress Eugenie, but this meant nothing to Jeanningros. The sentence was to be carried out. The doomed man asked to see the general.

"General, you know if I am shot my possessions will go to the government; that is the law. My mother is widowed and that would make things very difficult for her."

There was no response from Jeanningros, who turned and walked silently from the cell. At sunset an orderly delivered a bottle of cognac and a loaded revolver to the young officer. Calmly the man made out his will, wrote several letters to friends; then drank his fill of brandy and killed himself. The official report read "suicide."

At Monterey the command separated. Some went to Sonora and fought with the Liberals under General Corona; some went to South America; some joined Colonel Dupin to avenge the death of General M. M. Parsons between Matamoros and Monterey. Others went to California, Timberlake and Langhorne among them.

The death of Parsons and his party occurred after they had been captured by a band of Liberals while trying to bring in supplies from Matamoras to Monterey. General M. M. Parsons was under the command of General Jeanningros at the time, along with Colonel Standish, Colonel Conrow, and several Irish soldiers. The wagons were ambushed and captured in a narrow gorge, and the escort was driven back by the Liberals. General Parsons, who had led a brigade in Price's division in Missouri, managed to escape, but was captured and returned to camp. A few hours later he and his companions were shot and killed. Some Mexicans in the area buried the six bodies in shallow graves. Later, when eighty-two of Shelby's men arrived in that area, they learned of this massacre, sought out most of those responsible, and killed them.

From Monterey General Shelby and fifty of his men marched on through Parras, San Luis Potosi, Mexico City, and other towns, finally settling at Carlotta in Cordova. Later he returned to the United States and was appointed United States Marshal by President Cleveland. While in Washington he met General Sheridan, who said to him, "I begged General Grant to let me go over to the Trans-Mississippi Department and capture you."

Shelby replied, "I wish you had come General; it was mighty lonesome over there."

Shelby remained a close friend of the Jameses and Youngers during their careers of banditry. At the trial of Frank James in 1883 he was a witness in favor of the defendant. John E. Philips, defending Frank James in a long and eloquent speech, had this to say of Shelby:

"Mrs. James's mission to General Shelby for support was most genuine. Shelby's testimony is worthy of all credit. It is but frank in me to admit that the General's deportment on the witness stand was improper, as a matter of propriety [some reports said the general had been drinking]. . . . It hurt no one but himself, and I knew he regretted it. But he spoke truth. His high character needs no defense and no eulogy by me. His name is a household word in Missouri. As splendid in courage as he is big in heart, his home is the model of hospitality. No man, however poor or outcast, was ever turned from it hungry. Truth and chivalry to him are as modesty to the true woman, and azure to the sky.

"He had been denounced in public and private as a friend of Frank James. Smirking Puritans and lugubrious Pharisees have shrugged their shoulders at the fact of Shelby giving a bed and a glass of water and a pinch of salt to the defendant when he chanced to pass his door; and for extending the hand of assistance and a word of sympathy to Frank James's wandering, heart-sick wife. In the midst of so much moral cowardice and starveling charity in this age, I rather admire the quality of heart which prompted Shelby. It was not the promptings of a spirit of disloyalty to law and society, but it was a quick response of a brave and generous heart to that sentiment which makes us humane instead of savage."

On January 19th, 1875, General Shelby was asked to take over as warden of the Missouri State Penitentiary at Jefferson City. Three hundred men in the shoe shops had mutinied, refusing to work until their food was improved. Order was restored quickly, but the prison officials were criticized for alleged laxity of discipline. It was then decided to ask for the services of that tough ex-Confederate General Jo Shelby.

General Sterling Price, who had also gone to Mexico in a colonization scheme, returned to the United States in 1866. He died in St.

Louis, Missouri, September 29, 1867. Price served as Missouri's governor from 1853 to 1856.

Of the other generals who followed Shelby into Mexico we have this information: Cadmus M. Wilcox served as Chief of the Railroad Division of the General Land Office, Washington, D.C., where he died December 2, 1890; John B. Magruder went to Texas and died there February 19, 1871; Thomas C. Hindman went from Mexico to Arkansas, where he was murdered by a soldier of his command on September 28, 1868; Gustavas W. Smith died in New York on June 24, 1896.

In the summer of 1866 Timberlake returned from California to Missouri, choosing his home as Clay County. For two years or so after that he was peacefully occupied in the pursuits of farming and stock raising. In 1872 he made a trip to Texas and brought back a herd of cattle, which he disposed of in Kansas at a great profit.

In 1876 James Timberlake was appointed constable of Liberty Township and served for two years. So well did he perform the duties of that office that in 1878 he was asked to run for Sheriff of Clay County. He was elected handsomely and re-elected later on. His services while in that office marked him as one of the best sheriffs Missouri ever had. His pursuit of Jesse James and his band is a feat believed impossible by many people, even to this day. And his cunning and planning in the development of the outlaw's final days were examples of Timberlake's courage, cunning, and resourcefulness.

After his retirement as sheriff, Timberlake went with his brother to New Mexico, where they bought two ranches, becoming actively engaged in the cattle business. In 1883 he was appointed Deputy United States Marshal for the Western District of Missouri. Timberlake also ran one of the largest livery stables in the State of Missouri, at Liberty. On November 25, 1874, James Timberlake married Katie Thomason, daughter of Grafton Thomason, one of the pioneers of Clay County.

Former Sheriff James Timberlake died at his home in Liberty, Missouri, on February 19, 1891, around midnight. Death was caused by an accidental overdose of morphine, which he had taken to induce sleep. The funeral took place at 11:00 in the morning of the 21st, from the home of Thomas Gosney. The pallbearers were James F. Reed, circuit clerk of Clay County, F. V. Atkins, Charles Wymore, Senator H. F. Simrall, Antonious Brown, and William M. Burris, Jr. Elder F. O. Fannon, pastor of the Christian church, conducted services at

Emperor Maximilian.

General Sterling Price.

General Jo Shelby.

Captain M. M. Langhorne, went to Mexico with Shelby and pursued the Jameses.

Rare photo Dick Pool, McMurtry brothers, rode with Jameses during war.

Rare photo Mrs. Jo Shelby.

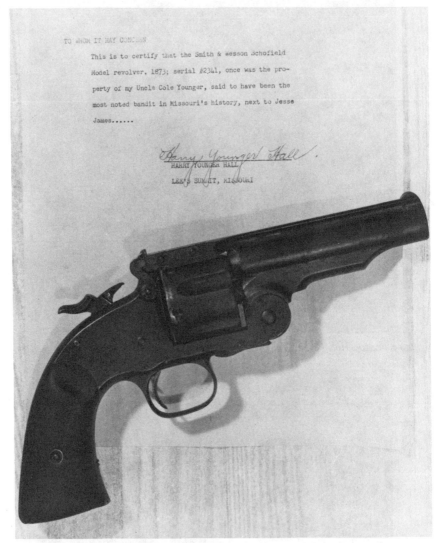

Cole Younger Smith & Wesson revolver.

the grave. Quite a number of citizens, ladies and gentlemen of the most prominent families in the city and county, attended. He was buried beside his wife, who died in 1886.

Timberlake was, to use ex-Governor Crittenden's words, "the truest and bravest man who ever lived." There was no question but that he was a man who knew absolutely no fear, and whose loyalty to the state and his office rid Missouri of the most dangerous and lawless gang of desperadoes and robbers that ever infested it. In ex-Sheriff Timberlake's death the state and Clay County lost one of the principal factors in the extermination of the James brothers gang and the killing of Jesse James, its noted leader. The other man with whom this credit was shared was Captain H. H. Craig, at that time a member of the Board of Police Commissioners of Kansas City and, at the time of Timberlake's death, a noted lawyer, at that time in Corpus Christi, Texas.

James Timberlake was the ideal symbol as a hero and fighter. He stood over six feet tall and was broad in proportion. He was a magnificent specimen of manhood. With the strength of three ordinary men and the courage of a lion he combined all the graces of an Apollo and was noted as one of the handsomest men in Western Missouri. His complexion was dark, made still browner by exposure, and his face lighted by a pair of black eyes that never flinched in the face of danger. A full, determined chin and over that a firm mouth, shaded by a black, drooping mustache, was his description in the days when his fearless and energetic pursuit of the James gang made him one of the best-known men in the country. His many escapades with the gang and members thereof would make a dime novel seem tame.

During the seventies when the James brothers were in the zenith of their fame, Timberlake was elected sheriff by the Democrats of Clay County. He inaugurated his term of office by a fierce, unflagging, and determined warfare on Jesse and Frank James and their gang, of whom nearly every other officer in the West stood in deadly fear. The intrepid sheriff was aided by an equally courageous man, Captain H. H. Craig. Together these two brave men rode night after night, carrying their lives in their hands, through all the wilds of western Missouri in pursuit of the gang of robbers. Several times Sheriff Timberlake almost lost his life in this endeavor.

When a daring bank robbery was committed, or a train holdup perpetrated, these two men were always among the first, if not the very first, at the scene. Keen and relentless was their pursuit of the outlaws. So unabating was their vigilance that Jesse and Frank both had to seek safety in flight to distant states, and Timberlake and Craig also succeeded in breaking up many a rendezvous of the gang and also frustrated several contemplated robberies.

Governor Crittenden finally realized and recognized the determined efforts of these two brave men and complimented them:

"If it hadn't been for the efforts of Sheriff Timberlake and Commissioner Craig the James gang never would have been broken up. These men were often out weeks at a time and in such close pursuit of the robbers that it was only the hardest riding that saved the outlaws. Every day I dreaded that I might hear that these two men had been killed by the James band. They seemed to bear a charmed life, and this very fact finally instilled a fear of these two men in the hearts of the desperadoes that they left Missouri for some time.

"Timberlake finally succeeded, after many a thrilling escape and encounter, in placing the muzzle of his revolver to the head of Clarence Hite, a member of the gang. He was brought back to Ray County, where he was sentenced to twenty-five years in prison, dying therein. So pitiless and relentless were they in their pursuit of the gang members that Dick Liddil, another noted member of the gang, surrendered to the authorities. Even the Ford brothers, Charley and Bob, two of the most daring of the James followers, finally opened negotiations with the sheriff, looking to their own immunity from punishment and the capture of the James brothers."

At the time just prior to the death of Jesse James there was a reward offered by the state of ten thousand dollars for the capture of either Jesse or Frank and turning them over to the marshal of Jackson or Daviess Counties. The latter rewards did not provide a "dead or alive" clause, for it was noted that Governor Crittenden opposed their being killed through treachery. During all this time and in the face of many efforts made to capture the James brothers, the governor never lost faith in Sheriff Timberlake and Commissioner Craig, and he firmly believed that the final extermination of the gang and the capture of the leaders would be accomplished only by them. He was kept closely posted on all their efforts and was informed of the overtures made by the Ford brothers. With his sanction,' on March 24, 1882, Bob Ford was detailed by Sheriff Timberlake to go from Kansas City into Clay County and get onto the trail of Jesse James, who was then believed to be somewhere in that county. Bob started out, and he was given ten days in which to either report or return. If, at the end of that time, nothing was heard from him it was to be taken for granted that he had failed in his objective or had been killed by the James gang.

Eight days passed and nothing was heard from Ford, and on the ninth day Governor Crittenden telegraphed Sheriff Timberlake his fear that Bob Ford had been "put under the daisies." In this fear both Sheriff Timberlake and Commissioner Craig shared, for none knew better than they the dangerous nature of the mission Ford had set out upon and the certain fate that was soon to overtake him if Jesse ever learned his motive.

When Bob Ford left Timberlake and Craig in Kansas City he proceeded direct to a rendezvous of the James gang in Clay County and, as he expected, met Jesse James. Accompanying the famous outlaw leader was Bob's brother Charley. Jesse had planned a daring robbery of the bank at Platte City, Missouri, and at the time Bob was hunting him he and Charley were in search of him to secure his cooperation in the robbery, which was set for April 3rd. There was at the time a famous trial in progress at Platte City—the Anderson murder case— and Jesse knew that everybody, not only in the city, but in the county roundabout, would flock to the courtroom. The concluding arguments in the case were set for April 3rd, and Jesse rightly guessed that on that day a bigger crowd than usual would be at the courthouse and that the bank would be left practically unprotected, or at the most with only the cashier in charge. They determined upon murdering him and, after robbing the safe, making a bold dash and escape. Then, before an effective pursuit could be organized, they would be safely out of reach.

To more fully mature the plan for this robbery, Jesse went to his home in St. Joseph and told the Ford boys to accompany him. It seemed that Jesse mistrusted the brothers from some marks corresponding with Captain.Craig's initials he had recently found on one of Bob Ford's underwear. He never allowed either of them out of his sight during the ten days of enforced waiting at St. Joseph. If the Fords went to the barn to curry and care for their horses Jesse was sure to accompany them. Under this constant guard neither of the Fords had the opportunity of sending a message to either Craig, Timberlake, or the governor, as had been agreed upon, and so the time wearily passed until the ninth day, when Governor Crittenden sent the message to Sheriff Timberlake expressing his fear that Bob Ford had been killed.

Bob and Charley Ford were not idle, however, and they might have shot and killed Jesse several times on any of the days, but their express orders were not to kill him, but rather to capture him alive or send word of their whereabouts to Timberlake, Craig or Crittenden. The latter they were unable to do because Jesse watched them like a cat watched a mouse, and the former they were incapable of doing at that time, anyway. They had both challenged Jesse James to wrestle, and, after throwing them singly, the outlaw leader easily threw them both together.

Convinced finally that they could not capture him alive, and realizing the hopelessness of getting any word to the authorities, Bob Ford finally determined to kill Jesse James at the first opportunity. On Monday, April 3, 1882, the tenth day, Jesse James was hanging a picture in his house. He got upon a chair, taking off his pistols and placed them on a nearby bed. It was the first time in the criminal career of the outlaw leader that he was ever known to remove his weapons from his person. Bob Ford, who was in the room, took this opportunity, snatched up Jesse's guns, drew his own revolver and fired at Jesse James before the latter had time to realize his danger. The shot was fatal and killed the outlaw instantly. Leaving the premises, Ford hurried to the nearest telegraph office and sent the following dispatch to Governor Crittenden:

I have got my man. What shall I do with him,
                    Bob Ford.

Governor Crittenden did not understand the telegram, and he telegraphed both Sheriff Timberlake and Captain Craig, asking them what the telegram meant and if they had received any news from Bob Ford. The governor had received the wire about noon on Monday, the 3rd. An hour and a half later he received a telegram from General John B. Carson of St. Joseph, at that time superintendent of the Hannibal & St. Joseph railroad, briefly stating that Bob Ford had killed Jesse James.

"The killing was never authorized by me," said the governor, "and neither did Timberlake nor Craig want the capture effected in any such manner. Bob Ford acted on his own responsibility. Every cent of the ten thousand dollar reward was paid to Sheriff Timberlake and Captain Craig, and of course Bob Ford probably got his share." (Bob and Charley Ford denied ever getting more than five hundred dollars of the reward money.)

Treasurer Cooley of the Ninth Street Theatre in Kansas City, who was once a resident of Clay County, said this of the deceased lawman: "Timberlake must have borne a charmed life. He was the only man the James boys went for that they did not get. Timberlake used to sit outside the old Arthur House in Liberty, tilted back in his chair against the wall with a pipe in his mouth. Not far away was a corncrib. Many a time did members of the James gang ride past that and from behind it empty their pistols at the sheriff. They never did hit him, either, and they were damned good shooters, too. At times pieces of the bricks would be broken out by the bullets, though. After that Timberlake would go into the hotel and prepare for a chase after the James boys with a posse and would soon be scouring the woods for them. Generally he would wind up at Mrs. Samuel's house near Kearney and bring her into town to interrogate her.

"Timberlake had recently been interested in the livery stable business with a brother and Mr. Bell. I was with him one day a summer or two ago driving over to the springs and he spoke of one of his horses. I asked him if the horse was of the James stock. He grew very angry at that and didn't speak again to me for over an hour."

Sheriff Timberlake's last famous chase after the James boys was during the days and nights of July 16th and 17th. On the night of July 15, 1881, at Winston, Missouri, a train had been boarded and robbed by a band of masked men, and the conductor, William Westfall, was killed. Timberlake firmly believed the James boys had had a hand in it, and organizing a posse in the belief of his theory, he scoured the country for miles around. The robbers had vanished, however, leaving no clue. As usual, the posse raided the Samuel residence, to no avail.

Not long after the Winston affair a stranger dropped in at the bank at Plattsburg, in Clinton County, adjoining Clay County. While there he recognized an acquaintance, nodded, took a parting look at a portrait of General Lee hanging on the wall, then walked boldly from the bank. This acquaintance met Sheriff Timberlake several hours later in front of the courthouse.

"You're too late, Jim, Jesse has been here and gone, and nobody knows in what direction," and he smiled a broad grin.

Timberlake just bit his lip and walked on.

At the funeral one of the citizens remarked about Timberlake: "Timberlake was a nervy man and did not fear danger, as his exploits with the James boys plainly show. On the occasion when he was barricaded in a barn by the gang, he showed great nerve and judgment, which saved him from what was a very close call. He was handicapped, however, by the sentiment of a great many people in this section of the state who believed the James boys to be wrongfully outlawed and driven to the deeds they committed, while others thought they were blamed with a great deal they did not do."

6 • • •

Charley and Bob Ford Meet Jesse James

In August of 1879, Ed Miller, another bandit, in company with a stranger, came to the Harbison place, which Widow Bolton had rented, and asked for Charley Ford. The Harbison place stood well off from any public road, and was surrounded by a large forest of giant oak trees. Ed Miller and his companion dismounted and walked toward the house. Charley arose from his seat on the porch and went to meet the two visitors.

"Hello, Charley, this is my friend, Mr. T. J. Jackson."

"How are you, Mr. Jackson?" said Charley Ford, shaking the stranger's extended hand.

"He is one of us," said Ed Miller, with a wink. It was no mystery to Charley what that meant.

"I am glad to meet you," said Mr. Jackson. "I understand you and your brother were nearly lynched some time back."

"Yes, that was some experience."

"Do you know who the men were?"

"Those who were going to hang us?" asked Charley.

"Yes."

"No, I do not. Neither do I know the three men who saved us."

Charley Ford apparently missed the strange looks and words that passed between the two visitors.

"You are situated in a good spot here," observed Mr. Jackson.

64

Mrs. Bolton came into the room at that moment and was introduced to Mr. Jackson.

Mr. Jackson appeared to be a sporting man and gambled and drank a little that evening at the home of Mrs. Bolton. This incident shows that Jesse James sometimes acted in a diplomatic role, and tried to be "all things to all men." He left a good impression on the Fords.

"Where is Bob tonight?" asked Ed Miller.

"Went up to the old man's place for a visit," replied Charley.

"Isn't that a little dangerous, considering everything?" asked Mr. Jackson.

"In a way, yes," grinned Charley, "but Bob's not afraid of anything or anybody."

"To a point of recklessness," agreed Ed Miller.

The night wore on, with Miller and Jackson playing cards with Charley Ford and his sister, as well as drinking a little now and then. The east was growing rosy with the early dawn when the game broke up, with Mr. Jackson a decided loser.

"Well, I must return home," said Mr. Jackson.

With that he and Ed Miller strolled to their horses, mounted, and left in a cloud of dust.

"Charley, who was that man?" asked Mrs. Bolton.

"I don't know yet. But somehow his name strikes me as not being genuine."

"He is not a farmer, I am sure of that," said Mrs. Bolton. "His hands are too white and soft."

Bob Ford was at his father's place on the night the mysterious stranger came to visit the Harbison place with Ed Miller. Since the effort to lynch them, Bob and Charley had made it a point to steer clear of that area. Bob tried to keep his various meetings a secret, but some weeks after Mr. Jackson's visit with Charley Ford, a young neighbor girl saw Bob at his father's home, went home, and reported it to her parents.

Late that same evening a dozen masked men approached the Ford farmhouse, heavily armed and carrying ropes. Bob was aroused from his sleep by the loud barking of the dogs, and at once sprang to his feet.

"Bob! Bob" cried his mother. "Someone is coming!"

"I know it," he replied, dressing hurriedly, and buckling his pistols about his waist.

He ran down from the attic room and took a look through a window to determine from what direction the barking was coming. This would indicate the location of the attackers. Soon he saw four or five dark figures stalking toward the house.

"Don't shoot," cautioned his father. "There are too many of them. If you should kill one of them they'll hang you for sure. They would also burn the house and all of us in it."

It was sound advice.

At the rear of the house was a narrow window, almost concealed by a large oak tree that grew near it. Through that window Bob made his escape.

Bob paused for a moment to listen, cocked pistol ready for action. The men were slowly advancing, driving the enraged dogs before them, until the house was reached.

There was a loud rap on the door, accompanied by a rough inquiry.

"We want your sons, Ford, we know they are in there."

"They left a while ago," shouted Mr. Ford.

"We know for sure Bob is in there. We were told."

"He is gone."

"Where is he?"

"I don't know."

"Watch every exit, and shoot to kill. Bob Ford is a wizard with his pistol."

Suddenly, and to the astonishment of the men, J. T. Ford walked onto the porch and invited the men to search the house.

All this time Bob was worming himself through the grass as silent as an Indian brave. He well knew that the slightest sound would bring the men outside tramping in all directions.

"Damn! I wish I had a horse," muttered Bob Ford.

"He's not in the house," cried one of the vigilante group. "Where do you suppose he is?"

"Try the barn and the hayloft," suggested another.

"He'd not be that stupid," suggested one member of the band.

At the same time Bob eased himself over a fence into a thick orchard. Slowly and carefully he moved about. The moment he was far enough from the scene, he ran. His feet seemed to hardly touch the ground as he sped toward the protection of a nearby forest. Only then did he slacken his pace. He knew that he would have to seek shelter for the night, but he was not sure in which direction the Harbison house was. At last he came upon a deserted log cabin. The cabin was not large, the door was closed but not locked, and he opened it and entered. He could wait there until daylight and then make his way out of the forest. He was lost, and he knew it would be a waste of time trying to find his way in the darkness.

Bob felt his way around the room, and finding a rude bench he decided to catch a few winks. He did not know how long he had been asleep, but voices outside the cabin caused him to leap up, fully awake.

"Let's go in and divide the loot," he heard one voice say.

Bob did not know who the men were; he was in a critical position, and every avenue of escape was cut off, since the only entrance and exit to the cabin was by way of the door. As he inched his way along the rough wall, Bob suddenly felt a ladder that led to a small storage space above the room. Just as the door opened he climbed up to the attic and flattened himself on the loose boards.

"Well, here we are, men, time to divide our spoils," said a man, apparently the leader of the group.

"Have you a lantern, Jess?"

"Yes, and I'll light it now."

"Who are these men?" thought Bob Ford. "Who is Jess?"

In several minutes he could see faint rays of yellow light shining through the spaces between the loose boards. He gasped.

"It's Ed Miller!"

The man addressed as Jess threw the booty down on a rude table in the middle of the room, divided out the money, and shoved each man a pile as they stood around the table.

"Now, each of you men go home and tend to your own business just as if nothing had happened. I think the law will have as hard a time of finding you as they are in finding Jesse James."

"Good heavens, is this the noted train robber?" gasped Bob Ford. The name was familiar all over the world; now, here below him stood the famous outlaw and some of his men. What they were doing was dividing the loot taken from the Chicago, Alton, and St. Louis train at Glendale, Missouri, October 8, 1879. Bob hardly breathed.

"Jess, what do you think of Charley Ford as a new member?" asked Ed Miller.

"He seemed all right to me. What about his brother?"

"He's only seventeen or eighteen, but as tough as they come. He can shoot like any of us. You remember him. He was with Charley the night we rescued them from the lynchers."

Having a natural desire to see the men who were talking, Bob crept along the boards until he reached the outer edge of the opening.

He peered down and saw three men seated on the bench directly below him, while four or five more were in another part of the cabin. The lantern light was dim but it gave Bob an opportunity to see the faces of the men below him. The man called Jesse James was about five feet eight or nine inches tall, straight as an arrow, high forehead, blue eyes, with dark brown well-trimmed whiskers. Seated on the bench with him were Ed Miller and Jim Cummins, also two well-known bandits, and also both known to Bob Ford.

Suddenly the board gave way, and Bob Ford came crashing down at the feet of Jesse James. Shots whistled into the loft above, for the robbers thought they were being attacked from above.

Ed Miller pounced upon Ford, throwing him to the floor and covering him with his body.

"Get out of the way, Ed, I'll put a quick end to this snooper," Jess cried.

"No, he's all right, don't do it!" yelled Ed.

"Why? Isn't he a detective or lawman?"

"Hell no, Jess, he's Bob Ford, brother of Charley. His uncle marmied Jim Cummins's sister."

"Kill him," suggested another of the band, "or let him tell us what he is doing here."

"All right, I was run away from home by a vigilante bunch tonight, and I found this place by accident. When I heard you approaching I did not know who you were, so I hid in the loft."

"That all you have to say?" asked Jesse.

"There isn't anything else."

"Ed, do you believe him?"

"Yes, I know the Fords, I am sure he's telling the truth."

"Then release him," ordered Jesse.

Turning to Ford, Jesse continued, "Do you know who I am?"

"Yes, you are Jesse James, leader of a band of reckless bank and train robbers. I would join your band, since it is not safe for me at home anymore and I'd like to get even with some of the people for causing us Fords so much trouble."

"You would volunteer to become one of us?"

"Yes."

"What do you say, Jim Cummins?"

"Hell, I know the Fords for years, even related in an offhand manner, I am sure he's all right."

"Are you prepared to die should you betray us?" asked the outlaw leader.

"Yes," was the solemn reply.

"I was at your home the other night with Ed Miller, and he introduced me to your brother Charley and Mrs. Bolton. They did not know who I was, since I was using the name of T. J. Jackson. I wish to also recruit Charley into the band."

The next morning Bob Ford found his way home, where he related his experiences to Charley and Cap Ford. Charley also agreed to join the James gang, and from that time on, the Harbison place was a regular meetingplace for the bandits.

Another scene of same room at Governor's Mansion.

Scene of room where Bob Ford talked with Governor Crittenden.

Oliver M. Spencer, Prosecuting Attorney.

Judge William H. Sherman, in the case of the Fords at St. Joseph, Mo.

Colonel John Doniphan, represented Fords at St. Joe.

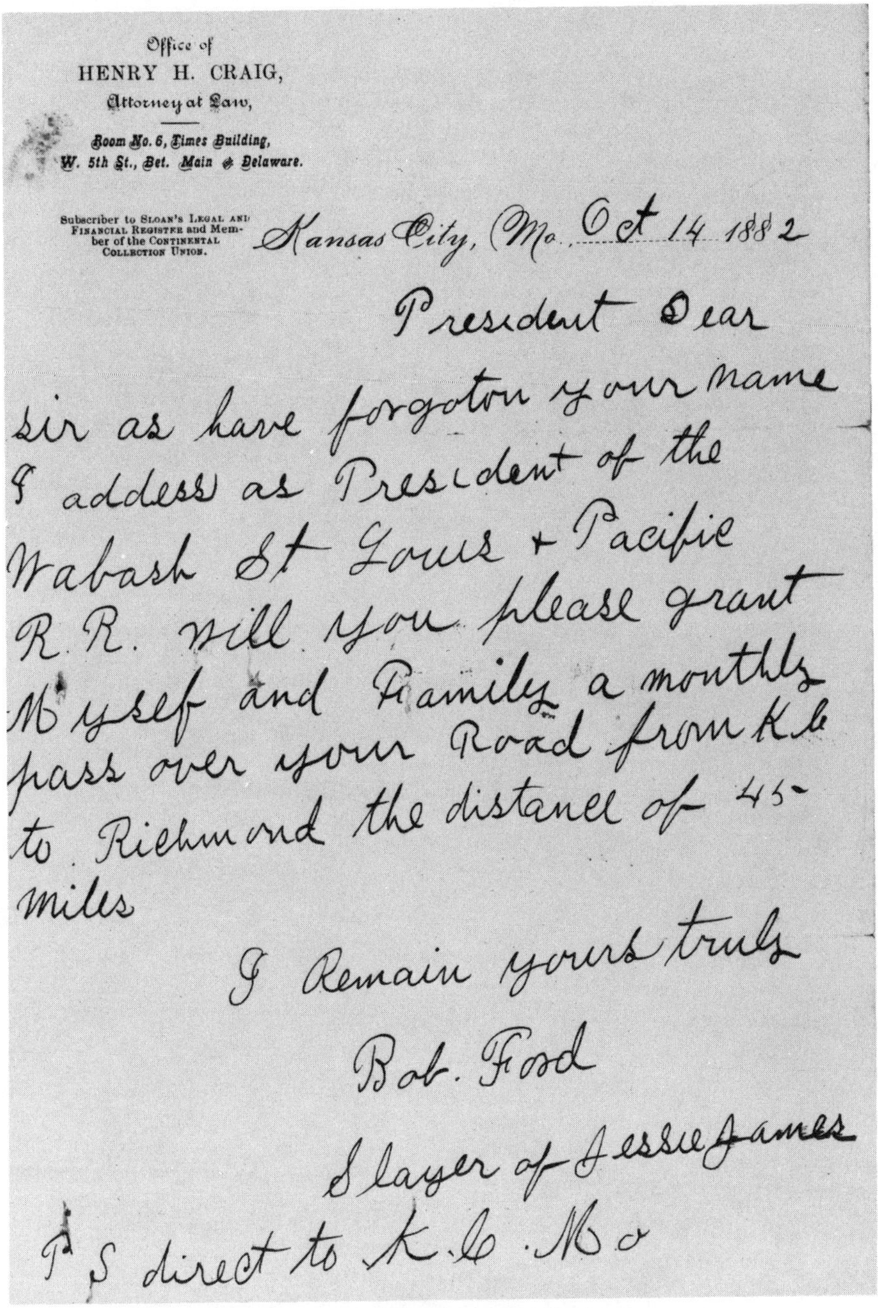

Office of
HENRY H. CRAIG,
Attorney at Law,

Room No. 6, Times Building,
W. 5th St., Bet. Main & Delaware.

Subscriber to SLOAN'S LEGAL AND
FINANCIAL REGISTER and Mem-
ber of the CONTINENTAL
COLLECTION UNION.

Kansas City, Mo. Oct 14 1882

President Dear

sir as have forgoton your name
I addess as Presicdent of the
Wabash St Louis + Pacific
R.R. will you please grant
Myself and Family a monthly
pass over your Road from K.C
to Richmond the distance of 45-
miles

I Remain yours truly

Bob. Ford

Slayer of Jesse James

P.S direct to K.C. Mo

Letter by Bob Ford to railroad company seeking free pass.

Courthouse, St. Joe, Missouri, 1880s.

Judge George W. Dunn, Plattsburg, trial of Bob Ford.

Joseph M. Lowe, Prosecuting Attorney, Clinton County, case of Bob Ford.

James W. Garner, Prosecuting Attorney, Ray County, case of Ford at Plattsburg.

Wichita, Kansas, 1880s.

Caldwell, Kansas, 1880s.

Caldwell, Kansas.

Upper Creede, Colorado, 1892.

7 • • •

The Winston Train Robbery

Winston, the scene of a train robbery on July 15, 1881, and the murder of two helpless, innocent men, and the robbery of the United States express car of the Chicago, Rock Island, and Pacific road, is today filled with wildly excited men, and the inhabitants of the hitherto quiet and placid village have not yet recovered from the first sensation of horror with which the infamous deed filled them. Nor is it likely that weeks or months will suffice to calm the excitement. The double murder was so cold-blooded, fiendish, and unprovoked, and the robbery so desperately done, that the affair last night would create food for speculation and material for conversation in a place where bloody deeds are frequent and sensations rife, especially, therefore, in a pastoral village like Winston. A place with such Sabbath-like stillness and wearisome, monotonous grind has few events of a startling character, an occurrence of the present nature is calculated to strike terror in the hearts of those accustomed to the commonplaces of life, and small wonder, indeed, that the details of the terrible affair were recited with bated breath.

Two young men who were so hurriedly cut down in the prime of their manhood were widely known and universally admired and respected in the town where their lives were wasted by the red-handed assassins, and the feeling of grief and sadness that is manifested by the entire community is earnest and sincere. The general expressed opinion concerning the villainous perpetrators of the horrible outrage is such that it is safe to hazard the conjecture that, if the ruffians are apprehended within thirty days, the hemp that will adorn their necks is already twisted.

78

It is not at all probable that the law's delay will be endured, but the primitive, yet sometimes righteous, judgment of Judge Lynch, spoken by popular clamor, will serve as writ and warrant for execution. Men armed with shotguns, rifles, and revolvers, and men armed only with a religious desire to see justice done, and evildoers brought to account, are scouring the country in all directions, and in all quarters, under the lead of sheriffs and peace officers, and traveling alone in bodies with no warrant save public spirit, and the present outlook is that the game will be run to cover in forty-eight hours.

Mr. Harry Thomas, an eyewitness and brakeman on the train, under Conductor William Westfall, said he took the train at Cameron for his home in Trenton, and between the former place and Winston he said the robbery occurred.

"All the shooting of which I had any knowledge occurred in the smoking car. I sat in the rear of the car as we left Winston. Several seats in front of me sat a tall, spare man with heavy, black whiskers; he wore a black slouch hat and a long lined duster, and had boarded the train in Cameron. Between me and their party Bill Westfall stood taking tickets from passengers. Suddenly the tall man sprang to his feet and shouted, 'Keep your seats; don't move.' I thought at first he was crazy and trying to play the Younger brothers and Jesse James act, and felt inclined to laugh at him. When I saw the two revolvers and heard them go off I began to think he meant business. Westfall, at the time the stranger jumped to his feet, was sticking a check-stub in a passenger's hat, and was leaning over. Before he could straighten up the revolver went off and I saw the wadding rise out of Westfall's coat. He staggered past me out on the platform, and that was the last I saw of him until I found his dead body by the side of the track.

"The shooting was kept up by the man who shot Westfall and by another man in the front end of the car. Where the last man came from I do not know. Another man who was standing on the platform was shot and fell from the car. The trouble began within a short distance from Winston station, but the second man was killed about three-fourths of a mile farther on. The train kept moving on at an increasing rate of speed for fully a mile. Then I shut off the automatic brakes and the train stopped. The point where we slowed up was the other side of Little Dog Creek trestle work. Mr. Ewing and I then got off the train and walked back to see what had become of Westfall. We found the body of the man shot last lying by the side of the track near the Dog Creek trestle work. It was nearly a mile from that place where

Westfall lay. His body had been taken into the section house, opposite where he was shot. Mr. Ewing and I put the body on the train going east and took it to Cameron."

When asked as to the character of William Westfall, Mr. Thomas was visibly moved, and stated that he was one of the most honest, upright, and companionable men he knew.

"I don't think," continued Thomas, "that the man shot Westfall intentionally. He was shooting recklessly around the car, and stood facing the south side so that he could command both ends. He shot principally into the roof of the car. When Westfall was shot the robber swung his pistol around over his head and fired as he brought it down, so that I think it was accidental. The bullet went in at Bill's right shoulder and came out on the left side of the chest, having passed directly through his heart."

C. L. Ewing, claim agent of the railroad, with headquarters at Winston, also took the train at Cameron, and gave his statement as follows.

"I had gone to the car in the rear of the smoker to speak to some ladies of my acquaintance, just before the shooting began; all at once the passengers from the smoker came rushing into our car wild with excitement, screaming that the train had been attacked by robbers. Everybody seemed to lose command of their senses, men piled toward the rear end of the car to get into the sleepers. They put their money, watches, and jewelry into their shoes, and crawled under seats, trampled over each other, and acted like insane men generally. I never saw anything like it, and will not attempt to give any description of the scene. Everything was supreme confusion, and description is impossible.

"I pushed forward to the smoking car, as well as I could, opened the door, and looked in; the car was full of smoke, and pistol shots going on all the time, and I concluded that I had no particular business in there just then. Soon the firing ceased, and the men in the car who had not already left came out. The last to leave the car was a little newsboy, who said to me as he came out, 'Did you know that Billy Westfall was shot?' That was the first I had heard of it, and afterwards, when Thomas had set the brakes, we walked up the track and found both bodies as he stated.

"When we got to Cameron, I went at once to the telegraph office, and called for G. F. Walker, the superintendent. After telegraphing to the police of Kansas City and other towns of the robbery, I caught

Mr. Walker at Washington, Iowa, and he gave orders by telegraph as to what disposition to make of the bodies. He told me to take West-fall's remains to Plattsburg, where his wife and three children reside, but to send it on this morning, since his wife is in delicate health, and I did not want to alarm her. I did not intend to let her know of her husband's death until this morning, but the telegraph operator at Platts-burg caught the news from the wire and reported it to her. The shock nearly overpowered her.

"Westfall was one of the kindest-hearted and best-natured men on the road, and very methodical in his business affairs. I searched his pockets at the station here and found his tickets, checks, and money all entered in proper form up to the minute of his death. He was a man of some property, owned the place in Plattsburg, where his wife and children live, had two thousand dollars in the bank and insurance policies on his life amounting to four thousand dollars. He will be taken down to Plattsburg on the next train, and the funeral will be held tomorrow.

"After leaving the smoking car, the robbers went into the baggage car, where they found Express Messenger Charlie Murray and the baggage agent, Frank Stamper. There were two who went in there. One of them put a revolver under Frank Stamper's nose and said, 'You get out of here.' Frank complied very readily. The other one put his revolver to Murray's head and told him to stay. This Murray did, and was induced to give up the combination by the threatened blowing out of his brains. There was three thousand dollars, I think, taken from the safe, which was all the cash it contained. A large quantity of bullion was untouched.

"As to the exact number of robbers in the gang I can't say, but I think there were not more than eight nor less than six. One of them took the train at Cameron. He was the man who shot Westfall. Billy and I took supper at Cameron, and this same man was there in the dining room. I think that two and perhaps more came through from Kansas City.

"Three more got on just after the shooting commenced, at Winston. Two of them went through the baggage car and told Ed Wolcott, the engineer, to hurry up his train. He refused to, and they began firing at him. Wolcott put out the lamps in his cab and returned the fire until his revolver was empty. He and Suggs, the fireman, then crawled along the boiler and hid on the pilot, after extinguishing the headlight."

The party furnishing these eyewitness notes stated that his relative next went to Winston. He described the area as follows: "The railroad tracks run down toward the east and, after leaving the depot, swing around on a curve to the southeast. About forty yards or more from the station is the section house; ten rods farther on is a steam shovel, used in excavating the bed for a side track, and about sixty rods farther on, or about one-third of a mile from the station, is the trestle bridge across Little Dog Creek; half a mile farther is a bridge across Big Dog Creek, but it is the stretch of track between the station and Little Dog Creek bridge that will remain forever historic. Between the section house and the steam shovel, the body of William Westfall, and just at the Winston end of the trestle work the remains of the murdered McMillen, were found. The latter, with his father, brother, and two Penn brothers, all of whom lived in Wilton, Iowa, had just boarded the train with the intention of going home. The senior McMillen is a contractor and had just completed a job of masonry at Winston, his two sons and the Penn brothers are stonemasons by trade, and had been working at Winston in Mr. McMillen's employ since early spring. They were consequently well acquainted, and Frank McMillen, a bright young man of about twenty-seven years, was a high favorite.

"At the section house Samuel Gibbons was contacted. He stated that he lived opposite the section house, heard the shooting, and ran to his door; he saw the conductor fall from the platform to the ground while the train was in motion; with the aid of others he carried him into the section house; he just breathed twice afterward.

"The way McMillen came to be shot was, I think, accidental," Gibbons went on. "He, with his partner, was sitting on the platform; a shot broke the window, and when McMillen lifted his head up to look through this window another bullet struck him in the forehead; his body was found at this end of the trestle work."

McMillen's body was brought to the Winston depot and laid out on the platform at 11:00 o'clock.

An inquest was held by Dr. D. M. Claggit, who in the absence of the coroner acted as such. Since no better account of the manner of McMillen's death can be had than the evidence before the coroner's jury, the substance of the same is given.

J. L. Penny, being the first witness sworn, said: "I live in Wilton Junction, Iowa, and I was on the Eastern-bound train on the evening of July 15; I was in the front car. Just after leaving the depot at Winston three men entered from the front door. Each was dressed in a dark suit of clothes with a high cap, and all were masked. The conductor was in the act of putting a check or stub in my brother's hat. Two of the men fired at the conductor. The conductor went toward the rear of the car, was in a stooping position as though he was shot. The men followed him, shooting at random in the car. The conductor and the three men passed out of the car at the rear end. I did not see the conductor after he left the car. The three men went into the next car, firing as they went. In few minutes they came back into the first car. They fired two or three shots as they came back through the car. One stood on the front platform and two went into the baggage car. When they first entered the car one said, 'Stop!' to the conductor. I heard several shots fired after they went into the baggage car. Frank McMillen and myself went to the rear platform of the car and sat on the steps; firing ceased. I raised up and looked forward toward the baggage car. One of them then fired at me, breaking a glass near me. I then sat down again.

"In a short time Frank McMillen rose and looked in at the window, and another shot was fired, and Frank McMillen fell forward off the platform. The train came to a stop at the Dog Creek bridge. While standing, I heard someone say, 'Move on further,' and the train moved on to Little Dog Creek bridge and stopped. In a few minutes three men passed me as I sat on the platform. They were going toward the rear of the train. They had revolvers in each hand and wore masks. One had a sack on his left side, and was putting something into it; it was papers and envelopes. They were on the south side of the track and went down the dump. I then got off in company with R. W. Penn and A. McMillen and started back to look for Frank. We came back toward Winston about a quarter of a mile; we met George Stewart and others with a handcar. A portion of us walked on each side of the track, looking for Frank McMillen; we found his body a short distance this side of the bridge, and some of the men put him on the handcar and brought him to town."

A. McMillen, being duly sworn, said: "I live in Wilton, Iowa. I was on the Eastern-bound train on the night of the 15th of July, '81. Shortly after leaving the depot at Winston three men entered the front car from the front door. I heard two shots fired at the conductor. The conductor started to run for the rear door of the car. He passed out of the rear door and I saw no more of him. Shots were fired in the front door of the car. I got behind the seats and remained until near Little Dog Creek bridge, where the train stopped at the bridge and I got off in company with the Penn brothers to hunt for Frank McMillen.

We found the body one-quarter of a mile west of Little Dog Creek bridge, on the south side of the track."

George W. Stewart, being duly sworn, said: "I was sitting by the boarding car about 9:45 P.M. and heard shots toward Winston. Myself and Mr. Steel started toward the shots to see what was the matter. We went about 150 yards before we met the train, and heard shots in the cars. We turned and followed the train with a handcar a little over a mile, and met Mr. Penn and Mr. McMillen, who told us that the conductor and Frank McMillen had been killed; so we started back to look for them and found Frank McMillen one-fourth of a mile west of the bridge. He was lying on his back five or six feet from the tracks. He was dead. We brought his body to the depot. I live in Cameron, Missouri, and am foreman of the construction gang at the Dog Creek bridge."

George Steele, being duly sworn, said: "I live in Cameron, Missouri, and am working on the steel gang three miles east of Winston; and I was sitting at the boarding car talking with Mr. Stewart about 9:45 P.M. on the 15th of July, 1881, and I heard firing in the direction of the bridge. I started there in company with George Stewart and others. We met the train about 150 yards from the boarding car. After waiting a while, Stewart came up from the east with a handcar. We went about a quarter of a mile west of the bridge, and found the body of Frank McMillen lying on his back about five feet from the track, on the south side. I then came on further looking for dead bodies, but found no more."

The jury, after considering the evidence, rendered a verdict in accordance with the facts brought before them.

Dr. H. E. Brooks, the coroner of Daviess County, arrived in the meantime, and with the same jury a verdict was rendered in the case of William Westfall. The verdict stated that William Westfall and Frank McMillen had come to their deaths by shots fired by persons unknown.

The grief of Frank McMillen's father was excessive and painful to behold. Instead of the merry quintette who started out the night previous with such pleasurable anticipation, the morning Eastbound train bore from the Winston depot four sorrow-stricken men accompanying the inert body of the fifth.

The local paper at Winston, headed by Mr. Martin, printed shortly thereafter an extra edition giving full details of the matter, and also stated that the robbers, after leaving the train, had mounted horses that had been hidden in a dense thicket about two hundred yards from the section house near the village cemetery. So great had been their haste to depart that they cut the bridle reins and left the thongs of leather dangling from the trees where the animals had been tethered.

On the night of the robbery the main portion of the people of Winston were attending a church social and immediately upon hearing the sound of the revolver shots ran from the church to the railroad tracks. Men and women rushed from their homes, all bent on ascertaining the cause of the commotion. The shooting had been done with heavy Navy revolvers, principally, and the sound could be heard a half mile away. After the bodies had been brought to the station a large number of men scoured the underbrush, but found no trace of the bandits.

The opinion of the people locally as to the identity of the robbers and killers is divided. Many thought the James boys were the leaders of the raid, and others did not.

One belief that had many followers is that the leader of the gang was a man who was at Cameron, Winston, and other places all winter under assumed names of Jones and Smith, and who, while in the employ of a farmer named Pefley, was arrested by a United States Deputy Marshal six weeks prior for various crimes, but who had escaped jail. However, the facts brought forth concerning this escapee led most people to finally believe that he was not the man at Winston.

Several days later a telegram was received by W. R. Hall, the station agent at Cameron, to the effect that a dispatch was sent from Station Master Wyman of Kidder, a town on the Hannibal road, six miles southeast of Winston, stating that seven mounted men had ridden rapidly by his house, and that it was believed they were the robbers. The impression was that they were making for the Crooked River bottoms, and would work their way down through Ray County to the Missouri River.

The remains of William Westfall were met at the depot by a large number of mourning friends who escorted the dead to the house of affliction and sorrow. He was buried at 9:30 A.M., at Plattsburg, July 17th, with full honors of the Odd Fellows Lodge.

William H. Westfall was born on January 8, 1843, in McLean County, Illinois, where his earlier years were passed upon a farm. Later, he was employed as clerk in several neighborhood stores; and in 1867 he was proprietor of a small confectionery at Kidder, Caldwell County, Missouri. In September of that year he married Miss

Eliza Sweeney, whose home was in Daviess County, near Gallatin, and at once engaged as brakeman on the Hannibal & St. Joe Railroad. After two years service in that capacity he was promoted to the position of conductor, which he retained until 1878, when he was employed for a few months as conductor on the Central Branch of the Union Pacific. It was in March of 1879 that he entered the service of the Chicago, Rock Island & Pacific Railroad, where he remained until the time of his death. He was a member of the Conductors' Union and also of the Ancient Order of United Workingmen, and also several other organizations.

The firm belief was that the triple crime was committed by the band of the notorious James brothers in pursuance of a vow made by them some years before. Everyone remembered the bombing of the James home, residence of Mrs. Samuel, their mother, at Kearney, Missouri. Frank and Jesse, on learning that their mother had been maimed by the bomb, and their half-brother killed, swore vengeance against those responsible. William Westfall had been the conductor on the Hannibal line at the time, and was in charge of the train that carried the detectives and the parties who stormed the Samuel home. It was thought that Westfall had been shot down for this reason, and it was not improbable that his death that Friday night was caused by a bullet fired from the pistol of one of the brothers.

Mr. Marcus M. Lowe, an attorney for the railroad, was asked whom he thought the robbers had been; this was his reply:

"I am confident they were headed by the James boys, and that their party also included Jim Cummins, Dick Liddil, Wood Hite, Clarence Hite, and probably the Ford brothers, Charley and Bob. Two of them have been positively identified as far as descriptions go by eyewitnesses to be Jesse James and Jim Cummins. Day before yesterday two men stopped by the house of Reverend Benjamin Matchett, three miles southeast of here, and dined with the family. They rode bay horses, both nervous, spirited, and Thoroughbreds. Last night they took supper at Mr. Montgomery's, south of Winston. Mrs. Matchett, in whose judgment I have implicit confidence, stated to me that she suspected that there was something wrong about her two guests, and for that reason she took careful note of their appearance. Remember that this occurred before the present excitement, and Mrs. Matchett did not know whom she was describing to me. One of the men, she said, was tall and spare, about five feet ten inches tall, brown hair, worn somewhat long, and thin about the forehead; he spoke in a slow, deliberate manner, and had a straight, thin nose, brown moustache, not very heavy, and side whiskers. Anyone who ever saw Jim Cummins will recognize the picture.

"The other man was of smaller build than his companion, and about five feet eight inches in height; he had a light blonde mustache and small, fuzzy side-whiskers of the same color; his nose was dished, or slightly crooked. This is a perfect description of Jesse James. Mr. Montgomery gave me a similar description. Sheriff Timberlake, of Clay County, told me that Jim Cummins and James's brother-in-law, Parmer, had been seen in Clay County within the last ten days. Polk Wells is wanted up in Sidney, Iowa, for horse stealing and bank robbing, the former offense having been committed on July 10th, the latter, the following night. Sheriff Sam Chandler, of Sidney, is here now looking for him."

There has never been any connection with Jesse James and Polk Wells insofar as is known, and it is doubtful that Wells had any part in the Winston matter. He was later captured and sentenced in 1882 for the robbery of a bank in Illinois and later for committing a crime in Iowa. He died in the Iowa State Prison in 1896, insane.

"Mr. Potts, the blacksmith at Kidder, put new shoes on two Thoroughbred horses," continued Lawyer Lowe. "Shortly after he again shod the first two horses in addition to three others. The men who rode them are unknown to him, but the two who came first and who came again yesterday are described as the two men whose descriptions I received from Mrs. Matchett. Five or more horses were hitched near the graveyard, and there is no doubt but the owners, with others, perhaps, are the wanted men."

"What has been done to capture these men?" my informant asked of Mr. Lowe.

"Sheriff Timberlake of Clay was up here today, and will send a posse of men through his county; Sheriff Crosbie will do the same for Daviess County, and the Rock Island offers five thousand dollars reward for all or a proportionate amount for the arrest of anyone of the gang. Constable Leard of Winston is out with a party of men, and numerous other lines are being laid. I received a telegram from Governor Crittenden today, asking what progress had been made toward the apprehension of the robbers."

At that particular time a messenger ran into the lawyer's office

and displayed a telegram sent by Agent Davis of Winston. Mr. Lowe
and James S. Conkling were, at that time, in a private office car,
parked on the siding at Cameron.

The dispatch informed Mr. Lowe that a letter had been found in
the thicket where the horses had been tied. The letter afforded valuable
clues, revealing that the robbers probably would head for Kansas City.
Chief Spears of Kansas City and Sheriff Timberlake at Liberty were
at once wired concerning the finding of the letter. The evening train
from Cameron, the same train, in fact, on which the murders and
robbery had been committed, brought Agent Davis and the letter
referred to.

The writing contained in the letter was poor and made more
illegible by the use of a purple indelible pencil by the writer. It was
at last figured out and read as follows:

Kansas City, July 12, 1881

Charlie: I got your letter all right to-day and was glad to hear
you had got everything ready in time for the 15th. We will be on
hand at that time. Bill will be with us. We will be on the train;
don't fear. Will be in somewhere at Winston. Have horses and boys
in good fix for the feast. We will make this point again [or work
this joint again—the writing was blurred] on the night of the 16.

All is right here. Frank will meet us at Cameron, look sharp
and be well fixed. Have the horses well gaunted, as we may have
running to do some time. Don't get excited but keep cool till the
right time. Wilcox [Wolcott] will be on the train. I think this best
to send to Kidder.

Yours till and through death

Slick.

This letter may have been dropped as a blind, or it may have
been a bona fide letter and lost. It was found in a very out-of-the-way
place where the horses had been tied.

An investigation of the train revealed the ceiling of the smoking
car riddled with bullets, and several large No. 42 cartridges were half
imbedded in the wood. The window that was broken when McMillen
was shot had not yet been replaced. The blood on the steps where
McMillen fell and the red spots on the floor told where Westfall's life
blood oozed away and were ghastly reminders of that awful night.

Toward the end of the day on July 17th, Winston appeared calm;
no robbers had yet been apprehended, but people were hoping that

in the next few days some new developments would occur that would put the perpetrators behind prison bars.

The Chicago, Rock Island & Pacific Railway offered a five-thousand-dollar reward for the arrest and conviction of the parties who stopped one of its passenger trains on the night of July 15th, killed the conductor and another employee, and robbed the express car.

President Riddle, of the Rock Island line, received the following dispatch from Davenport, Iowa, about the train robbery:

> After the train had left Winston it was boarded by twelve armed men. One party of the robbers took control of the engine, while another gang went to the smoker car and completely overwhelmed the passengers. Conductor Westfall met them at the front end of the train, when one of the robbers fired a shot which wounded him in the arm. He immediately ran to the rear of the car followed by two of the men. Two shots were fired at him in quick succession and he dropped dead on the rear platform. Several of the desperadoes entered the baggage car, and holding revolvers to the head of Express Messenger Murray, commanded him to open the safe. Murray did it and the robbers obtained between two thousand dollars and three thousand dollars. The train ran along about three miles under the direction of the gang and when it slowed up they departed.

Mr. Treat, manager of the United States express office at Kansas City, was questioned regarding the amount of money taken from the express car, but was unable, or at least unwilling, to state the amount. He said it might have been three thousand dollars or more, but that he would consider fifteen thousand dollars too high a figure. He would report nothing further, and, as in many other robberies, the newspaper and witness accounts usually were much less than the companies involved would be willing to admit. Agents of other express lines were interviewed, but they professed to be densely ignorant of the amount of loot taken. One of their number stated that it would be impossible to gain the desired information from officers of the express company, for it was as much as a man's head was worth to divulge. From the office boy to the officers of the company, all were under strict instructions to observe the most perfect secrecy. At the Rock Island office only meager details could be obtained.

Marshal Murphy had officers throughout the county notified of the robbery. He telegraphed to Liberty, also, but could learn no particulars except that Sheriff Timberlake was in hot pursuit. One report stated that the robbers had been overtaken ten miles north of Liberty by Timberlake, and were surrounded in an area of woods ten acres in extent. The report was unfounded. Marshal Murphy doubted the theory that the band was led by the James boys.

Chief Speers was of the opinion that the robbers were new hands at the business, and would probably be apprehended in due time. The chief stated further that a man answering the description of the black whiskered man was known as a professional in that region. He added that the country where the crime was committed was filled with desperate characters. Other peace officers had theories of various nature, but, in the end, none of the bandits was captured.

NOTE: In his testimony at the Frank James trial at Gallatin, Missouri, Dick Liddil stated on the witness stand that the following men were at Winston: Frank and Jesse James, himself, Clarence and Wood Hite, and Charley Ford. For some reason he did not mention Jim Cummins or Robert Ford, both of whom were also thought to have been present. Liddil further stated from the stand that Jesse James killed the stonemason, Frank McMillen and Frank James killed William Westfall, the conductor.

8 • • •

Pursuit of the Robbers after the Winston Train Robbery

On the morning of July 16, 1881, railway and express circles were greatly excited when the details of the Rock Island train robbery at Winston, Missouri, became known. The useless killings of Conductor William Westfall and railroad employee Frank McMillen added additional horror to the whole affair. The robbery was noted as being the worst train robbery in Missouri for many years.

During the robbery of the Kansas-Pacific at Muncie, Kansas, on December 8, 1874, the bandits had taken time to fire some shots at Conductor Brinkeroff, but no one was killed. When the James gang robbed the Missouri-Pacific at Otterville, Missouri, on July 7, 1876, again, no one was killed. And at Glendale on the Chicago, Alton, and St. Louis Road, the outlaws were content to rob the train on October 8, 1879, but did not molest the passengers. Several ruthless murders occurred during several bank raids perpetrated by the James gang, such as Gallatin, Missouri, Northfield, Minnesota, and Columbia, Kentucky. Why the robbers deemed it necessary to kill two innocent victims during this raid at Winston is a matter of conjecture and speculation.

As to who comprised the gang at the Winston affair there were numerous opinions, but it was felt that the gang consisted of Frank and Jesse James, Dick Liddill, Jim Cummins, Ed Miller, Clarence and Wood Hite, and possibly Bob and Charley Ford.

91

The robbery was well planned and executed. The bandits, knowing every foot of ground they had to cover, showed that they were not greenhorns but professionals. Many comments were made about the cowardly shooting of Conductor Westfall by the bandit in the smoker, many people claiming it was done to protect the bandits in the express car, others claiming it was an act of revenge because Westfall had been on the train that guided the Pinkertons to the James farm at Kearney in 1875. It was during the raid of these detectives that the mother of Jesse and Frank James was maimed, and their half-brother Archie killed.

Early on the morning of July 16th all sorts of exaggerated rumors were abroad with regard to the pursuit and capture of the robbers by heavily armed posses of men. Other reports stated that parties of armed men were enroute to Clay County to meet Sheriff James Timberlake, where he was waiting with a party of fifty men. It was known that Timberlake had gone to Cameron by way of the early Hannibal & St. Joseph train, and was returned in the afternoon as fast as a special train could bring him to Kearney. Armed men waited and started out from Liberty, all of the opinion that the train robbers would try to reach Clay County, where the lay of the land was well known to them.

Conductor Wyatt, who arrived in Kansas City the day after the robbery, stated that it was thought at Cameron that two of the bandits boarded the train at Kansas City and others at Cameron and Winston. At the depot and in the ranks of the railroad men it was thought that a portion of the gang was on the train from the time it left Kansas City, for the purpose of becoming acquainted with the layout of the cars. At Cameron, where the dark-whiskered man boarded the t.ain, he was seen to converse with two or three men who got off the cars, and then all three of them entered the smoking car.

John R. Treat, manager of the United States Express office at Kansas City, refused to give any details of the loss sustained by the company. He thought the amount secured by the robbers was not so large as had been stated, but until all the waybills had been received and the report of the messenger checked, nothing positive could be stated. Mr. Treat was very emphatic in denouncing the, robbery, stating that nowhere else in the country except Missouri could such a high-handed piece of business go unpunished. He thought that Governor Crittenden should at once issue a proclamation offering a reward for the robbers, dead or alive, since the robbers would always be safe unless something like that was done. Such a proclamation was issued a short time later.

Considerable excitement was created in official circles on July 16th, the day after the robbery, by the receipt of a telegram stating that a letter had been picked up near that point giving full particulars of the robbery and plans of the gang. The letter was dated Kansas City, July 12th, and was addressed to a certain name, and the letter went on to detail certain plans of the party after the robbery, and from it, it was thought the gang might go to Kansas City. With that idea in mind, the officials telegraphed the authorities at that point to be on the alert for members of the gang. Many thought that the letter was not genuine, that it had purposely been planted so to mislead the officers. Even so, Chief Speers of Kansas City made plans to watch every avenue in and out of the city, in hopes that some of the bold robbers might ride into his jurisdiction. The letter did not confirm pertinent information regarding the actual train robbery, however.

William Westfall, the murdered conductor, was a man in his early thirties, and a man who was well known to railroad men around Missouri. He was formerly in the employ of the Hannibal & St. Joseph and Central branch, but had been running a passenger train for the Rock Island for nearly a year. He was married and left a sorrowing wife and, two children. William Westfall was buried at his home town of Plattsburg on Sunday, July 17th at 9:00 o'clock, by members of the A.U.O.W. Lodge, of which he was a member.

Many telegrams were sent to the Executive mansion, urging the governor to issue rewards so large that the bandits would be forced to flee from the state. Governor Crittenden, however, was permitted to issue rewards in the amount as allowed by law, so other monies were promised by the railroads. Mr. A. Kimball, general superintendent of the Rock Island Road, issued the following statement:

The Chicago, Rock Island and Pacific Railway Company will pay a reward of $5,000 for the arrest and conviction of the parties who stopped one of its passenger trains near Winston, Daviess County, Missouri, on the night of July 15th; killed the conductor and another employee and robbed the express, or a proportionate amount for the arrest and conviction of any one of them.

When asked what action he was going to take in the matter, Marshal Murphy stated that he was waiting advice from Clay County. If he

received information that his services were required, he would activate
his men at once. Otherwise, he would await information that the bandits
were coming into Jackson County, his jurisdiction, and then he would
take action.

Of course, most everyone agreed that there was no man better
acquainted with the ways of the robbers or with the old gang itself
than Deputy Marshal Whig Keshlaer of Jackson County. He knew the
men and every inch of the ground they traveled. When asked who he
thought was among the robbers, he replied, "Well, I suppose it was
some of the old bunch, Ed Miller, Dick Liddil, Jim Cummins, and
perhaps one of the Coffman boys. I rather doubt that the James boys
were present. Perhaps the Ford brothers also were there. Winston is
on the prairie, and they probably wanted to stop the train at the edge
of the timber that surrounds Gallatin, and begins a few miles beyond
Winston. You know, the boys always had a fondness for timber."

At Liberty the news created much excitement. No sooner had the
news of the Winston robbery and double killing been received at
Liberty than most of the old-timers readily agreed that Jesse must have
been the leader of the bold bandits. With that thought in mind, Sheriff
James R. Timberlake secured a special train and raced to the scene
of the robbery and double tragedy. There he learned enough to convince him that the old gang had begun operations again. The outlaws
were reported to have gone south after the train robbery, and Sheriff
Timberlake found traces to convince him that such had been the case.
From Winston he went directly to Kansas City, where he gathered a
posse of reliable men, consisting of Deputy Sheriff Reed, W. H. Wymer, and Lank Adkins, to accompany him in the pursuit of the robbers.
He stated that he would pick up more fighters on the way to Clay
County.

Going to Winston, Sheriff Timberlake and his men followed the
trail of the outlaws along Crooked River, this route reassuring the
sheriff that his guess as to the identity of the robbers was correct. The
trail led to Greenville in Washington Township, then on to Clay
County, and then on to Kearney Township. Sheriff Timberlake was
under the impression that the whiskered robber who had killed Westfall
had been Jesse James; some others believed it had been Frank James.

One prominent citizen gave this remark, "Well, Jim Cummins was
seen in the vicinity for the past week or so. When you see him you
know others of the old gang are about, up to no good. They always
come back to their old haunts, but Timberlake will never catch them.

They will steal a wagon and hitch their horses to it, pretending to be Nebraska settlers and will move on unmolested. Once they reach the river they can cross over to Boonville and take their sweet time getting away. I know the sheriff is in high hopes of intercepting them, but I'll wager that he won't get close to the boys."

This time the speaker would have lost his bet, for Sheriff Timberlake was soon to experience the most hair-raising incident of his entire life.

"I'll either get him or he'll get me," growled the sheriff. "I'll tell you what I think. If we cannot get the men we want right here in Glendale and aroundabouts, we'll look elsewhere in Jackson County."

He then turned to Sheriff Thomason and told him to wire Kansas City, Lee's Summit, and several other points for a posse to trail the outlaw Jesse James, and for them to be ready as quickly as possible.

The sheriff did not expect his move to be a surpirse to Jesse James, who had spies all around—people who were willing and anxious to assist the famous outlaw for the so-called honor of doing so. And Timberlake was right in his thinking; Jesse was as familiar with the officer's movements as he was of those of his own men.

After galloping away from the scene of the train robbery, and when there was some distance between them and that spot, Jesse James motioned for the band to slow down. Just ahead of them lay a small creek, and into this Jesse drove his horse, followed by the rest of the gang, in Indian file. Up the stream they rode until at last they found themselves among a dense growth of alders, and there a halt was called.

The lair of the outlaws was not more than twenty rods from the main road and was surrounded by an open field. At first it appeared as if the bandits had made a bad choice, for if they were attacked, they could not hope to find cover for man and beast under a half mile at least. Yet the neighborhood of the Sni Hills, near the breaks of the Little Blue River, always afforded a good hiding place. Using his Civil War guerrilla tactics, Jesse James usually was able to provide security for his followers.

Bob Ford and his brother Charley objected.

"They will drive right here. Timberlake can follow the trail as well as you or I can."

"Perhaps that is what I want the posse to do," grinned Jesse.

"Then why did you take the trouble to hide your trail by following the creek in?" asked Jim Cummins.

"Your question shows that you do not know Timberlake as well as I do," grunted Jesse, his face drawing down into hard lines that boded ill for the representative of the law should he try to make Jesse a captive.

For the remainder of the day, the band loafed away the time in smoking and sleeping, for the previous night they had had little or no rest at all. But all during the day, Jesse James kept a sharp lookout toward the road. At last he came back to the camp with a smile on his face and threw himself down for a brief rest, not to arise again until the shades of night had fallen and a cool breeze blew up from the Little Blue River not far distant.

Taking a bit of hardtack—for Jesse would permit no fires—the desperado slipped away in the shadows, and was gone for more than an hour. That he was possessed of grave information of importance the others instantly realized from the actions of their leader. In the darkness they were unable to see his face clearly.

"Lead your horses up the stream and tie them as far to the west as you can. Be quick about it!" Jesse ordered.

Not understanding the object of their chief, the men hesitated, then proceeded to carry out his orders, Frank James nodding to do so as well. They were back in a short time.

The flats on which they were located were covered with a tall growth of rank flatland grass growing to the height of a man's waist, but all through which trails had been made by horsemen making short-cuts to the road leading to Glendale.

Bidding his men to follow, James led them out on one of these trails nearly parallel with the course that had been followed by the horses and within a few rods of them. Spreading his men out in the shape of a fan, Jesse told them to crouch down just off the trails and wait. He gave each man a few terse directions, then the band settled down to silence, waiting for the lawmen. And they had not long to wait.

Bob Ford had been lying down with his ear to the ground.

"They're coming," he announced, getting to his feet and peering over the surface of the waving field of verdure. A half dozen or more rifle barrels suddenly appeared about the tops of the rank grass.

Now the outlaws could faintly make out the forms of the body of horsemen, some fording the creek while others were moving up in the field. A small portion of the band rode straight up one of the trails leading to where Jesse James and his men were in hiding; so close did they pass that the outlaw chief could have reached out and touched their horses with his Winchester.

But the time for action had not yet arrived.

The long, blue barrels of the bandits' rifles had now sunk below the level of the grass tops. A slight commotion in the alder patch told the bandits that the officers had found their empty camp.

"Surround the field!" cried the sheriff. The command came sharp and clear, and the noted bandit smiled grimly.

Quickly the posse led by Sheriff Timberlake swung out; but instead of beating up the untrod grass, they followed the trails in. Smaller and smaller grew the circle in which they were moving, and as it contracted, the outlaws fanned out also, in a circle. But the latter, instead of moving in the well-beaten paths, worked their way in from the tall rank grass, inch by inch and foot by foot.

Now the posse let out a yell of triumph. They had discovered a hat poked just above the surface of the waving field. It was the hat of one of the desperadoes.

With a shout the members of the posse turned their horses in.

"Look sharp," warned Timberlake. "They will fire a volley into you the moment they can. Have your guns ready."

But the hat had been perched on a stick, stuck in the ground, to deceive the officers.

"Damn that Jesse James!" muttered the sheriff in an undertone.

Thus warned, the lawmen dropped the bridle reins on the necks of their mounts and threw their Winchesters down in readiness for instant action.

"Steady there. Now move slowly."

They were moving more cautiously now.

"Halt!"

"Not a man moved.

"Take aim!"

"Fire!"

A sheet of flame belched from the heavy rifles of the possemen as the weapons crashed in the midnight air.

"Once again!"

Another volley raked the grass all about the spot where the bandit's hat had first been observed. But now it had disappeared, and not a shot had been fired in return. Had they killed every man of them, Timberlake asked himself, or had they made a mistake?

"Spread out in a half circle and rake the grass with your fire. Then we'll fire until you have completed the circle!" was his next command.

If Jesse James and his men still lurked amid the rank growth they could not fail to feel the sting of the bullets. The firing had become almost incessant, bullets mowing down the grass like an invisible scythe.

Timberlake, with a sense almost as keen as that of the outlaw chief himself, felt sure that their prey was within easy reach. He was sure that they could not escape him now. The sheriff worked his Winchester almost with the regularity of the ticking of a clock.

The distant hoot of an owl was faintly heard in a lull of the one-sided battle. Instantly it was answered by a hoot from the opposite side of the field. But so busily engaged were the possemen in their battle against the rank grass, that they gave no heed to the weird calls —if they heard them at all.

"Keep firing and increase your range slowly so that not an inch of ground may go uncovered," directed the sheriff.

The firing was begun with renewed force. All of a sudden the landscape was lighted up with a bright glare that threw the forms of the men up in bold relief.

"The prairie has been fired!" came the alarmed cry.

"Make for the road. This grass will go up like powder!" warned another lawman.

Even as they whirled toward the road, a slender thread of flame ran along that side of the lot, rapidly shooting up into a wall of solid flame. With a cry of fear the manhunters dug in the rowels of their spurs and dashed madly toward the creek, only to be met there by a sudden blast of flame.

"We are trapped!" yelled Sheriff Timberlake.

"They have fired the whole prairie! It is more of Jesse James's damnable work; what shall we do?"

But Sheriff Timberlake was a resourceful man, and was not yet at the end of his wits.

"Dismount and start small back fires all around us. But be careful they do not get away from you. The moment you get a space cleared begin your back fires. We will outsmart those bloodthirsty devils yet!" he shouted.

"There's a place over there where the fire hasn't caught," called one of the posse. "Maybe we can get through there before the flames get to it."

"We'll try that first. Mount and ride for your lives."

The words had no more than left his lips before every man of the posse was in the saddle, digging the sharp rowels of his spurs into the quivering hide of his mount. Rearing and plunging, in a vain effort to clear their feet of the tough grass that wrapped around them, the frightened animals dashed away.

Few of that herd of faithful animals but sensed the danger that menaced them from those constantly increasing flames. The sheriff was leading the way. Steadily the flames were eating their way into the black gap ahead and closing it fast.

"Faster!" yelled the sheriff. "We can make it yet, but you will have to ride as you never rode before."

And they did. At last they reached the opening, just as the lapping flames were reaching out their all-devouring hands to complete the circle of death. With a mighty leap, Timberlake's animal cleared the barrier; he was safe, but the horse of the man behind him stumbled and went down, hurling its rider into the consuming flames.

The unfortunate man uttered a yell of terror, then his voice was stilled. The rest of the posse brought their horses up standing—the gap was closed.

Just then a rattling volley crashed from the opposite side of the wall of flame, and half of the horses of the posse went down and disappeared in the tall grass. Pandemonium now reigned among the manhunters. The sheriff had not yet come up and they were at a loss as to what to do next.

A pall of smoke had settled down on them, and their breath came short as they plunged blindly toward the center of the field, choking and reaching frantically for a breath of fresh air. But their cries of ·terror were growing less and less distinct and finally were heard no more. A second volley had dropped the rest of the horses, so that now they had no reliance save their own feet to carry them from the deadly element.

How many men perished never was published, some of them made it; some did not. In any event, a cry of horror went up all over the country on account of it.

Sheriff Timberlake—where was he? Had he knowingly deserted his men who had agreed to faithfully serve him as posse members?

As the lawman's horse leaped through the gap and to apparent safety, a rope sang through the air, and a great loop dropped over his head and slipped down over his arms. He felt its gentle pressure, then all at once his rapid progress was suddenly checked.

The sheriff had ridden into the trap that had been laid for him by

Jesse James. No matter what they said about Jesse's education, he was a match for anyone in a game of wits. His ability to get others to follow him was uncanny.

"Great! You got him, Jesse!" cried young Bob Ford, waving his hat.

With a jolt that, for a moment, seemed to knock the breath from his body, Timberlake was hurled from his horse and lay stunned and senseless on the ground.

"Get the horses," snapped Jesse. "We can take care of the sheriff later. I want him to see who's got him. Right now, we must get out of here, for in less than an hour the whole darn country will be after us like a pack of hungry wolves."

The fire was roaring over the field, still lighting up the landscape for more than a mile around them. It would draw scores of people to that location quickly. Haste was now imperative.

The unconscious body of the sheriff was quickly bound to the back of his horse, which also had been captured, and the bandits, swinging into their saddles, took him in tow. Their horses, fresh after their long rest, sprang away at a fast gait and were soon out of sight of the telltale flames.

The moon was rising as the band came to the precipitous banks of that section of the Little Blue. Never pausing for this, the desperadoes slid their horses down the steep sides and plunged into the water with a mighty splash, holding the pommels of their saddles with one hand and bearing their weapons aloft with the other, lest these become water-soaked. They could not afford to be without weapons at this critical moment.

As yet, there were no sounds of pursuit back there, but the light of the fires they had kindled threw all the sky into a red glow. No attention was paid to Sheriff Timberlake, who, more dead than alive, was being dragged through the water, his head submerged part of the time, and at others high and dry. But the shock of the rapid movement through the cool stream had brought him back to consciousness.

He tried to think what had happened to him. Then memory came back with a rush. He had been roped from his horse as, he was leaping the gap. Had the others escaped? He wondered vaguely how many of them this band had killed, but not the slightest inkling of the awful truth did he have.

The outlaws reached the opposite side of the river, drenched and bedraggled, as they scrambled up the bank. Jesse James, who had pinned a box of matches in his hat before crossing the river, lit one, and held it over the face of his victim.

"So, you are awake, are you, Timberlake? You'll wish you had never heard of Jesse James before we are through with you. Anybody know of a place around here where we can get some dry clothes?" Jesse then asked his men.

"Old John Jones and his daughter live about a mile farther to the west of here," replied Bob Ford, who was acquainted with that part of Missouri.

"Who's he?"

"A rich old miserly farmer."

"He'll do," agreed Jesse.

"And the daughter is a knockout, take my word for it," said Frank James, who was acquainted with the family.

"Well, if some of you fellows know this family, we'd better just split up for a spell and meet later at Hudspeth's place," said the outlaw chief. "Bob, you and your brother and Jim Cummins take Timberlake with you; the rest of us will divide up. That way we can better outwit the posse that is sure to come. And be sure the prisoner does not escape."

Charley and Bob Ford, Jim Cummins, and the prisoner left their comrades, following a trail that could have been followed on the darkest night.

Charley Ford rode up the trail to the farmhouse with Cummins and knocked on the door. An upper window was suddenly thrust open.

"What in tarnation do you want this time of night?" demanded a surly voice.

"We want to use your kitchen fire, for which we will pay you well," replied Bob Ford. "We are officers with a prisoner, and we were obliged to ford the creek in order to capture him."

"No, you can't come in here," snapped the old man viciously and slammed closed the window with a loud bang.

Then Cummins struck the door with the butt of his rifle, and all but wrenched that part of the building from its hinges. Once more the window was thrown open and a double-barreled shotgun was thrust out.

"Will you all get out of here? Clear out and fast."

Bob Ford's rifle cracked and the gun in the old man's hands was hurled free as if by some mysterious force, falling to the ground, where it exploded harmlessly. Jones was so stunned for a moment that he could only gasp. Another head then appeared at the open window.

"What do you ruffians want here?" a feminine voice wanted to know.

The three outlaws became all gentlemen at once, for they always were gallant toward women, although there is not much record of their being connected with them very much.

"Madam," said Jim Cummins, "we are officers of the law, and we have a prisoner here. We were obliged to ford the creek and all we ask is a chance to dry out by your kitchen fire and have an opportunity to question the culprit in quiet. We will pay you for the privilege, believe me. And we are sorry that we had to shoot the shotgun from your father's hands."

"Is that all you want? I can see no objection to such a request. If you will be patient a bit longer, I will come down and build a fire for you." The girl seemed right nice, they all agreed.

"Thank you, madam; I felt you would accommodate us," said Charley Ford, bowing. "And we all best keep a civil tongue in our heads unless they suspect things are just turned around. Stick a gag in the sheriff's mouth so he cannot give us away."

Cummins performed that task; shortly after, Miss Jones opened the front door and bade them enter. But they held back for some reason. "Madam, best we come through the back door as we would not want to drop water on your parlor floor," said Bob Ford.

"You are welcome through the front door; please come in," the pretty girl requested. She bowed politely and stepped aside as the desperadoes walked into the lighted room.

"You are most kind, and we appreciate your kind hospitality," smiled Cummins. Bob Ford nudged his brother, this was something new for Jim.

At that point Jesse James, Wood and Clarence Hite, and Andy Ryan appeared at the front door. The cold night had forced them to seek shelter, so they had followed the Fords and Cummins to the Jones place. Frank James, Ed Miller, and Matt Chapman remained outside, some distance from the house, since they were known to the Joneses and they also acted as lookouts for the rest of the gang.

"Oh yes, these are members of our posse," said Bob Ford to Miss Jones. "This is Sheriff Thomason," he went on, pointing to Jesse James.

"Yes, I am Sheriff Thomason, and we have been after this man for a long time. If you will excuse me, I will let them bring him through the other door."

"The other way, please," stated Miss Jones, as Jesse stepped to a door that he thought led into the kitchen. Correcting his mistake, he opened the door to the kitchen and, lighting a lamp, threw open the outside door and motioned his men to enter with the prisoner.

"Get some wood, Bob," said Jesse, "and we'll have a fire in a jiffy, and will roast him to a turn," he added significantly.

Timberlake was placed in a chair and some of his bonds loosened so that he would be more comfortable. His face was flushed with rage.

"What a horrible looking man," gasped Miss Jones, and at the same time backing away from Timberlake. "Who is he?"

"That, miss, is supposed to be the terrible outlaw, Jesse James!"

"Jesse James!" she uttered the name in almost a whisper.

"Yes."

The sheriff's face almost grew purple as he made a desperate effort to dislodge the gag, so that he might tell what really was taking place. He was amazed at this treatment from Jesse James; the outlaw hadn't done anything like this before. Perhaps he was becoming deranged, or just plain furious at being hounded by the forces of the law. Yes, Jesse was a criminal and deserved only what criminals of his type should and eventually did get.

Bob and Charley Ford and Cummins turned aside to keep from laughing in the poor girl's face. By this time the fire was burning rapidly and their soaked clothing was beginning to dry out. With seven men, beside the prisoner and the girl, bunched in the small kitchen, it is no wonder they began to dry out quickly.

"What are you going to do with the prisoner?" the girl asked.

"We haven't decided yet, miss. You know what we are supposed to do with a vicious train and stage robber like Jesse James."

"Oh, my goodness," the girl wrung her hands, "surely you would not kill him." This experience was all so new to the girl that she seemed almost ready to swoon.

"Well, something of that sort, I guess. Have you a place where we can safely store him for a spell?" asked Jesse, not wishing the sheriff to be present while they had their little visit with the pretty Miss Jones.

"We have a spare bedroom," said the girl.

"No, nothing with windows in it. How about the woodshed; is that rugged enough?"

"Oh, yes, I had forgotten that. It is a safe place. No windows and strongly padlocked."

"That will do," said Jesse. "Men, throw the prisoner into the woodshed."

This was done, while Jesse sat in the parlor, talking to the young girl, who seemed to have captivated him. She talked of some of her visits to California and like places, and he told her of his war experiences with Quantrill's raiders. Acting out his role as a law officer, he also told her weird tales of stalking desperate criminals and bringing them to justice. A mighty different role for the crude Jesse James, but he seemed to enjoy it.

"Are you really going to kill your prisoner?" implored Miss Jones.

"Such a matter should not concern such a pretty girl. He is a most desperate criminal. He has robbed trains and stages and may have taken many lives. We must act quickly, or his gang will come upon us and we will have a terrible fight."

At that moment, Bob Ford appeared in the room and beckoned his chief outside. Jesse saw that the young man was worried. Quickly Ford informed James that the lookouts they had left at the creek had returned with news that a body of men was approaching the other side of the creek. Jesse James placed his fingers between his teeth and three shrill whistle blasts echoed through the clearing. As if by magic, all the bandits were in the saddle, where they sat calmly awaiting orders.

Jesse looked at Miss Jones. "Kindly favor us by allowing our prisoner to remain in your woodshed a mite longer. News has come that some men are nearby and it may be the James gang."

At that moment, old man Jones entered the room and his daughter called him outside and introduced him to Jesse James. The old man was surly and had taken his good old time in dressing—hence his late appearance upon the scene.

"Father, this is Sheriff Thomason of Bay County."

"Glad to know you, Jones. I think you know a couple of my possemen. Sorry I have to rush now; we'll be back later."

The horses of the robber band plunged forward and were off like so many shells from a giant cannon. As they approached the creek, they slackened their speed and proceeded with more caution until within a few yards of the bank, and then halted. Halfway across the wide creek, a number of black objects were seen swimming toward the shore where the outlaws were hidden in the deep shadows. Jesse ordered his men to remain quiet until the party was close to the shore. Then he made known their presence.

"Hello, there, who are you?" he shouted.

"We are officers of the law looking for Jesse James. I am Sheriff Duncan of Jackson County, and have been searching for Jesse James and Sheriff Timberlake of Clay County for some hours now. Might we inquire as to who you are?"

"I am Jesse James!" roared the outlaw. "Take aim, men, fire!"

A volley roared out as a sheet of flame belched from the desperadoes' Winchesters.

The outlaws could not tell the effect of their firing, and cared less since it was apparent now that all pursuit from that quarter had been called off. They could have killed them all, no doubt, but this was not Jesse's way particularly.

They found the Jones home in complete darkness when they returned, and Jesse decided to not reawaken the occupants, telling his men to get some rest and that morning would be time enough to decide what to do with Timberlake. He did not necessarily want to kill the lawman, but certainly wanted to make an example of him in some manner.

The entire band had a restful night, and the first thing Jesse saw early the next morning was old man Jones coming out of the farmhouse. Jesse arose and went to the pump for some cool water and found Miss Jones also drawing water there.

'Good morning, Mr. Thomason," she smiled, "I trust you slept well."

"Very well, Miss Jones."

"We shall have some breakfast, but your prisoner cannot indulge in same with that horrible gag in his mouth."

"You prepare the breakfast; I'll see that he gets it."

"I do hope you have reconsidered about taking his life. He should be turned over to the authorities. You could collect the reward, too, then," remarked the girl.

"The devil with that; he has caused us lawmen too much trouble and he might escape us again."

"It seems so strange that you, as a sheriff, would take the law into your own hands, when you are sworn to preserve it and to prevent law and mob rule," argued the girl.

"Please, madam, the meal," interrupted Jesse. He saw that he was going to get nowhere with this woman, and had to act fast and get out of there before she realized the truth of the whole affair. Without further ado, the girl walked to the house. In the meantime, Jesse had obtained the key to the woodshed padlock and opened the door. It was still inky black inside and he began groping about for Timberlake. A sudden yell of rage told the others that something was wrong.

"What is it?" called Miss Jones.

At that moment Jesse James appeared in the doorway, not the smiling, agreeable young man, but now a vicious-looking outlaw, whose appearance now so stunned the girl that she shrank against the opposite wall of the kitchen.

"Is this some of your doings?" he at once demanded.

"I don't understand."

"Oh yes, you do. You were so anxious to save the life of our prisoner all along. Now he is gone, aided by you or your father."

"What in thunder is taking place around here?" Old Man Jones wanted to know as he stormed into the room, irritable as could be.

"Your daughter has seen fit to release a dangerous criminal."

"But I did not," she tried to explain.

"No respectable man—police officer or otherwise—has the right to take the life of another human being; I set . . ." Old Man Jones began, but his now thoroughly terrified daughter cut him short and quickly asked him to fetch a pail of water before he could finish the damaging sentence.

Straight as a string she now faced Jesse James. "Yes, I set him free and am glad of it; I could not see you stain your hands with the blood of this man."

"You lie! You are sheltering someone—your father, no less," demanded Jesse.

"I am trying to shield no one. He tried to tell me before I released him that . . ." and she stammered in utter confusion. Jesse knew he had her trapped; he knew that Timberlake would have explained the matter—and that he was the sheriff and this man standing before Miss Jones was the notorious and hunted outlaw, Jesse James.

Jesse wheeled and strode from the room. In several minutes he returned, dragging Old Man Jones by the collar.

"Last night I said you and your band was a bunch of ruffians, now I am sure of it," said Jones defiantly.

"But I did it," protested the daughter.

"You keep out of this matter," said Jesse, and turned to see Jones beginning to boldly walk toward the door.

"One more step and you are a dead man," warned the outlaw, and Jones heard the menacing click of a revolver hammer.

Jones turned, now frightened by the menacing weapon and the terrible look on the bandit's face. He knew now that here was a man whose like he would never meet again, and he was right.

"Jones, your time has come. You have done a thing to me that no other man has done and you must pay for it," declared Jesse.

With a cry of despair, the daughter threw herself at Jesse's feet and implored him to spare the life of her father.

"Can't you see he is old and feeble, and gradually losing his mind? He has not been right since Mother died several years ago. He probably did not know what he was doing, and what he did he thought was right. I am the only one he has left and he is the only one I have left. I promised Mother that I could care for him and watch after him after she was gone. Please understand."

But Jesse was stern and unyielding. His had been a hard life from the very beginning. He had had to fight his own battles, and to make his own way in a rough world, scorned at times, ridiculed at others. Now he felt, as an outlaw, he was in the driver's seat—for a while anyhow; seldom had he been called upon by a pretty girl.

Jesse James had not much pity, but somehow this girl affected him in a manner he could not explain. Perhaps it was the reference to the girl's mother, for Jesse was very close to his own mother. Yet, he did not wish to lose face with his followers and others who would become members of his notorious gang at a later date.

"Go to the woodshed, old man," ordered Jesse, and throwing the key to Bob Ford, instructed him to lock the man therein.

Jesse turned to Miss Jones. "I feel that there are some things you should know before I leave. I am not what I claim to be."

She looked at him in surprise.

"I am what is called a badman, an outlaw. I am hunted by day and by night, seeking shelter where I may, asking only those I know I may trust. It is too late to turn back to a decent life, too far gone to surrender to the law and take my punishment like a man. Many crimes are laid at my door that I did not do. A large reward is out for me, too. Strange that I should be telling you this, yet it seems I am compelled to do so. Perhaps I am seeking sympathy—who knows?"

"I understand," she said quietly. "Please go on."

"This man your father freed has hounded me for some time, and I knew him before I became what I am. It is hard to see those who once were your friends take the trail against you. Yet such is the case and so it must be and so it must end, in violence. I don't know if I would have killed him or not, but I doubt it. A good scare might have done him some good, but this man is very courageous and a good man and a fair fighter."

"If you are not what you claimed to be, what then?" she inquired with a tone of sympathy in her quiet voice.

"Miss Jones, I am the man the country is looking for. I am Jesse James!"

If Jesse expected her to recoil as having seen a rattler, he was mistaken; she looked deep into his eyes without flinching.

'I am sure they misjudged you. Perhaps your destiny lies in your life being what it is. My faith in you shall be confirmed by the fact that you have spared my father, but now that I have heard your story, I doubt if you could have killed the sheriff in cold blood."

"Perhaps you are right."

And that was the first and last time that the Joneses ever saw Jesse James until they later read the news of his death in the *St. Joseph Gazette* in 1882.

A sudden crash of Winchesters smote their ears. Jesse's form froze to rigidity.

"We are attacked!" he cried, springing back into the house.

"Attacked by whom?" inquired Miss Jones.

I don't know yet," replied Jesse. "But it is a large posse and from what I hear a mighty determined one."

"Who can they be looking for around here?" the girl asked.

"Need you ask such a question?" Jesse looked at her.

"Oh, I forgot. Then it could be only one person who brought them here."

"Yes, that's right, madam—the man your father freed—none other than our lawman friend, Sheriff Timberlake."

"So that's who he was. I was going to ask you, but couldn't get up the nerve to do so," stammered the girl.

"We'll give them a hot reception all right; see, some of my boys are swapping lead with them now."

And even as he spoke, a volley crashed from the heavy Winchesters of the retreating desperadoes, and several members of the posse appeared to have been hit.

"Have you a Winchester in the house?" asked Jesse.

"No, the only gun we ever had was the one Father tried to use on you. But you must hide and quickly, or they'll surely get you and kill you. Look at them now—some of the men are pointing to the house."

"Then all the reason more that I should leave," agreed Jesse, looking for a quick way out.

"What will you do?" inquired the girl.

"I must leave at once," replied Jesse, looking at her with a gentle smile. It was a different thing for Jesse to be worried about a woman or a woman worried about him, except his own Zee, of course. Perhaps his notorious reputation had hypnotized the poor girl.

"Oh, but you must be careful and you must return quickly," cried the girl.

"Why?"

"Becase I love you, Jesse James, for some reason myself I cannot explain."

"It is only fancy, madam," and he put her from him almost sternly. "I was never meant to be loved by anyone but Zee; you must cast it from your mind."

"Where are you going, how will you escape?"

"I don't know, but I must be gone before Timberlake gets too close to the house, for otherwise he will know that you have aided a criminal and you will find yourself in jail."

With that he sprang through the doorway. It was not long after that a yell from the posse told her that they had discovered him. She could hear their horses bearing down on him and she feared for his life. Yet, the girl knew little of Jesse and his workings. Calmly he turned to look at his pursuers, a revolver in each hand. Then at the psychological moment he leaped aside, the bullets of the posse plowing up the ground where but a moment before he had stood. Then the heavy Colts in Jesse's hands barked viciously and several of the foremost horses were brought to the ground, causing those behind to tumble over them in mass confusion.

After reorganizing, the posse divided into two parts, one going after the band and one taking after Jesse himself.

"There he is!" cried Sheriff Timberlake. "Don't let him escape. We'll get him for certain this time." The man who had so lately been a captive of the desperate Jesse James was intent on getting revenge.

A sarcastic grin played about the lips of the outlaw as he fired, and another posse member fell with a broken shoulder. Usually Jesse did not shoot to kill, for murder was not part of his makeup.

Then he did a mighty strange thing. He turned and sprang at the foremost horseman and dragged him from the saddle. Then he leaped therein and dashed off.

"Shoot! Shoot!" yelled Timberlake, almost beside himself with rage. "He is escaping!"

But in their excitement the possemen fired too quickly and as a consequence missed their target.

So rapid had been Jesse's work, and so unerring his aim, that the band was thrown into confusion; and in the brief respite before Timberlake could start them off again in organized pursuit, Jesse had roweled the frightened animal beyond pistol range. With a yell of determined rage, the manhunters again took up the chase.

Jesse was heading for a heavily wooded area that he saw lying to the northwest of him, and he figured that if he was able to get within the protection of the trees he would be able to make the river and thus escape his pursuers. He could hear the battle between his men and the posse raging off to the left of him, the crash of their rifles growing more and more intermittent. It told him that they were either getting away from the posse, or else that there were few of them left to offer resistance. Jesse would have ridden straight to them but for the fact that his pursuers were between him and the point where he heard the guns. He would be unable to go around and reach his own men, and he was too far-seeing to attempt it.

Instead of spreading out, Timberlake's men were massed in a bunch, so close they were together that their horses actually touched sides as they ran. Jesse smiled at the lack of leadership. That one man could so utterly disorganize a force of fairly well-trained men was almost beyond belief, and the fact that he had done so did not help to increase their peace of mind.

They were using their Winchesters on him now, but the shots went far of their mark, because he was following a zigzag course that made the mark doubly difficult to hit.

Sheriff Timberlake was in a fuming rage. Was he to lose his prize right from his grasp?

"Shoot! Curse you all, shoot!" he yelled. "Don't you see he is making for the woods. If he gets there, we shall lose him. Fire in volleys and you will stand a better chance of hitting him."

But try as they would it seemed that Jesse had a charmed life. At last his horse crashed over the brush fence and plunged into the woods. It was like the old guerrilla days all over again. Jesse smiled in satisfaction; he had made it. There were no trails to follow, and the density of the woods made his progress slow; yet he was well in the brush before he heard the posse at the edge of the clearing. Jesse recalled that either side of the river was lined with heavy timber, so he decided to make for the river. He could still hear the thrashing of the posse as he turned in the direction of the Little Blue.

Jesse kept going in the general direction of the stream when the dampness in the air told him that he was near, and so he was. In a few minutes he found himself in the open, with the broad stream slipping by at his feet. The river was rather wide at this particular point and Jesse wondered if he should try to ford it here and possibly give the posse a chance to come upon him in midstream.

There was no time to lose in making a decision, and he could not afford to lose this opportunity to escape. Suddenly putting spurs to the horse he plunged in. And no sooner had he reached the water before he slipped from the back of his mount; with a firm hand on the bridle and saddle pommel, he floated by the side of the plunging horse, which, under his urging, was making frantic efforts to escape from his continued grueling commands.

Before taking to the water, Jesse had drawn the cartridges from his guns and had placed them within a small, waterproof sack that he carried, all of which he stowed away in his clothes. Keeping his body as low in the water as possible, and steering a diagonal course across the river, he was able to shield himself from anyone who might chance to observe the swimming horse; but his eyes were continually sweeping the wooded shore line in search of the sheriff and the determined posse.

Suddenly a shout told him he had been discovered; and as he ducked beneath the water, a volley of bullets pelted the water like so many hailstones. His mind was working like a triphammer now. The posse had followed his example and were following alongside their swimming mounts. Quickly Jesse released his hold on the animal and began to swim underwater as far as he could in the opposite direction of the posse. Only at intervals did he allow his nose to poke above the surface of the water in order to draw in deep breaths of fresh air.

Although Jesse James was not an educated man, in times of emergencies he was no dunce. Quick as a wink he turned about and began to swim for the shore he had just left. He was safe from observation for the time being, for the posse did not turn to look back, but were intent on the horse of Jesse's, which was still trying to gain the opposite shore.

A shout of rage greeted his ears when his mount trailed up on the bank, riderless. In the meantime, Jesse had reached the safety of a fallen tree in the water and was watching the posse with a grin on his face.

"We've lost him!" shouted Timberlake. "He has escaped again!"

"Perhaps he was killed in the volley," suggested a member of the posse.

A fruitless search was conducted by the posse for some time; then apparently deciding that they had shot Jesse James, or that he had been drowned, the manhunters decided to give up the search and return home.

Later, Sheriff Timberlake told the people of Clay County a story that sounded hard to believe; yet it was true.

Also later, back at the Hudspeth farm, the outlaws got a big laugh out of it all while they divided the loot from the train robbery. This was one of the most talked about train robberies throughout the nation due to the unbelievable aftermath.

Sketch of Jesse James.

Jesse James, 1875.

Sketch of Jesse James.

Exceptionally good photo Mrs. Zerelda James Samuel.

Frank James, age thirty-three.

Old cabin where Jesse James was born—front view.

Newspaper item, Jesse's birthplace—mother in yard.

Overall photo of Jesse's birthplace, Zerelda Samuel and Mary James shown.

View of Samuel-James home just after Pinkerton raid.

School Jesse and Frank attended.

Jesse James home in St. Joe on original site.

Home at St. Joe where Jesse James was killed—as it appears today.

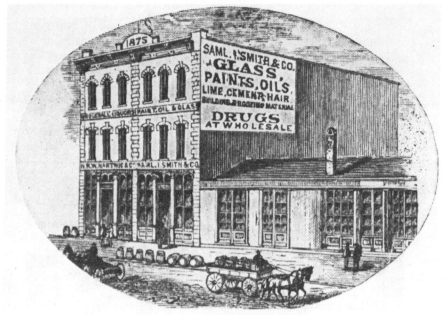

1880, corner and 3rd and Edmond streets, St. Joe.

From Studio photo, Mrs. Jesse W. James.

Taken from studio photo, Mary and Jesse Edwards James, children of Jesse.

9 ● ● ●

Jesse James and the Fords Capture a Bank Official

Early one spring morning in 1881, three well-dressed men approached the home of John Simpson, one of the wealthiest men in St. Joseph, Missouri. These men bore the appearance of prosperous cattlemen or rich farmers of Buchanan County.

One of the men, slight in build, about five feet, nine inches tall, gave the door clanger cord a yank, thus summoning the maid to the front door.

A stout, short woman opened the door and asked, "What is it you want, gentlemen?" What her question would have been had she known these men were actually Jesse James and Bob and Charley Ford, can be left to one's imagination.

"I am Thomas Howard," smiled Jesse James, "and these two men are my associates, John and William Johnson."

"What is your business?" asked the woman.

"We want to chat with Mr. Simpson," replied Jesse James.

The three outlaws were ushered into the handsome drawing room of the banker's fine home, the luxuries of which they were totally unused to, by the manner in which they tested the elegant upholstery of the chairs before finding suitable ones into which the three men thrust themselves.

"What a great place to live," said Bob Ford, with a sickly grin. He was a short, blond-haired young boy, but with plenty of experience under his belt.

121

"Forget such thoughts," reminded Charley, "this ain't for us."

Jesse James just grinned broadly.

The three felt safe enough. Their disguise would be sufficient to fool this banker, probably anyone else as well, since they were not known in that city at all.

"Well, gentlemen, what can I do for you?" asked the banker, as he stepped into the room. To whom do I owe the pleasure of this visit?"

Damn! What a pompous, overbearing bastard. This was the immediate impression the stout, prosperous-looking man cast upon the three visitors.

Jesse's eyes glittered with amusement, keenly sizing up the banker, as did his two companions.

"Don't know about the pleasure, but I am Mr. Howard and these men are the Johnson brothers as I stated before. I have a cattle ranch near the Andrew County line, and wish to discuss some business with you."

It was easy to see that the banker was in a mood to make some easy money. As he rubbed his chubby hands together he repeated, "What can I do for you?"

"Well, let's put it this way," said Jesse, as he winked at the Fords without the movement being detected by the moneylender. "We plan to go to Colorado in the morning to buy up a bunch of cattle. It is an opportunity to make a lot of money, since this particular place is going under the sheriff's sale and the stock should sell for perhaps less than half price."

"I suppose you need some ready cash to make the purchase."

"That's right."

"How much do you require?"

"Fifteen thousand dollars."

"My, that is a lot of money," said the banker, raising his eyebrows noticeably. "I'd have to have security, of course."

"Of course, my ranch," smiled Jesse, with the Ford brothers hardly able to keep straight faces.

"That sounds like fair collateral. I'd like to examine your deed, naturally," smiled the banker, dollar signs dancing in his eyes.

"Sorry, I do not have it with me, it is at the ranch."

"It is after banking hours," objected the man, "but I have heard of the Howard ranch, and I should have a look at the property. I could not allow you to have the money right now. You said you were leaving in the morning?"

"That is correct. But I have a fast horse and a rig outside. Why not come along with me now and we can return in the early evening?"

"But the money—" protested the banker.

"We'll wait for you here until you can get it from the bank," suggested the noted outlaw. "Also, you can have the papers made out while we are gone, or you can have them made out and taken along so that I can sign them."

"That is a good idea. There are four of us and I don't believe any bandit will molest us on the way. Besides, it is a nice drive to Clay at this time of the year; it's only some thirty miles."

Jesse nodded. Bob and Charley Ford turned their heads to one side to keep from laughing out loud.

Mr. Simpson gave Jesse a set of papers to be taken to the Justice of the Peace so they could be properly notarized and recorded.

"That will save time and I'll get the money and meet you back here at my home."

"Fine by us," agreed the three daring robbers.

The three actually did go to the justice and had a mortgage drawn on the property, using a fictitious place for the farm. When the papers had been made ready for signatures of all parties, the three outlaws went back to the home of the banker. There he sat on the porch, puffing away on a fat cigar, an envelope containing the money stuffed in a safe pocket.

Soon the four men were driving briskly from St. Joseph toward the little town of Clay, banker Simpson in a good mood.

"Been a long time since I've been this way; sure hope you know the way," he grinned.

This was much to Jesse's liking, since he had intended to turn off the main road long before reaching their proposed destination, and he was pleased to see that the banker was unaware of landmarks and the like.

Many subjects were discussed as they rode along. Eventually the conversation turned to the subject of Jesse James and his ruthless band of outlaws.

"I remember Jesse James very well," grinned the outlaw. "I was once his prisoner and would have been killed had I not escaped."

"I've read some terrible things about him," chimed in the youthful Bob Ford. Charley said nothing at that point.

"Well, I'll tell you this," bragged the banker, "they'll get him soon; there's a posse on his trail this very moment."

"They'll never take him," assured Jesse.

"Why not? What makes you so cocked sure?"

"Because Jesse James is slick as an eel. He'll outwit those lawmen again as he always does, mark my words."

"I'm surprised at you, you seem to talk like you'd be glad if he got away."

The Ford brothers kept quiet, for fear they might queer the little game.

"He's a holy terror and woe to the man who sets a posse on his trail. Jesse is very revengeful, don't forget that."

The banker started, apparently well shaken in his boots.

"What do you mean?"

"Well, I sure wouldn't want to be the one who tries to turn him in, that's all."

Jesse James and the Fords seemed to take pleasure in the man's apparent fear, for he was trembling visibly.

"Well, anyway," continued Jesse, "whoever set Seth Jones onto Jesse's trail is going to be mighty sorry."

The fat banker almost rolled to the ground and Jesse had to reach out to grab him to keep him from falling from the front seat of the buggy.

"What's that?" exclaimed the banker. "What did you say?"

"I said Jones," replied Jesse, smiling. "What's there to get so excited about?"

"How'd you know about that?"

"Just a wild guess. I know Jones and the other day he told me he was going on a manhunt so I presumed he meant Jesse James."

"Oh, maybe so, maybe so . . ." stammered the banker.

Banker Simpson was so instilled with the fear Jesse had induced that he had no reason of time or direction. It was nearly twilight when they drove into a small clearing with a small house on it.

"I want to speak with my foreman before we go to the house," said the outlaw leader. "Here, have a cigar, it will calm your nerves."

"Hey, Dick," cried Jesse, "C'mon out."

Dick Liddil poked his head through the door and welcomed the men to his place.

"No doubt Mr. Simpson will want to check some things with you, Dick, he's going to loan me flfteen thousand dollars on the ranch. Oh yes, Mr. Simpson, Dick is my foreman."

No sooner had they entered the place, than Jesse softly closed the door and locked it, standing with his back to it.

Simpson at first had no cause for alarm, and on Dick's invitation, seated himself in a chair and began to ask questions about the ranch. All at once he noted there was another man standing in the shadows of the room.

"Had we not better discuss this in private?" asked the banker.

"Oh, it is all right; that man is my brother."

"Bring in a lamp, Dick, we must get the business done since Mr. Simpson will want to return home yet tonight, I suppose."

"Yes, by all means. I did intend to remain overnight, but it is best that I start back immediately after the transaction has been completed."

As the lamp rays dispelled the shadows around the room the banker could see several other heavily armed men standing around.

"Don't be alarmed," said Jesse. "These men are all my hired hands."

"I must say, Mr. Howard, you certainly cater to an odd and rough-looking bunch of ranch hands," said Mr. Simpson.

"Well, anyway, this here man is my brother, Frank."

By now the banker was getting madder and madder.

"I said this is my brother Frank . . . Frank James!"

Had a bomb exploded in the room, the astonished banker would not have been more shaken up.

"Frank James . . . you can't mean the outlaw Frank James."

"Exactly," replied Jesse, "and the two men who came to your home with me are Bob and Charley Ford."

"Then you must be . . ." stammered the shaken man.

"Yep, you hit it right. I am Jesse James, at your service."

The banker sank back into his chair, weak and trembling.

"Did I not tell you that Seth Jones would never take Jesse James, and I might add that he is dead as he'll ever be."

"You mean to kill me?" gasped the poor man.

"That depends. You deserve more than that, but since we have made a business bargain, I mean to keep it."

"A bargain?"

"Yes, the loan on the ranch. You can have the ranch if you can persuade the real owner to give it to you."

"Well, Mr. Banker," said Bob Ford, "you big money people have posted rewards for Jesse if he is apprehended. Well, you got him, so pay the reward."

"You would rob me?"

"No, just completing a business transaction as we agreed."

The banker knew he could expect no sympathy from the men in that room; the only thing he could do was to turn over the envelope to Jesse James.

"Count it, you cannot trust bankers," said Jesse.

Frank James did so and reported the fifteen thousand dollars intact.

"Now, come with us," Jesse ordered the unfortunate victim, as he jerked the banker from his chair. "Make a sound and you die."

Late that same night the jailer at the Clay jail was awakened by a loud pounding on the door.

"C'mon on out, sheriff, we've got a prisoner for you. He's bound and gagged so he cannot cause any trouble or create a disturbance."

As the excited jailer opened the door he exclaimed, "Sheriff ain't here this time of night. Who's your prisoner? Who are you?"

"I'm the sheriff of Clay County and have an important prisoner here. We want him held until morning and we'll then be on our way."

With the help of the jailer, Jesse threw his prisoner into a cell, still bound and gagged.

"Remember, now, he's not to be touched until I return."

"Yes, but that is somewhat irregular. Who is he, anyhow?"

"Will you keep it a secret until we have left town?"

"Of course."

"The prisoner is none other than Jesse James. We cannot let the word get out or his brother and gang members would be upon us at once. Understand?"

"Good heavens, you can't mean it," said the jailer.

"Yes, and if you don't want to be killed tonight by his men, you'd best keep quiet and keep away from him."

In a little while the daring band of robbers dashed from town, laughing and roaring at the joke they had played on money-bags Simpson.

It was no laughing matter for poor Simpson, bound and gagged as he was, propped up against the cold wall of his cell. The jailer respected Jesse's orders and did not approach the prisoner. However, when the "sheriff" did not return, he decided to summon his own boss.

The sheriff at once recognized Banker Simpson and set him free.

"Best joke of the year, Simpson. How the hell did you get in such a fix?"

"I was put in there."

"I can see that, man, but who was the man who did it?"

"Jesse James brought me here and told your man that I was Jesse James."

Banker Simpson was the butt of many jokes of the whole state of Missouri for many weeks to follow. Although asked many times what had brought about such a situation, he refused to tell anyone about the matter of the fifteen thousand dollar loan to Jesse James.

10 • • •

Bob Ford Visits Commissioner Craig and Saves a Girl's Life

A short time after the Winston robbery, and a few days before the Blue Cut affair, a young man called at the private office of Police Commissioner Henry J. Craig of Kansas City, and asked to see him.

"The commissioner is very busy today. What is your business with him?" asked a clerk in the outer office.

"My business is personal and most urgent."

"Write your name on this piece of paper."

Bob Ford took the piece of paper and in a clear, bold hand simply wrote "Bob" thereon.

Puzzled, Henry Craig allowed the young man to be admitted.

"What is your business with me, young man?"

"Do you want to capture Jesse James?"

Certainly an odd question from a mere youth. It excited the imagination of the commissioner.

"Naturally, we do."

"What will be paid?"

"Governor Crittenden has offered five thousand dollars for him."

"Dead or alive?"

"You would have to speak with Governor Crittenden about that stipulation. Nothing was said of it in the last reward proclamation issued from Jefferson City."

"He can never be taken alive."

"I think he can," disagreed the commissioner.

"You are wrong. I know he cannot."

"Can you take him dead?"

"Perhaps, with the proper opportunity presenting itself."

"Call again in a few days."

"That I will do and I can assure you the reward for Jesse James will be higher then," said Ford.

Commissioner Craig sat in silent meditation long after the brazen young man had left.

"Such a mysterious young man," he finally muttered.

After leaving Kansas City Ford made his way to the stable on the Harbison place in Ray County, their base of operations. There he obtained a fresh mount and started down the long lane from the barn to the woods. It was safer to ride the wooded trails than it was to be seen on the country roads.

Familiar with every path that wended through the forest, Bob Ford soon was in the backyard of the Hudson place.

"Perhaps some of the boys are around," he mused. "I'd better let them know that I'm here, too, since they might think I'm a Pinkerton or an officer of the county."

With that Bob Ford gave four hoots of the nightowl. He waited several minutes, receiving no response to his signal. Bob finally decided that the James boys were not in the immediate vicinity.

Before Ford could decide on whether to repeat the familiar call again or not, he heard a window raised and a woman call out, "Who's there? Who's in the barnyard?"

"It's Bob Ford, Jane."

"Good grief! I thought you were a hundred miles from here. What brings you back to Ray County?"

"Many things, Jane. Also, I wanted to congratulate you on your recent marriage. Martha told me about it."

"You're the only one of the bunch I've seen for a few days. Put your horse up in the barn and come up to the porch roof."

"Why? What's the trouble, Jane? Is there a lawman waiting in the kitchen?"

"Heavens no, Bob, but George is on a drunken rampage again. I'm afraid to go downstairs and he told me I'd better not," replied the young woman, apparently much afraid.

Bob thought the matter needed looking into. He knew that Jane was a high-spirited woman, usually not afraid to stand up for her rights before anyone. "George must really be in a terrible mood," he muttered to himself.

Ford walked his mount to the barn, where he unsaddled it and gave it some hay and barley. He then walked silently to the house and scrambled up the latticework to the roof of the porch, from which point he could easily reach the window from where Jane had called to him.

"Oh, Bob!" she cried. "George has been awful these past few days. He promised never to drink another drop after our marriage; this is what I get for listening to him. My heart is broken."

"Well, Jane, you should never have married him, why don't you leave him right now?"

"Been thinking about that."

"Tell me what happened. George used to be a rather sensible guy as I can recall," said Bob.

"I can agree with that. Well, anyhow, when one of his aunts died not too long past, he came into several thousand dollars or so. That gave him the idea to go to Kansas City or Independence to buy some cattle and raise them here."

"Sounds like a good plan to me," interrupted Bob.

"Yes, I was thrilled with the idea, too," continued Jane Hudson, "but he refused to allow me to accompany him on the trip; said it was no job for a woman. I wish now that I had insisted."

"Why? What happened?"

"Well, when George got to Kansas City he met some of his old cronies. They enticed him to take a drink and then more and more. Before long, George was soused and bragging of all the money he had. They told him he could make a mint with such an investment. They took him to some crooked gambling hall where he lost it all."

"Who were these men?" asked Bob.

"No one knows, and George won't tell me."

"Perhaps if I meet with them one day I can get the money back."

"To make matters worse, when George did come home Frank and Jesse James and your brother Charley were in the house, discussing some matters. George guessed who they were and I am sure he saw them many times before. He rode into town and said he was going to tell the sheriff they were here."

"Did George really tell the law?"

"Yes. They came later with a posse of quite a few men. Jesse wanted to follow George and kill him before he could get to town, but they just saddled up and left."

"What happened then?"

"After the posse left, George became so mad that he took his rifle and began firing it everywhere. Lucky I was out of his way or he'd have killed me sure."

"Why didn't you run off to our place or elsewhere?" asked Bob.

"I couldn't. He ran me upstairs and told me to stay there. That was almost a day ago. I'm still here."

"Did the boys say where they were going?"

"Jesse said they probably would stop off a spell at Tom Clark's place, and if I got away to come there."

"All right, Jane, gather some of your belongings while I take care of George."

"Don't kill him," pleaded the girl. "He's still my husband, and the boys did get away from the posse all right."

"Damn!" muttered Ford, "If you women ain't the limit. Here he almost kills you, squanders the money, sicks a posse on our friends; yet you still plead for his worthless life."

"I know that I would be better off without him," agreed Jane, "but I'd never get over the thought of a dear friend like you killing my husband, regardless of his manners."

"Oh, all right, but let's get moving. I've got business with the boys over at Clark's."

With some of her clothing in a pillowcase, the girl crawled through the window onto the porch roof, then down to the ground, being assisted by Ford.

Bob Ford saddled up his horse and one for Jane. However, before they could ride off into the darkness, the figure of George Hudson appeared at the window so recently vacated by Jane. He was angrily waving two pistols.

"Stop!" cried Hudson. "Or I'll shoot!"

Bob Ford pointed his rifle toward the window.

"Don't, Bob, let him shoot. He cannot hit the side of a barn the condition he's in."

Bob Ford and Jane Hudson had just started to ride from the barn lot when a pistol shot rang out.

"My God! You've shot me!" cried Jane. "Bob, I think it's a fatal shot." With that the girl reeled and fell to the ground.

Bob Ford snapped off two fast shots toward Hudson. The man

straightened up, then pitched headlong through the window to the ground. He was dead!

Ford quickly picked up the limp form of the girl and discovered she had been shot in the shoulder. It was not a fatal wound, but the shock had rendered her unconscious. Quickly he gave her a little whiskey, reviving her.

"Bob, what happened? I feel faint, just awful."

"You should, you have a shoulder wound."

"Did the sheriff attack us?"

Not wanting to inform the girl that he had killed her husband, Bob replied, "Yes, that's it, we were fired upon by several men passing by, but my guns drove them off quickly. We'd better get to Clark's right off."

Jane's mount had darted into the woods so Ford raced back to the barn, saddled another horse, and brought it to the girl. Jane was too dazed to know what was going on, so Bob told her to hold onto the saddle horn and he would take them to Clark's.

The six miles between the Hudson place and the Clark home was covered in good time. In a nearby woods Ford gave the signal—four hoots of the nightowl. This time the calls were answered. The door of the house opened and four men walked out.

"That you, Bob Ford?" asked Jesse James.

"Yes, Jess."

"Who's that with you?"

"Jane Hudson."

"What the hell did you bring her along for?"

"Never mind. Help me take her into the house. She's wounded. I'll give you the story later."

"Have a run-in with that posse?" asked his brother Charley.

"Dammit! I told you I'd tell you later. Now help me get her into bed."

Jane Hudson was carried gently into the bedroom, where she was placed on the bed, her clothing loosened, and the wound bathed and treated. She was then covered with blankets. This chore completed, Bob Ford, the young bandit, rejoined the Jameses and his brother and several other members of the gang in the kitchen of the Clark house.

Quickly and concisely Bob related what had happened, informing the men not to advise Jane that she was a widow.

That matter set aside, the robbers began discussing plans for another holdup. Charles Ford, who had been standing near the window, said quietly, "There's a bunch of riders coming through the woods. No doubt they'll stop here."

"Dammit! They can't even let us plan in peace!" cried Jesse James. "I'd just as lieve meet them right now and shoot it out."

"Hell, no, Jess, there must be fifty of 'em," disagreed brother Frank, as well as the others chiming in with the same sentiment.

"What about Jane?" asked Bob Ford. "Do we take her along?"

"What for?" asked Jesse. "They won't hurt her and she's no outlaw. We'll leave her here for her own good."

They all agreed, so Bob Ford told Clark to watch after her.

"Let's have some fun with the posse," suggested Jesse.

"How can we do that, they've got enough fire power to wipe us all out for good. If we shoot they'll know just where we are," complained Frank James.

"Who said anything about shooting at 'em?" grinned Jesse.

On reaching their horses, the bandits turned toward the lane through which Bob Ford had just before approached the Clark house. The men followed, anxious and curious to know what their leader had in mind. Upon reaching the entrance to the lane, which had two large posts on the sides, Jesse directed Bob Ford to take his lariat and tie one end around the upright, about ten inches or so from the ground, and then run the rope to the other post across the path, wind it around the post, then bring it back again to the other side of the path. That left a double rope across the path the posse must use.

"That ought to upset them plenty," grinned Jesse.

Bob Ford chuckled. "Jesse, let's wait to see what happens. This should be hilarious."

The men thought it was a good idea, so they hid their horses and waited behind a stone wall that bounded the lane. It was also decided to startle the posse more by firing a couple of volleys over their heads, Jesse giving strict orders that no lawman should be shot.

"We just want to scare the hell out of them," reminded Jesse. "So be sure to fire over their heads."

So near were the lawmen that the sounds of their voices could be heard distinctly, and it was quickly determined they were moving forward at a brisk gallop.

In a few minutes the moving forms of the possemen grew visible as they dashed through the lane, thinking they soon would have the terrible outlaws in their grasp. Soon they were near the trip rope.

Suddenly the animal hoofs came in contact with the strong rope.

In a mass of noise and confusion they struck the ground, piling upon each other until a vast, tangling heap was the result.

"Check your speed!" yelled one of the posse members, as the others rode forward. But it was too late. More of the mounted men were thrown into the heap of animals and men already on the ground.

To add to the confusion the pistols of the outlaws roared. Every lawman thought he had been shot. After a few minutes of this added bedlam caused by the laughing outlaws, Jesse and his men rode off into the night.

"It would be better that we split up again," suggested the bandit leader, and this was done.

Bob Ford told them that he was not really suspected of being connected with the James gang as yet, so he was going to ride on to Seybold's Tavern, near Excelsior Springs, where he had spent many pleasant hours during his early years.

Some of the bandits found their usual sanctuary in the Crackerneck region of Missouri. This area was west of Blue Springs, Missouri, and southeast of Independence, Missouri, and a little north of the old U.S. Highway 40. The old railroad maps will show it as Selsa Station on the C & A, where some train holdups occurred.

11 • • •

The Blue Cut Train Robbery

On the morning of September 8, 1881, great excitement prevailed in almost every town along the right-of-way of the Chicago & Alton Railroad due to the reports of another daring robbery having taken place on the evening of the 7th.

Not only that, but reports had circulated that several of the train robbers had already been caught. That seemed an impossibility—to most Missourians especially. Yet Creed Chapman and John Bugler had been arrested as having been part of the gang who had robbed the train a few miles from Independence, Missouri, near Glendale, the scene of another such robbery in October of 1879. These two men were arrested by Sheriff Casen and his posse from Saline County, near the scene of the robbery. It was said that a brother of Chapman told the officers about Creed's participation in the affair. With further information being obtained, it was expected that other arrests would follow. When arrested both men were heavily armed and were carrying pieces of cartridge patching material such as had been found at the scene of the robbery. Besides, the brass spurs of Bugler were found where the train had been stopped.

Both John Bugler and Creed Chapman resided in the area of the robbery, and it was generally believed that Jesse James had been their leader. So all the adjoining counties as far as Jackson were being scoured by heavily armed bodies of men, all searching for the bandits. Sheriff Casen instructed Sheriff Timberlake of Clay County to be on constant alert for Jesse and Frank James, since it was expected that they would seek refuge in the vicinity of their mother's home at

Kearney. Several days later Sam Chapman also was arrested and accused of having been one of the robbers.

Some accounts stated that Messenger Fox had been killed, but such was not the case. However, his injuries were serious. Reports from people who had been on the train claimed about fifteen thousand dollars had been taken by the robbers, considering what was taken from the passengers in cash and valuables. Some thought the amount taken from the express safe may have been just as large, although the express company, as usual, refused to divulge the exact amount stolen. They indicated that the amount taken was quite small.

Witnesses stated that they never saw a more thoroughly frightened and disgusted lot of people than those who had occupied the train that night. Many of the passengers were from the East, and it was strange and discomforting to be stranded in Kansas City with no money or friends. Many of them stopped at the local hotels, anxious to tell their stories to eager listeners. They also lamented that they were afraid to go farther West for fear of being robbed again if they could muster more finances somewhere. Many of the victims wept. Some of them were women who remained hysterical the greater part of the night. By morning, however, most of them had reconciled themselves to the situation, either telegraphing for aid or going on to their destinations where help would be available to them.

Normally, the list of the victims would not be presented here. Yet, as people read this account I am sure they will be keenly interested should the name of some relative appear in the listing. Therefore, here is a list of the persons robbed on the Chicago & Alton train on the evening of September 7, 1881.

> John Evans, Topeka
> S. M. Maas, Ottumwa
> M. J. Cameron, and
> Jerome H. Cameron, Slater, Missouri
> R. McCormack and
> A. H. Powers, Cambridge, Missouri
> A. G. Perry,
> Jane B. Hulz,
> Tura Palette,
> Samuel Steèl, Oak Grove, Missouri
> Dr. George W. Streeter, Waco, Texas
> Dr. Louis Strom, Milwaukee, Wisconsin
> Alex Galt and niece, Blackburn, Missouri
> J. H. Wagner, San Marcos, Texas
> M. Mead, Savannah, New York
> Nancy Johnson, Olathe, Kansas

A. S. York, Council Bluffs, Iowa
Mary B. Stafford, Humboldt, Nebraska
George Lampling, Sterling, Illinois
Robert Carthe, Berry, New York
J. J. Smith, Fort Smith, Arkansas
Peter Berry, Iowa
J. F. Cannon, Oxford, Kansas
William Hayes, Gunnison, Colorado
J. E. Long, St. Louis, Missouri
Mrs. H. P. Betts and
Mrs. S. M. Smeut, Hillsdale
E. F. Spedlaberger, Hamilton
Mrs. L. A. Yerkes, Detroit, Michigan
Julia and Dannie Smith, Indianapolis, Indiana
W. C. Slocumb, and
Frank J. Mattler, Kansas City, Missouri
G. H. Edgeworth, Ottawa
W. P. Haley, Kansas
Mrs. Feet, Ohio
Mrs. Edington, and
Mrs. Haley, Kansas
Mrs. Duncan, Leroy, New York
P. R. Peets, Holyoke, Massachusetts
Thomas Shields, Chicago
J. R. Tarbush, Chicago, Illinois
Nathan Perry,
John O'Brien, wife and daughter, Penn Yan, New York
Charles H. Brown, Jordan, New York
O. H. Grimanald,
W. Willis, Chicago
John Blackhart,
Col. James Harris, Chicago, Illinois
A. S. Davis, Albany, New York
Charles Garfield, Osborn City
Mrs. Martin, Hancock County
T. S. Mason and wife, Topeka, Kansas
T. A. Smith, Chicago, Illinois
F. G. White, Burlington, Iowa
E. C. Benson, Quincy, Illinois
R. H. Clifford, New York
R. A. Ingersoll and his two children, Helena, Montana
R. N. Keene, Lexington, Missouri
C. S. Trimball, Mexico, Missouri.

Mr. C. R. Camp stated that his party from the New York land-buying company lost $4,021. One woman had $1,500 and her watch in her stockings and offered the robbers her purse as they passed her seat. They refused to take it. In the seat just behind her a woman was robbed of a diamond ring, earrings, and a pin, and her baby's shoes were checked for hidden valuables. John High of the L.E. & W.

lost fifteen dollars. Mrs. C. A. Dunakan from Avon, New York, was made to hold up her hands, but the robbers did not search her. One of the bandits said, "The next time we pull off a job like this we'll have a lady along to search you female passengers."

To this the determined woman replied, "You might have a woman with you or a man dressed as one, but you'll never have a lady."

John O'Brien of Penn Yan, New York, lost one thousand dollars and saved seven hundred dollars he had hidden in his trousers. Just as the robbers passed by, that hidden money slipped to the floor. His little girl grabbed it and exclaimed, "Here's some money, Papa." The bandits overheard that remark, returned, and took it from the child.

Again trying to keep the report of their losses at a minimum, Express Agent Treat at Kansas City stated that about four hundred dollars had been taken. Other sources claimed that nearly three thousand dollars had been taken from the express safe.

The Alton & Chicago was due at Kansas City at 9:00 on the evening of September 7th. Several miles east of Independence and almost twelve miles from Kansas City there was a sharp curve and a grade on the road. It was the custom for the engineer to keep a careful watch on the curve, since accidents had occurred there several times due to stalled freight cars on the grade. Therefore the train was kept under slow control at that point. This fact was certainly known to the robbers. The engineer was on the outside of the curve looking ahead when he noticed a dim red light. A tall man waved the light across the track, and as he did so the stream of the headlight fell on him and revealed that he was masked. The first thought of the engineer was that there was a stalled freight train ahead, but as he caught a glimpse of the mask and at the same time saw a pile of stones across the rails, he at once understood the situation.

There was nothing that Engineer L. Foote could do but stop the train and submit to the robbers. The engine came to a complete stop just as the cowcatcher touched the pile of rocks. The locality was called Blue Cut, a spot where the Missouri-Pacific line crossed the track of the Chicago & Alton line. Immediately the robbers, about twelve in number, came running down the banks from either side, surrounding the train. The leader covered the engineer with his revolver and compelled him to break open the door of the express car. Messenger Fox of the U.S. Express Company had left the car, but he was found. Under threat of instant death he was forced to open the safe. No doubt the amount obtained from the safe was small, and this fact may have

prompted the robbing of the passengers, as well as the knocking of
the messenger to the floor by several vicious blows to his head. Immediately the contents of the safe were dropped into the proverbial
grain sack, and the robbers started for the passenger cars.

A guard was posted on either side of the coaches, while five or six
of the bandits went through the whole train, one carrying the burlap
sack while the rest, with drawn revolvers, demanded the passengers'
valuables. As fast as these items were handed over they were dropped
into the bag. The robbers carted off nearly a bushel of wallets, pocket-
books, papers, watches, rings, and so forth. There was a party of
vacationers from Penn Yan, New York, on board, in the charge of
C. Roland Camp, general travel agent and land manager for the Fort
Scott road. From these people alone the robbers took over four thousand dollars. It was estimated that altogether between fifteen thousand
dollars and twenty thousand dollars was taken from the frightened
passengers, while it was supposed that the express safe had not contained more than two thousand dollars, even though all sorts of speculations about that were floating around.

After the robbers had gone through the train they marched back
to the engine and told the engineer to get his train moving. Then they
climbed up on the bank and disappeared in the heavy woods. The
entire operation had taken less than a half hour to complete, and it
was generally agreed that the Blue Cut robbery turned out to be one
of the best executed by the James gang.

L. Foote, also known as "Chappy" Foote, the engineer of the illfated train, gave the following story as to what had happened:

"We were coming round the curve in a cut about three miles east
of Independence, Missouri, running twenty-five miles an hour, when
I saw a dim red light waving across the track just a short distance
ahead. Freight trains often got stalled there, and I supposed that was
what the trouble was this time. I began to slack up and soon saw
that the man who was flagging the train was masked. I also saw him
set the lantern on a pile of stones between the rails. I turned to my
fireman and told him we were going to be robbed. As the train stopped
two men came down the bank, and one of them, presenting a cocked
revolver, told me to come down out of the cab and to bring the coal
pick with me. I said, 'Don't shoot, boys.' The leader replied, 'All right,
we won't hurt you if you get down and out of that right lively.' I didn't
move very fast because I knew what they wanted with that hammer,
and I didn't know but a little delay might help the messenger a little.

They commenced to swear and say, 'Do as we tell you, or we'll shoot your damned head off you.' All this time I heard orders from someone to the gang telling them to do this and do that.

"The leader was a tall, rather good-looking fellow with dark, heavy beard. He had a slight crook in his nose as if it had been broken some time, and he wore a broad slouch hat. He came up and shook hands and said his name was Jesse James. He then introduced one of his gang, a short, heavy fellow, as Dick Little [Liddil]. I heard him call him Dick afterwards. Of course, I don't know whether this was Jesse James or not. I had never seen Jesse James and had no idea what he looked like. Well, they took me to the express car and told me to break open the door. I struck a few blows and then opened it. In the meantime the express messenger and the baggage master had slipped out of the door on the other side and were trying to conceal themselves. The robbers asked me where the messenger was and they were very angry at not finding him. I told them I didn't know where he was.

"The leader said, 'Find the messenger, or we'll shoot you.' I didn't like the look in his face, so I called to the express messenger he must just as well give up. The leader told two of the men to get into the car. The messenger was very slow about opening the safe, and they struck him over the head with a revolver. I understand there was only a small amount of money in the safe, and they seemed to be mad about that, for they struck the messenger again. I guess they hurt him pretty bad.

"They dumped the contents of the safe into a sack and started back to the train, saying, 'We'll go through the passengers, and don't you move till we tell you.' We had passed a freight train at Glendale, and there was danger of its running into the rear of our train, so Conductor Hazelbaker sent a brakeman named Burton to flag it. The robbers saw him start with a lantern, and they commenced to shoot at him. I guess there must have been as many as forty shots fired at him. I told the leader what Burton was going back for, that unless the freight train was flagged it would run into us and maybe kill a lot of people. He threw up his hands and ordered the firing to stop, and it did stop instantly. They had started to run after Burton, and would certainly have killed him if they hadn't been stopped just when they were.

"I think there were six in the party that went through the car. The others were stationed along on either side of the train. Everything was quiet after they quit firing at Burton. While the robbery was going on, the fellow who stood guard over me asked me if the engine would need any attention. I told him it would, and he went back with me while I fixed her so she would stand all right. When the thing was over, the robbers came back to the front of the train. The leader shook hands with me and gave me three dollars, saying, 'You're a good one. Take this and spend it with the boys. You'd better quit running on the road. We're going to make it so hot for this damned Alton road they can't run.' They then vanished over the bank. I did not see any horses, but I suppose they had some there somewhere. They had held us up about half an hour."

Conductor J. N. Hazelbaker related the circumstances of the robbery as follows:

"We were about three miles or so the other side of Independence, in what is known as Blue Cut, when the train suddenly stopped. I went out to see what the trouble was. I saw the train surrounded by a number of masked men heavily armed. I at once started back, passing through all the cars, warning the passengers to secure their valuables, since a gang of robbers was aboard who would spare nothing of value if visible. I passed to the rear platform when a man with two revolvers pointed at me commanded me to halt. I told him an approaching freight train would smash into us directly, and I was going back to flag it unless I was killed before I got there. I took a lantern and one brakeman and, stepping off, started back around the curve to signal the freight. The man on the platform did nothing to stop me, but a number of men hidden in the bushes on the banks shot at us repeatedly. Some of the bullets whistled unpleasantly near, and I must confess to a little nervousness. But I was determined to stop that freight, for if it came into us I knew somebody in the rear cars would get hurt. They were so close to us that I only had to go about ten rods—just around the curve—and after I saw them stop I went back and took a seat in the sleeper. Just then the robbers came into the car, and if the passengers had kept away from me I don't think I'd have been recognized. But everybody crowded around me for protection, as though they thought me a government arsenal. Of course I was spotted and had to give up pretty liberally. I had hid my watch and seventy-five dollars in a water tank as I passed through the cars, and I had kept about fifty dollars, which I gave up. Another man pulled out a gold repeater and a roll of about seventy-five dollars.

"After the train was gone through, the whole crowd of robbers

went to the front and told the engineer to move on, that they were
satisfied. We moved out while the robbers ran up the bank and disappeared in the woods. There were sixteen of them that we counted,
but it is probable there were more hidden in the bushes, as the shots
fired at us came from the bank, and I saw no one approach the train
after it was stopped. They had made a second trip through the sleeper,
turning up cushions and ransacking things generally. It was the worst
looking car I ever saw after they left, and I guess the passengers had
given up everything they had.

"I went forward after we started up and found the express
messenger had been hit on the head with a revolver and slightly cut.
The wound bled some, but I don't think he was badly hurt. I guess he
fought for the money he had and tried to hide it. The boys told me
the engineer had been forced to go back and break open the door to
the express car with a coal pick, so I presume they felt a little wrathy
with the messenger. I don't think they molested the mail car or, rather,
that portion of the car used by the government. We have one car for
baggage, express, and mail, but they tumbled the trunks around and,
I think, they broke open a few. The passengers were badly frightened,
and when I went through the train to tell them what was up, a good
many crawled under the seats and everybody sought out some kind of
a hiding place for their money. It was a tough gang and they meant
business, you can bet on that."

The passenger train arrived at the next station about thirty-five
minutes behind time, due to the robbery. There were other witnesses
who were anxious to give their accounts of the adventure. Three of
them gave accounts worthy of reading. These were Otis P. Mellor, the
mail agent; H. A. Fox, the express messenger for the U.S. Express
Company; and Charles Williams, a black porter.

The porter appeared to have an excellent memory and gave his
account as follows:

"I don't know exactly what time it was, but we were going up
Independence hill, where there is a sharp curve, and the train had to
slow up a little. All at once she stopped, and I heard some shooting
outside. I looked from the platform of the ladies' coach and saw three
or four men at the engine making the engineer get down. I stepped
down off the platform between the ladies' coach and the chair car with
my lantern. I was going to skirmish around to see what it was all
about, but someone yelled at me three or four times, 'Get back, you
black bastard.' When I didn't appear to get it through my head quick

enough, there were three or four shots fired. I don't suppose they meant to hit me, but I got back, you bet. I looked in the smoking car and yelled to the passengers that there were robbers on the train, and they all stampeded into the chair car after me. I stood in the door of the chair car and told them the same thing, and all the ladies commenced a-pullin' down the curtains. The car was pretty full—in fact, after the smoking car passengers came into it every seat was filled—and there was about half of the passengers ladies.

"They behaved might well. There wasn't a single one of them screamed. They just scrounged down into the seats and pulled the curtains over the windows. I helped them do it, not that there was any use as I know of. Finally I come to one tall, old grey-haired man who stood up. 'Looka-here now,' he says, 'Are you all going to set here and have half a dozen men go through you and walk off with all you got?'

"There wasn't anybody said a word. Everybody was busy chuckin' away their money so's the robbers wouldn't get it.

" 'Are you all going to sit still?' says the old man.

" 'Do you want to fight?' says I.

" 'Yes, by damn, I do.'

"He runs his hand into his pocket, and I thought I'd best get away from there quick as I could. He stood out in the middle of the aisle, and I went to the door.

"There were three men standing outside, and one says to another, 'Go and ask them hadn't we better go through the cars.'

"The man he was talking to went up to the engine and spoke to the man who had the engineer in tow. He was the leader, I guess. The one who had gone to him started back, and one of the fellows happened to look around and see me. 'Better get in, you black devil, or you'll have your head blowed off.'

"I got in as fast as I could and told the man who was so anxious to fight that they was a-comin'. He appeared to weaken like, and just as I dodged behind the cooler there was a shotgun barrel stuck in the door, and he could look right down into it. 'Throw up yo' hands, you sons-a-bitches.' When the robber said that, the man who had been so brave held up his hands so high it looked like he was a tiptoin' to touch the top of the car. He looked so funny I could 'a' laughed at it had it been any other time. Then three men came into the car all masked. Two of 'em 'peared to be young men, dressed like farmer boys.

"They wasn't 'sperienced, I know from the awkward way they went at it. One of 'em had a big Colt's pistol and the other had a musket and a bag. The third fellow was an older man. He was in his shirt-sleeves and didn't wear any vest. He had on a navy-blue shirt, and that's about the only description I could give of him. The man who stood at the door just let enough of himself past the edge to hold a shotgun trained down the aisle. Soon as they came into the car one of them said to the man who wanted to fight, 'I'm Jesse James, ye damned yellow dog. Gimme your money.' And the old man let 'im have his money, you bet, and he wasn't long about it either. He lost seventy-five dollars and a gold watch. Then they shoved him into a seat and commenced robbing other passengers. One of them would hold the pack and the pistol, the other would keep his eye on the rest of the car, and the third, the man in the blue shirt, would take the money and chuck it into the sack. They took money, watches, and rings.

"They robbed the ladies of their jewelry whenever they caught them trying to hide it, but they didn't stop to search anybody. It was 'Gimme your money, ye damned dog' (or something like that), 'or I'll blow off yer damned head.' And the money came. If it didn't look like enough they held the pistol to the fellow and told him to shell out. One man had to give up eight hundred dollars this way. He gave them part of it at first, but they 'spected from his looks that he had some more, and they made him give it up. This was the biggest haul they made. There was an old Dutchman who was asleep; all the noise an' the shootin' hadn't waked him up. He was snorin' away when one of the robbers punched him.

" 'Damn you, gimme your money.'

" 'Vat for? I bays my fare a-ready.'

" 'Gimme your money, you Dutch fool, or I'll blow a hole clean through ye.'

"The Dutchman looked at the pistol and then I reckon he sorta came to the right conclusion.

" 'You rob me, hay?'

" 'Yes, you. I'm Jesse James. Give it up quick.'

" 'All I got?'

" 'Yes, every damned red cent of it.'

" 'But I goes to Joplin to buy a farm. Vat vill I do?'

" 'Beat your way there, and hire yourself out when you get there.'

"They took three hundred dollars from him.

"The next man was a Jew. He begged 'em to let him take his insurance papers out of his wallet, but they called him a fool and asked him if he sposed they were goin' to stay there all night to accommodate a damned Jew.

"They struck the conductor on the Pullman. He had gone and hid all his own money and the company's money and his gold watch in the cooler. When they told him to shell out he said he didn't have nothin', but they put a pistol to his head and made him run his hand into the cooler and pull it all out. Oh, he was the sickest man you ever saw, and it was his own fault too. All the sensible passengers had put away part of their money and kept the rest out to give 'em.

"Some of the passengers put away their money in the spittoons, but there wasn't no use for it, as they didn't search 'em. I got a good look at that flour or grain sack they carried, and it came from a house in St. Louis. I know it because they had their name printed on the outside. I can't zactly recollect what the name was now, but I thought of it once today. It was some brothers, grain merchants. They dragged this sack along after 'em, and I saw one of the passengers on the outside of the aisle fool with it with his foot. He told me afterwards that he thought it had about a couple of pecks of things in it.

"There ain't no one yet who's found out how much they got from the express safe. You see, he daren't tell. But they seemed disappointed at what they got in the cars, for they cursed about it. They took all the watches, silver, and gold, but they gave one silver watch back to a boy who was going out West, telling him it was not worth enough to steal. They didn't rob all the passengers, for one man who was sitting about the middle of the car was overlooked altogether. I heard him say on the platform at Kansas City that he had over a thousand dollars on him."

The porter was asked, "Could the men in the car have wiped out the robbers?"

"Well, yes, I guess so, easy enough, but they didn't feel like it. There was about thirty men in the chair car, about twenty of 'em that had pistols, I'll bet. One of the robbers didn't have nothin' but a common old musket, and the other's pistol wasn't a good one. The man that wore the blue shirt had a great big fine pistol.

"I counted eight robbers when I first went out. There was three to the car and two 'tendin' to the engineer. But there was some more came up afterwards and stood 'longside the coaches. If they were the James boys they lied, for the man with the engineer said he was Jesse James, and the man in the blue shirt said he was Jesse James, too.

They kept us waitin' I guess around forty-five minutes, and then they disappeared. After they had gone through the car, one of the slim young fellows wanted to go back and search the passengers, but the man in the blue shirt said he wasn't goin' to stay there all night. Then he went out the door and they had to follow him.''

Immediately upon reaching the depot, O. P. Melloe went to the post office, where he gave his report as to what he had seen during the Blue Cut robbery:

"I was standing in the mail car, looking out, when I saw several men at the engine in conversation with the engineer. They were all heavily masked. They made the engineer leave the cab and go with them to the express car, which is separated from the mail car section by a partition. Passing the mail car one of them caught sight of me and cursed me, calling me vile names. They pointed a pistol at me and I heard several shots from outside the car. There seemed to be a lot of confusion going on. When they found out that I was not the express messenger they went around to the door of the express car and made the engineer break it in. Then they struck the express agent over the head with the butt of a pistol and knocked him down. When he got up they sat him on a chicken coop and pointed a pistol at his head until he opened the safe. They took the money out and struck him another blow to the head. Then they left the express car and went to the passenger cars, robbing the passengers and taking the ladies' jewelry away from them. The booty was not what they appeared to expect, and after swearing and firing their pistols they left.

"When I fully realized what was going on, I threw the mail registers among some sacks on the floor, and they made no attempt to rob the mail. The postal authorities thought they did not overlook it but were afraid to rob it for fear of having the U.S. Government get in on the search for them. Postal Superintendent Dunn thinks it a good reason for believing that the James boys were not managing the robbery."

As had always been the case, when the U.S. Express Company lost any money in a robbery it was almost impossible to determine the exact amount lost. Every employee of the company, had been forewarned of such possible happenings. Each was told if he knew the exact amount to forget it. Messenger Fox had declined to even discuss the matter with anyone in Kansas City. Now, back in St. Louis, he was equally anxious to avoid any publicity regarding the matter of how much money was lost. From the Union Station he raced to the post office at 500 North Fourth Street, eager to find a suitable hiding place from the curious. Eventually, Mr. Fox was found at bay by persisting police officers, reporters, and the morbid curious. In the lobby of the building they found several men discussing the Blue Cut affair. Among them was a young man wearing a bloody bandage around his head.

"Mr. Fox, I presume?" suggested one of the visitors.

"Yes, I'm Fox. What do you want?"

"Were you not the express messenger on the train robbed several days ago?"

"I was, but I know as much about it as you do."

"We have seen reports of a number of the witnesses. Yours was not among them, yet you surely are an important cog in this wheel."

"All right. What do you want to know?"

"I am glad to see you are not as badly hurt as I at first thought."

Fox seemed to ignore that statement. He was not yet thirty years old, and his physical stamina had been sufficient to ward off any serious complications as a result of the strikes on his head.

Then he made his statement.

"As we were going up the Independence grade, the engineer saw a red light on a pile of rocks in front of his engine. The rocks were piled across the tracks, as he could see, and so he stopped. There were several shots fired on the outside, and two men made him come down out of the cab and bring the crowbar or pick along with him. I was in the express car with the baggageman, who thought we ought to bolt the door on the inside, and we did that. They made the engineer commence breaking down the door, and when it became evident that they would get in anyhow, it was opened for them. I stepped outside, but they brought me back. I was struck over the head with a pistol twice, I think, and a pistol was fired off in the car, the bullet going close to my head. They didn't set me on a chicken coop and knock me off, for I sat down on a box myself."

He continued:

"I had to open the safe, which was a small hand affair, and they took everything out, even to the waybills. But everything wasn't much. When they left I hid behind some boxes, for I heard them talking about coming back. From the express car they went to the passenger coaches, and when they were through robbing them, they gave the engineer several dollars and left. I don't know whether they rode away or not. I didn't watch them. Since I did not know how badly I was hurt, I telegraphed for a doctor to meet me at the next station."

In addition there were several circumstances on which Fox might possibly have thrown some light had he felt so inclined. But he did not, probably acting under orders from his superiors.

The Blue Cut robbery appeared to have been managed with a foresight covering the smallest details. However, one detail had been missed. Under a pile of chicken coops was an Adams Express Company safe en route to Kansas City, and it contained a fairly large sum of money. How much was actually in that safe will probably never be known.

The pursuit of the Blue Cut robbers was taken up in earnest throughout the state of Missouri. The sheriffs of Jackson County and adjoining counties took up the search in a diligent manner, scouring the countryside far and wide. Chief of Police Speers of Kansas City had been in the saddle for several days, returning to his home on September 9th, after having failed to locate a trail. At Glendale a posse was formed under the leadership of John Boothe, who led his men to Oak Grove, where they met another posse under the command of Jackson County Marshal Cornelius Murphy. There Marshal Murphy assigned Boothe to lead the officers of Saline County under Sheriff Casen in an effort to run the outlaws to earth. The posse left Marshall, Missouri, riding all night and meeting another group of Jackson County officers near Lee's Summit.

Back in the vicinity of Glendale and Blue Cut no one could find any satisfactory answers to questions that would assist in identifying the robbers. Several citizens had silly and evasive answers when questions were posed with regard to the stopping of the train. No one seemed to have seen any suspicious characters or strangers in the neighborhood. One family, however, whose name could not be used, stated that they had noticed a fine-looking man riding an unusually fancy horse. This man, as far as they could remember, was clean-shaven with the exception of black whiskers and mustache. Where he came from or where he went remained a mystery.

The best information was obtained from James Sneed, who resided close to the scene of the robbery. He stated that the train was nearly on time and his attention was attracted by the train's coming to such a sudden stop. His first impression was that the train had been derailed and he, in company with others, started at a full run for the scene. But as they neared the spot, they were seen by the robbers who opened fire on them. As Mr. Sneed put it, "We lit out."

Mr. Sneed further stated that he noticed the signal for the freight train to stop and heard some more shots fired besides those fired at him and his party, one of which struck his house. He stated that, as far as he could guess, the train was held for three-quarters of an hour, perhaps a little less. The next morning he visited the scene and learned that about two tons of rock had been placed on the track as an obstruction. He could not tell in which direction the robbers had gone, but he had heard them yelling a defiant yell. He went to the place where the horses had been tied, there finding a small spur that one of the bandits had lost.

On the evening following the robbery, Governor Crittenden arrived in Kansas City, where he went into immediate conference with local and county officials. No plans of any consequence were made that evening, since there was little or nothing to go on. However, the Governor did, on his return, issue the following statement:

> Executive Mansion
> City of Jefferson
> September 8, 1881

TO THE PEOPLE OF MISSOURI

We are again shocked by the intelligence of another express and train robbery, which occurred on the Chicago and Alton Railroad near Glendale, in Jackson County, on the evening of the 7th last. But a few weeks since, a similar atrocity was perpetrated near Winston station on the line of the Chicago and Rock Island Railroad. The frequency of the perpetration of these highhanded and outrageous crimes is alarming to all good citizens and is disgraceful to our state. The law officers of Missouri charged with the preservation of the public peace have evinced courageous zeal in their endeavors to vindicate the outraged laws of our state, by apprehending and bringing the perpetrators of those crimes to justice, but so far their efforts have been fruitless. It is said, and I fear with truth, that these outlaws are secreted and protected by a class of citizens who reside in the western counties of Missouri. I am reluctant to believe that any citizen of the State could so far forget his duty to society and to the law, which is his own safeguard and protection, as to furnish aid and comfort to these public enemies. No honest man will do this.

The ordinary processes of the law and the extreme authority of the Executive, supplemented by the utmost vigilance upon the part of county officers, have been exhausted in endeavoring to bring these outlaws to justice. The only result, so far, has been a repetition of their shocking crimes.

This alarming condition of affairs demands prompt, summary, and decisive action upon our part. If ordinary remedies are unavailable, heroic treatment must and will be resorted to. This foul stain shall be wiped from Missouri's fair escutcheon if the honest people of the State will but aid me in my endeavors. But in order to do this there must be such an expression of sentiment upon the part of every citizen who favors the enforcement of the laws and the protection of life and propety as will compel the secret friends of these outlaws to reveal themselves. Not only this, but the people of the State must rise en masse and apprehend, not only the criminals themselves but every known ally. Those who furnish asylum to the robber must be taught that the laws recognize but one treatment for crime—swift punishment.

Let no citizen of Missouri refuse to do his duty. If he does, all good men should regard and treat him as an enemy of the State. Such a policy proved speedily effective in the capture of the Northfield bank robbers, and our people should show the same determination and diligence.

I call upon the people of Missouri, especially in the counties adjacent to the robbery, to rise in their might and wipe out this stain. Let not the pursuit be abandoned by day or night until the entire band is either captured or exterminated. The good name of our State and your counties and your own safety demand it.

I again call upon the people of the State to stand by the law officers of the State in the endeavor to eradicate and exterminate these desperadoes, as the good name and reputation of the State depend upon it. In doing this they are but acting upon the elevated ground of self-defense.

THOS. T. CRITTENDEN
Governor

On the morning of September 9th a telegram was received in Kansas City by Marshal Murphy from Blue Springs, Missouri, requesting him to arrest William Murray for alleged participation in the Blue Cut train robbery. About three o'clock that afternoon alert deputy marshals noticed Murray on Delaware Street, where he was arrested. When Deputy Marshal Hays informed Murray he was under arrest, he claimed innocence, stating that he had been a passenger on the illfated train but had no participation in the holdup. He later stated that he could prove that he came into the city Wednesday on another train. However, he was lodged in jail to await further developments.

At the same time a heavily armed posse left Kansas City under the leadership of the able Deputy Marshal Maurice Langhorne, a former Confederate soldier under General Jo Shelby. New arrests were expected momentarily, as stated by Officers John Boothe and Oscar Cogswell.

William Murray was the son of John Murray of Independence, an ex-county treasurer of Jackson County. He was about twenty-three years old but already a hard customer to deal with. The telegram leading to his arrest was not explicit but merely stated that he was wanted as one of the robbers. Murray had been in Kansas City since Thursday, as was later proved, but it was also noted that he had not been home since Wednesday, and such an alibi would be flimsy indeed. Some people claimed that several of the outlaws were seen coming toward Kansas City on Wednesday night. Perhaps Murray had been one of them?

At three o'clock in the afternoon of September 9th, information was received from Independence stating that three more of the robbers had been captured near Little Blue and that they were being sent to Kansas City. Whether or not the report was authentic at the time, it was followed by the following communication:

A posse of officers from Kansas City have three of the robbers surrounded near the covered bridge on Big Blue on the new Kansas City road, and their capture is only a matter of time. The officers are close upon their men, and they will undoubtedly have them before this reaches the reader. Considerable excitement prevails. At six this evening six supposed robbers have been arrested and three are being closely pursued.

On the 9th of September Governor Crittenden returned to Jefferson City, where he told the people that Jackson County had awakened to the necessity of putting an end to outlawry and appeared determined to vindicate the fair name of their community; that their officers, as well as those of surrounding counties, were making every effort to capture the outlaws. He further stated that the people had risen in their might and that their efforts would be successful. He did not believe that Jesse James had had anything to do with the Blue Cut matter but was under the impression that Dick Liddil (alias Charles Siderwood, of Vernon County, who had already served time in prison) was one of the ring leaders and that the remainder of the gang were residents of Jackson County. Governor Crittenden further stated that he would lend his aid and assistance to the extreme limit of the law in assisting to bring the criminals to justice and that he was determined to leave nothing undone to accomplish that goal.

Crittenden, on learning that Sheriff Casen of Saline County was about to return home after arresting two of the suspected robbers, wired the sheriff to relinquish all other business of his office and to remain in the chase against the bandits. Besides, in learning that an officer in Lafayette County was unable to procure riding horses at Lexington, he sent eight horses via special train from Kansas City to a given point in Lafayette County.

Some prominent citizens throughout the state, on hearing that Crittenden perhaps planned to call a special session of the State Legislature in order that higher rewards might be offered for the arrest of the bandits, wrote him letters protesting the extra expense that would be added to the state if this were done. He replied that he was not inclined to add additional expense for the state but that, if the people wanted him to do so by calling the special session, it would be done.

On September 10th it was reported from Independence that nine arrests had been made in the Blue Cut matter. The six arrested on the 10th included Andy Ryan, a brother of Whiskeyhead Ryan, who was serving time for his participation in the Glendale robbery, and John Land, both of whom were captured at their homes in the Cracker-neck region one mile from Glendale by Deputies Laughlin and Brown. Earlier in the evening William Murray and James Wilkerson had been arrested in Kansas City actually around midnight on the 9th. Charles Fisk and William Stillwell were arrested in the Sni Hills near Blue Springs on the evening of the 10th. Fisk was a mere boy, but he had the reputation of a genuine hard case. Stillwell was a hardened desperado and showed signs of resistance when accosted, but, taken by surprise, he submitted to arrest without much of a struggle. The officers said he was heavily armed and also that they found on his person some of the merchandise stolen at Blue Cut.

Andy Ryan, Creed Chapman, and John Bugler kept insisting they were innocent of the charges. Some of the men claimed that Land was one of the leaders and Wilkerson another. People began to feel that perhaps Jesse James had not been present at all that night. The general impression was that other young men of Jackson County had partici-pated in the robbery at Blue Cut. The county was still alive with pur-suing parties expecting to make more arrests.

Who were the actual robbers? Were they misguided young men, caught in the successes of the James and Younger brothers, inspired and anxious to emulate the deeds of the great outlaws?

Matt Chapman, first to be arrested in connection with the Blue Cut robbery, stated that Jesse and Frank James were there. Later, Dick Liddil, also a member of the gang, after his surrender confessed that both the James boys had been there, together with Jim Cummins, Wood and Clarence Hite, and Charley and Bob Ford. Several others implicated by Liddil were Andy Ryan, Ed Miller, and the Chapmans.

On March 27, 1882, John Bugler, one of the Crackerneck citizens involved, was arraigned at Independence. In the meantime John Land, also under indictment in the same matter, made a full confession, implicating those as indicated by Dick Liddil in his confession. Land had this to say:

"Ten days before the robbery I was interviewed by Creed Chapman and John Bugler, who told me that Jesse James and Jim Cummins were going to rob the Alton and Chicago at Blue Cut. They invited me to go in with them, but I refused at first but gave in later."

His lengthy confession carried most of the details already related.

Land, Bugler, and Chapman were released due to insufficient evidence to convict them of their part of the crime, in spite of their confessions.

If the James brothers were involved in the Blue Cut robbery, it was the last spectacular assignment they ever undertook.

Although the time element involved seems to preclude the claim that they could have been in Texas on September 8th, the day after the Blue Cut train robbery, nevertheless another robbery was laid at their door. This later crime was perpetrated on the old Fort Worth road at Mountain Creek fifteen miles west of Fort Worth. There the victims were forced to raise their hands and deliver. Mr. J. J. Thomas stated that he and two of the Norman brothers and two of the Reinhart brothers, all of Tarrant County near Arlington, were on their way home after selling their cotton in Dallas. About four o'clock that afternoon they reached the Mountain Creek bridge, which was surrounded by dense undergrowth.

As the lead wagon started onto the bridge two men rode from the underbrush, exclaiming, "We are the James brothers."

With a pistol in each hand the outlaws called out, "Get down and huddle together, and be damned quick about it."

The farmers knew the outlaws meant what they said, so they lost no time in complying with the order. One of the men took off on a run, but he was quickly caught and returned to the group with a dire warning not to try it again.

One robber held two cocked pistols on the men while the other passed around his hat, and the contributions were given reluctantly. The loot amounted to seventeen hundred dollars and one gold watch. Bidding each man to return to his wagon, the two robbers calmly rode off. There is no doubt that these men were not Jesse and Frank James, since Mr. Thomas stated that they were two men he had hired in Dallas on Wednesday night to pick cotton for him. This was confirmed by the statement of one of the men when a victim stated he had no money.

"Didn't I see you counting it last night by the fire in the wagon yard?" asked one of the robbers.

With that the man was forced to "pony up" what cash he had. This is just another instance where someone else committed a crime that was laid at the doorstep of the Jameses.

After this episode Mr. Thomas flagged the Eastbound train near Dockman and rode into Dallas to report. Sheriff Jones and five of his men rode to the scene of the crime, trying to pick up the trail of the bandits without success. It was assumed that they had headed north into the Indian Territory.

12 • • •

Death of Wood Hite
and Ed Miller

The Blue Cut train robbery was the last bold act of the infamous Jesse
James gang; no more would there be pursuits by lawmen in their direction; no more would the newspapers all over the country carry the
stories of their daring exploits, for this robbery brought about a rift
between several of the most important players in the game.

One day, near Adairville, Kentucky, at the home of Jesse's uncle,
George Hite, Dick Liddil, a traitor and one-time member of the gang,
accused Wood Hite, Jesse's favorite cousin, of holding out on him.
Dick denied the charge, challenging Hite to a duel over the matter.

Strapping on their pistols they walked alone to the barn to do so.
The ground was selected, and they stood back to back and stepped
toward their places, each man to turn and fire when he had reached
his stand. Before Hite had time to return to his position Liddil wheeled
and fired at him. Hite immediately put a tree between himself and the
would-be assassin. Liddil did the same, and emptied his pistol, Hite
reserving his fire. When Liddil ceased shooting, Hite began, and his
antagonist broke and ran for the house Hite after him and shooting at
every step. Neither man was hit or hurt in the cowardly escapade, and
the matter was, for the time being, compromised by members of the
family. This doubtlessly contributed to the cause of Wood Hite's death
later on.

It was also about this time that Jesse became more and more
irritable, harder and harder to get along with. He knew that Ed Miller

and James R. (Windy Jim) Cummins had been talking about the Blue Cut affair, so one dark night he surprised Ed Miller in Saline County and killed him. The body was not found for several months; then it was almost unrecognizable. In fact, many claimed it was the body of Jim Cummins. However, Jim showed up and stated the body was that of Ed Miller; furthermore, he was positive that Jesse James must have killed him.

Jesse decided to shut Windy Jim's mouth once and for all. One sure way to keep him from talking was to kill him. Jim high-tailed it into Arkansas. Dick Liddil and Jesse James were hot on his trail, so he doubled back into Missouri. He rested at Bill Ford's for a few days, then on a hunch, saddled his horse and left. His hunch proved correct, for he had scarcely turned a bend in the road when Jesse and Liddil rode up to the farmhouse.

Bill was not at home, but his wife and fourteen-year-old son, Albert, were. Jesse inquired about Jim Cummins and was told that he had not been there for some time. Not at all satisfied that he was getting the truth, Jesse took Albert into the woods and tried to torture the information from him. Neither Liddil nor Jesse could pry anything from the plucky lad. Before Jesse could carry out his threat against Cummins that fateful day in April arrived. Cummins was spared, to end his days peacefully in the Confederate Home at Higginsville, Missouri (now razed), where he died in 1929.

Jesse's torture of young Albert Ford was one reason his cousin Bob decided to turn against Jesse. Another deciding factor was Jesse's favorite cousin, Robert Woodson Hite (called Wood), son of George Hite, Sr., of Adairville, Kentucky. In 1878 Major George Hite, Sr. had married the charming young widow Peck (nee Norris), after the death of his first wife, Nancy James, sister to Jesse James's father. The entire Hite family protested against the marriage, and most of them left the house when she entered it. Within a year she deserted the major and went to live with her father.

This stepmother hated Wood Hite and made no bones about it. Shortly afterward, Liddil became a member of the gang and went to Kentucky to hide out with Jesse James after one of the escapades. Liddil, a typical backwoodsman of the Cracker Neck region of Missouri, considered himself something of a ladies' man, and the sprightly young Mrs. Hite did not altogether repulse his advances. Wood Hite told Liddil in no uncertain terms to leave his father's wife alone or there would be serious trouble. In fact, only by the interference of other gang members was gunplay between the two avoided one day in the barn loft of the Hite farm, even though the two took several pot shots at each other, both missing. Liddil then hurried back to Missouri.

Wood confronted his stepmother with an accusation that she was playing fast and loose with his father. She retorted that she was not entirely unaware of his connection with Jesse James. She warned him that if he meddled with her love affairs she would tell the authorities about him.

One day Wood intercepted a black man named John Tabor as he was carrying a note to one of Mrs. Hite's lovers. Wood took the note and told Tabor that if he ever caught him on such an errand again he would kill him. The black man was badly frightened, but again Mrs. Hite induced him to act as her messenger. Wood caught him, searched him, found the love note, and simply shot and killed Tabor. He dragged the body into a fence corner and covered it with brush. Several days later it was hardly recognizable because the hogs running loose in the area had found it.

Mrs. Hite swore out a warrant for Wood's arrest. She declared she had witnessed the killing of the black man. Wood, unaware of his step-mother's actions, was fishing in the small creek that ran through his father's farm when two officers from Russellville drove up one afternoon' in a buggy. At that time the police had no suspicion that either Wood or Clarence Hite was a member of the famous Jesse James gang. Their having a lot of money at times did not excite comment because Major Hite, their father, was known to be pretty well fixed.

When the two officers drew up in front of the Hite home in their buggy, no one was there except Clarence, or Jeff as he was called. Jeff was a younger brother of Wood, a stoop-shouldered, consumptive, a half-wit of nineteen.

"Where's Wood?" one of the officers asked.

"Down on the creek a-fishin'," Jeff answered.

The officers had no difficulty in locating Wood, and they told him they had come out to get him to go bird hunting with them. Wood, entirely unsuspicious, told them he would go to the house after his shotgun. They started up the path toward the house, walking single file, Wood between them. About halfway to the house the officer in the rear eased a gun into Wood's back.

"Get 'y hands up, Wood, an' keep 'em up. You're that bird we aire a-looking fer. We've got a murder warrant agin ye."

When Marshal Jeter arrived in Russellville with his prisoner, he placed Wood in an upstairs room of the city's hotel instead of placing him in jail. Of course a guard was left at the door of the room, but in some unexplainable manner Wood simply walked out. He went down the stairs, through the hotel lobby, out the front door, and mounted a horse conveniently waiting in front of the hotel. He even rode around town for a while, offering one hundred dollars as a reward for the return of his "guard." Such a sum may have been given to someone beforehand.

Several old-timers who personally knew the Fords report that Wood, after his "escape" from the hotel-jail, went to Missouri, where, on December 4, 1881, he walked into the Ford home in Ray County. In the lean-to kitchen Martha Bolton had just gotten up and was preparing breakfast, and Elias Cap Ford was out feeding the stock. After the first greeting, Wood inquired if any of the boys were about.

"Charley and Bob and Dick are asleep upstairs," said Martha.

"That dirty Liddil!" Hite exclaimed. "He's got a helluva nerve to hang around after stealing that money out of the bag before it was divided after the Blue Cut job."

Martha told Wood that Dick was mad at him on account of his accusations.

"I don't give a damn, and I'll tell Liddil to his face!" cried Wood. "There's been a lot of talk among us about the way he filched that money."

Martha tried to act as peacemaker. "It will only cause more trouble. Don't go upstairs and start a ruckus."

But Hite would not listen to her. He stomped up the stairs and into the bedroom where two beds stood. In one slept the two Fords and in the other Liddil.

Dick Liddil was a native Missourian about thirty-five years old and as daring as any of the band. He was five feet eight inches tall, had blond hair and a blond mustache, with pale blue eyes and a short nose. Two of his brothers, James and John, had ridden with the Jameses during the Civil War and both had been killed.

Wood awoke the three men and addressed Liddil angrily, "You've a damned nerve speaking to me after all the lies you've been a-spreadin'."

With that Liddil drew a pistol from under his pillow, and the shooting became general. Bob Ford saw that Liddil was wounded in the leg, so he took a shot at Wood Hite, the bullet striking him in the head and killing him. Charley Ford did not get in on the affray; he had been sleeping on the wall side of the bed and quickly jerked up a window and jumped out onto the roof of the lean-to. There were several inches of snow on the roof and Charley slid to the ground, severely spraining his hip and ankle.

Elias (Capline) Ford was called in to help get rid of Hite's body, because Liddil was wounded and Charley Ford was hurt. So Elias and Bob Ford dug a shallow grave into which they threw Hite's body, wrapped in a dirty horse blanket.

Now the Fords had another reason to want to get rid of Jesse James. They knew what would happen to them when he learned that his favorite cousin had been murdered by Bob's shot. However, Jesse never did learn of Wood's demise. The body was not recovered until April 5, 1882, in an old spring several hundred yards from the Ford residence, covered with a slight sprinkling of earth and some stones. Then it was nude, and the features were almost unrecognizable. On the right side of the head was a bullet wound, and there was also a wound in the right arm. Some people have questioned as to why the body was nude, but in those days many people slept in the raw. The fight took place before anyone of the participants could get dressed, and it was useless to clothe the body after Wood was dead. At the inquest on April 6th Martha Bolton gave this version of the killing:

I recognize the body before me as that of a man who frequently went by the name of Robert Grimes, but his real name was Wood Hite. He was killed in the house in which I live about the last of November or first of December, 1881; I do not know who killed him, though I was present when he was shot; it occurred between seven and eight o'clock on a Sunday morning. I had prepared breakfast and called the boys into the dining room; there were present Dick Liddil, Bob and Charley Ford, and Capline Ford, Wood Hite, and my little daughter. There had been some difficulty between Liddil and Hite a few months previously in Kentucky, but they appeared friendly while at my house until the shooting occurred. My back was toward the two men when they commenced shooting in the dining room, but I quickly turned and saw Liddil and Hite, the former standing near the kitchen door and the latter perhaps ten feet distant, on the east side of the room. Three or four shots were fired so quickly that the room was filled with smoke and I could not even see the men, but there were perhaps as many as ten shots fired in all. When the firing ceased I saw Wood Hite lying on the floor dead, and Liddil was holding his hand over a wound in his hip, from which the blood was flowing freely. Hite was shot in the head and must have died instantly. I do not know whether Robert Ford fired at Hite or not, but his pistol was in his hand and I suppose he shot at Hite one or more times. After the killing my brothers carried the body upstairs and left it there until after night, when Capline and Charles Ford wrapped the body in the blanket and carried it out of the house to the place where it was found. Liddil was badly hurt and was assisted to a bed upstairs in the north room.

There is no explanation of the conflict between this story and the one related by Bob Ford. No doubt Martha Bolton lied for some reason best known to herself, or Bob had, since all the evidence at Bob's trial at Plattsburg pointed to the theory that the death of Hite had occurred in the dining room.

Aside from their enmity over the near duel in Kentucky, Wood Hite and Dick Liddil had hated each other because each was trying to win the attention of Martha Bolton's fourteen-year-old daughter. Naturally enough, Martha would not implicate her brother more than was absolutely necessary.

During Governor Hardin's administration nearly all the rewards for the Jameses offered by the State of Missouri were withdrawn, and when Governor Phelps took office he withdrew all the remaining offers. This caused the various corporations to withdraw any rewards they had offered. Yes, it is true, for some time the notorious James brothers were without a price on their heads.

However, when Governor T. T. Crittenden took over the office of governor, he called a meeting, at the Southern Hotel in St. Louis, of representatives from the regions through which the principal railroads ran into Kansas City and St. Louis. The result of this conference was the governor's proclamation that fifty-five thousand dollars would be awarded anyone effecting the capture of the entire robber band, or five thousand dollars for the arrest and conviction of any separate member. In the case of Frank and Jesse James, an extra five thousand dollars apiece was offered for conviction.

13 • • •

Bob Visits the Governor--
Raid on Harbison Place

Several days after the death of Wood Hite at the Harbison place Bob Ford was in Kansas City, anxious for another talk with Police Commissioner Craig. Ford had originally planned to kill Dick Liddil as well, for he knew that he must try and eliminate some of the gang members before "attacking" Jesse James. With Wood Hite out of the picture now, the odds were looking better. As it was, Dick Liddil did receive a nasty leg wound in the fight at the Bolton home. Who inflicted it—Wood Hite or Bob Ford? We know that Ford killed Wood Hite. All this time Bob Ford made it a point to avoid contact with T. J. Jackson, in reality Jesse James, for he well knew what would happen to him if Jesse learned of Wood's death.

Now the Fords had three reasons to betray Jesse: the reward, revenge, fear.

Bob walked up to the office of Commissioner Craig and asked the clerk to admit him. He entered Craig's office and announced a visitor.

"This late in the day? Who is it?"

"It's that Bob fellow again."

"Well, tell him to come in, since I am interested in what he has to say."

In a few moments Ford was ushered into the plush office.

"I have new information for you, Mr. Craig."

"For me? Well, let's hear it."

161

"Not so fast. My time has caused me much thought and sometimes agony in deciding to go through with it."

"All right, young man, but get on with it, time is wasting."

"Well, for one thing, if someone should tell you how to capture a robber, and goes with you to a house where he lies wounded, what would it be worth?"

"Frankly, five thousand dollars if the man is Jesse James."

"What if he is a member of the gang?" asked Ford.

"Well, I suppose a smaller amount would be paid."

"I suppose that would mean on conviction."

"Of course."

"What if a fellow should be accused of such crimes himself in trying to make such an arrangement?"

Commissioner Craig grinned. "Yes, I can see what you mean, and I would guess you are that fellow."

"All right, what have you to say then?" laughed Ford.

"Well, I'll certainly say for a young fellow you have a lot of spunk. Your coming here proves that. I believe all this could be arranged to your benefit. Governor Crittenden would agree I am sure, for he wants to break up this gang once and for all."

"Suppose I would lead you to the wounded outlaw, even though I, myself, was a member of that band, now acting in good faith, would I be pardoned by the governor?"

The commissioner did not reply at once. Finally he said, "Yes, I believe you would. My orders from the governor are to break up the band at all costs. If he feels your arrangements are on sound ground I am sure he would grant you amnesty after all is done with."

"That sounds fair to me. My brother Charley will help me. I would like to be appointed a detective on the record so that my work will be classified as such; not that I am just an outlaw."

"That can be arranged on a temporary basis," assured the commissioner. "But if you bertay us you will suffer the consequences."

"I understand."

"Now you must tell me your real name. You are known to me as Bob and have been reported to the governor as Bob. We will have to know your real name."

"All right, just so you and the governor are the only two who know it. If this got out our plans would be destroyed. I am Robert Ford."

"And your brother?"

"He is Charley Ford."

"Now what about the wounded outlaw?" asked Craig.

"I believe that a raid on the Harbison farm in Ray County might produce this man."

So it was arranged. It was agreed to start at once with a number of officers in order to reach the Bolton-Harbison place about daylight. On the arrival of the officers, Liddil, who was awake, heard them, and escaped into the brush. Bob Ford, in disguise, had led them to the place.

"Well, now that this has failed, I'll return to Kansas City with you. I cannot afford to be seen around here until all this has been taken care of," Bob told the leader of the posse. He agreed.

The news of the raid was kept as quiet as possible, since the police did not want any publicity at that time. Ford remained in Kansas City several days, then went to Mrs. Bolton's home. Dick Liddil was still absent, for now he was in double jeopardy, since he was as much afraid of the law as he was of Jesse James since the death of Wood Hite. But the noted outlaw never learned of the death of his favorite cousin, and that it had been Bob Ford who had killed him.

Governor Crittenden had promised the people of Missouri that he would destroy the outlaw band at all costs. However, this had not been done. Missouri was known around the country as "The Robber State," with thousands of emigrants bypassing it to settle in Kansas and Nebraska. Millions of dollars in various revenues were denied the state due to the presence of these bandits. The outlaws were ruining the state as well as the Democratic party, which controlled it at that time. Why were these outlaws permitted to exist? This question was on the lips of thousands of law-abiding citizens. Some said that the party in charge of the official powers of the state of Missouri had allowed a horde of outlaws to remain within the borders of the fifth state of the Union, not because they sanctioned their methods, but because some of the bandits were ex-Quantrillians, as were many men in high places.

Governor Crittenden, not realizing at the time that his destruction of the bandits would also destroy his future political career, did not hesitate to form plans to rid Missouri of Jesse James.

On January 8, 1882, a bleak and dismal night, Governor Crittenden sat alone in his study at the executive mansion. A rap on the door by his servant brought him out of his thought.

"What is it?"

" There is a lady to see you, governor."

"At this time? What does she want?"

"She would not say. She is veiled and I do not know who she is."

"All right, show her in."

A few moments later a woman walked into the governor's study.

"Be seated, please," said Governor Crittenden.

Without a word, the visitor sat down in the plush chair, at the same time handing the Governor a sealed envelope.

The governor opened the letter and read, "Trust the bearer, he is working to break up the Jesse James gang.—Craig."

The governor looked surprised. This was no "he" before him; it was a woman.

Throwing off the veil and revealing his face, Bob Ford explained the secrecy that had to be employed in the matter.

"Who are you, sir?"

"I am Bob Ford, the man who has been talking with Commissioner Craig."

The conversation between the governor and Bob Ford was long and in deep earnest. Although Crittenden did not approve of parts of the plan, he decided that the end would justify the means.

"I can manage to break up the band, I think, but you must stand ready to grant me a full pardon. I must say this, for there is only one way to take Jesse James—dead. Either I must kill him or you must arrange an ambush with Sheriff Timberlake to do so."

After Bob Ford left the executive mansion he managed to remain out of sight for some time, not revealing his presence until his next meeting with Governor Crittenden in Kansas City on January 13, 1882.

A few days after Ford's visit to Jefferson City, another veiled woman called on the governor.

"What's this? Has Ford returned for more bartering?"

But when the visitor was ushered into his office Crittenden could see by the slender form and her small size that the visitor was indeed a woman. She was heavily veiled, but at the request of the governor, she removed the veil, showing the face of a pale and nervous woman, somewhat on the pretty side.

"Madam, will you kindly tell me who you are and the purpose of this visit?"

"May I ask a few questions first?"

"By all means."

"Will what I have to say have any bearing on the person I came here to represent?"

"I can assure you that all you reveal will be considered without taking advantage of anyone," the governor assured her.

"I have been following your comments and reward notices with regard to the James gang. Would a member of that band be permitted to turn state's evidence, and pardoned, providing he surrendered voluntarily and used what he knew to capture the bandits?"

"Yes, I would make such a promise, providing all transactions are made in good faith."

"This will be the case," said the woman.

"Now, then, what is your name?"

"I am Martha Bolton, sister of Bob and Charley Ford."

"Whom do you represent?"

"My brothers and Dick Liddil. Liddil will surrender to Sheriff Timberlake and remain in the background, while Bob and Charley will handle Jesse."

"And will Liddil give Sheriff Timberlake and Commissioner Craig a full confession?"

"Yes, I feel sure that he will."

"Then return and tell Liddil to surrender to Timberlake at the opportune time. I will contact the sheriff and give him his instructions on how to act when that time comes."

However, before a surrender could be arranged, the frustrated officers in Kansas City, together with Bob Ford, decided to make another raid on the Harbison place in Ray County. They had learned that Dick Liddil and Jesse James and Jim Cummins had been seen in that area during the first week of January. Consequently, on the morning of January 6, 1882, a determined group of men marched into that county. On Thursday a high official had received a communication from one of his spies and it stated, "Have located Jesse James, Ed Miller, and Jim Cummins, and they can be easily captured." This message does not ring true, since Cummins and Jesse were not on good terms at that time and Ed Miller was killed by Jesse in 1881.

This information was passed around, and preparations for an expedition were begun at once. The police spy had returned to Kansas City by this time, his name never divulged, for fear he would be slain by some of the gang members. Sheriff Timberlake and several others were at once summonded to meet at a certain place with several of their most trusted and bravest deputies. Eleven picked men from the Kansas City police force, headed by Commissioner Craig, were ordered to report at midnight of the 5th and to be ready for a quick move. All the evening Sergeant Ditsch and a few of these men were busy around the police station, holding frequent consultations and loading and examining the weapons to be used by the raiders. Shortly before midnight a bag full of guns was passed out of the side door of the clerk's office and hidden at a spot near the bridge depot. The men all congregated at a point on the other side of the bridge, and at 12:15 o'clock a dark train, consisting of an engine and two cars, crossed the bridge, took the men on board, and sped away.

Not a light was seen on the train, which sped along at a fast rate of speed, probably forty or fifty miles an hour, and this was kept up until they reached Lexington junction. At that point the train was switched and ran to within a short distance of Richmond. There it stopped, and the men disembarked and formed in single file, ready to move. Sheriff Timberlake, in company with the spy who had given away the hiding place of the robbers, headed the party, and a silent march through the woods was begun. The sheriff's companion was familiar with every foot of the ground, and he guided the party to a small cottage in the woods about three miles from where they had left the train. There they halted and the men were stationed at regular intervals on every side until the house was completely surrounded.

The men were cautioned to keep a close watch on the house, but under no circumstances to make the slightest sound. In that position of suspense and discomfort they waited until daybreak, when they closed up on all sides of the house and stood ready to shoot at the first sign of an outlaw. In walking up to the house they made considerable noise, and this brought a young man to the door to investigate. As soon as he caught sight of the officers he retreated inside and closed the door. The men then made a grand rush, and the twenty or so that composed the raiding party formed a line around the house a few feet away. Captain Craig called out to attract the attention of the persons inside the building, and the young man who had previously appeared came out again, accompanied by his brother. They proved to be brothers of the widow who owned and occupied the house, and of them the officers demanded admission, and the same time explaining their mission. The young men denied any knowledge of the James gang and invited the officers to come into the house. Captain Craig, Sheriff Timberlake, and several others entered the house and, after a thorough search, failed to discover any of the outlaws in the building.

The raid was one of the most sanguine of any that had ever been made, and a betting man could have gathered big odds on the certainty of its success. The disappointment of the posse was beyond belief.

They had been almost certain that they had been on the right track. From what had been gathered later on it was determined that had Timberlake and Craig been a few hours earlier they would have captured some of their prey. There was no question but that Jesse and two of his companions had slept in the Harbison home sometime during the night prior to the morning raid.

The occupants of the house were very nervous, and an investigation of the surrounding area showed where three horses had been stabled, and where they had been ridden away. During the early part of the night it had rained, then turned colder, causing a sleet to settle on everything. From the stable the three horses were tracked to the main road a mile and a half away, where the trail was obliterated by the passage of some cattle. Perhaps, had the officers started at once to Ray County on learning that their suspects were at the Harbison place, they might have succeeded in capturing them.

Probably never before had an effort to capture the outlaws approached so near to success, and in all probability such an opportunity would not present itself again. Of course, subsequent events negated the necessity of further pursuit. Even so, that raid was one of the best planned and executed of all that had been carried out to date, with the exception of the delay in putting it into operation. The men involved were all known to be brave and fearless officers, ready to brave any danger for the benefit and safety of the people of Missouri. The officers from Kansas City were Sergeant Ditsch, Detectives Bryant and O'Hare, Constable Rucker, and Officers Snow, Hartley, McCormick, Nugent, Clarkin, and Lovett. They were all armed with heavy revolvers and a rifle each, and they would have made it almost impossible for the outlaws to have escaped from the house, had they been there.

The special train carrying the posse returned to Kansas City about noon on the 6th, where they disbanded for the time being. And, as might be expected, with the failure of the raid, some citizens were quick to criticize Craig and Timberlake. One of these, who wished to remain nameless, had this to say, "The popular amusement among police circles nowadays is to inaugurate and carry out a raid after the James boys. Whenever a fresh scent is placed in front of them a general scramble is made by all hands for the arsenal, and squads of armed men depart in every direction, riding at full speed, or are carried rapidly over the rails. In a few hours they return worn out, without having spilled any blood or captured any train robbers. These raids have been called farces and are enacted every so often. It would take a lot of work to calculate the time and money wasted on these so-called raids.

"Right now is one of the periods of the epidemic, and within the past sixty hours the country for fifty miles around has been traversed by armed bodies of men searching through the ravines and beds of dry creeks for the bodies of Jesse James and his companions. Last Thursday evening a party comprised of officers from Jackson and Clay Counties made a bold midnight dash to Richmond, surrounded a house where the notorious Jesse James was said to be, and failing to find him there, returned. They reported that it was a close scratch and that they had nearly laid hands on him, but that he eluded them by a hair's breadth.

"To begin with, Jesse James was not within two hundred miles of that house at the time, and hadn't been for several weeks. The only foundation, in fact, for the report that he was there, was the presence in that locality of a couple of his go-betweens, who came up this way to learn the particulars of the shooting of young Samuel, Jesse's half-brother [John Samuel had been wounded just prior to the raid in a dancehall brawl].

"They were there a day or two before the raid, and probably visited the Samuel home, but Jesse was not in this state nor within hundreds of miles of that house that night. When the authorities ought to have distinguished themselves, if they want to, by the capture of these men, was when they arrested the colored man, Strickland, a day or two later after Christmas. That day Dick Liddil was in town and stayed here twenty-four hours. He came here that day, a little before noon, and I know all about it. He left two big revolvers with a lady in Clay County, because he was afraid to wear them into Kansas City, for fear he would be arrested for carrying concealed weapons. They were so large that he could not hide them under his coat. The place where he left them was just across the river, and he then came over the bridge on foot, accompanied by a woman. Mattie Collins, his alleged wife, was in town at the time, and he went right to where she was and stayed all night. Strickland, the colored man, came afterwards by appointment and purchased the pistols [for which he was arrested for carrying same] for Dick Liddil. When Dick learned that his go-between had been caught, he struck out at once, recrossed the bridge, got his old pistols, and rode away, leaving Strickland holding the new pistols and also in jail. If the police had followed Mattie Collins when she paid the colored man's fine and started off with the pistols they could have caught Dick without any trouble."

When Chief of Police Speers of Kansas City was asked about the raid and the above incident, he said, "It is all very amusing to me, really. Jesse James might not have been at the Harbison farm, but you can bet that Jim Cummins and someone else was there. I cannot believe that Liddil was in town to get the colored man to buy new guns for him, since I think I know where he was that day, at least nearly where he was. People must think we are a bunch of blockheads in not being smart enough to shadow Mattie when she went away with the pistols. We thought of it, but we also knew it would get us nowhere. Mattie was smart enough to lead us on a wild goose chase had we tried to follow her."

Captain Craig stated that he thought Liddil had been in the city as stated, and if any reputable citizen knew the fact and did not report it, he was as bad as Liddil. Although to no avail, patrols were sent out for several more days, since it was feared that another train robbery would soon take place.

14 • • •

Mattie Collins

When the newspapers printed conjectures about the "veiled woman" who had been to see Governor Crittenden at Jefferson City, nobody knew they were referring to Martha Bolton. It was with her that the governor completed the arrangements in the James matter. The Fords were to be active in the capture; but Dick Liddil was to remain in the background, since Jesse was already suspicious of him.

Soon after Martha's visit with the governor, Jesse again called on the Ford brothers at the Harbison place and explained his plans for another robbery. Dick Liddil was not present, for he had skipped to Kentucky, waiting news from Mattie Collins about the governor's decision.

Several sources claimed that the veiled woman who visited the governor was Mattie Collins, but such was not the case.

Some years back, an old friend of mine, as a young policeman in Kansas City, stated that one day he and a reporter were discussing the death of Jesse James when a woman dressed in black and heavily veiled passed them on Main Street.

"There goes Mattie Collins," remarked the officer.

"Who is she?" inquired his reporter friend.

The officer looked surprised. "I thought everyone heard of her; she's supposed to be the wife of Dick Liddil, the man' who rode with Jesse James. He was supposed to have been mixed up in the plot to kill Jesse, too."

"Say, that's interesting!" exclaimed the newspaper man, as he started off to follow the veiled woman. "I think I'll chat with her, perhaps she can tell me something of the mysterious visit of the veiled woman to the governor's office."

"You'd better not bother her until she reaches her home or hotel or wherever she's staying. She might create a scene here on the sidewalk."

"Good thinking, I'll follow her and see what happens."

With that remark, the young reporter started to follow the woman to her living quarters.

On being advised that someone wished to speak with her about Dick Liddil and related matters, Mattie Collins readily consented to an interview.

"Are you Mattie Collins?" asked the young man.

"Yes, I am Mattie Collins. What can I do for you?"

"I'd like some first-hand information about your supposed visit to Governor Crittenden."

The question seemed to disturb the woman.

"Well, in the first place, I'm the wife of Dick Liddil, whose real name is James Andrew Liddil. Stories have been circulated of late that I visited Governor Crittenden in behalf of Dick, and asked that he give the outlaw his liberty if he would tell the whereabouts of the gang with which he has been connected. Now that is a damned lie! I have not been near the governor, nor have I ever seen him in my life, nor have I ever seen Captain [Commissioner] Craig. I saw Sheriff Timberlake once, when he was introduced to me as the brother of Bob Ford, the man that was with him. Why, I've never been to Jefferson City. I do know the woman, though, that did call upon the governor. She is the Widow Bolton, a sister of Bob Ford, and she lives in Ray County, this state. Dick Liddil has made her house his stopping place for the past eleven months, and it was he who sent her to see Governor Crittenden."

"Well, that will set some records straight, anyhow," said the reporter. "Can you tell us something of your wedded life with Dick Liddil?"

"You know when I was in trouble, accused of killing my brother-in-law? Well, Dick would come to the trial and watch all day sometimes. That is how we met. He took a liking to me after first seeing me. In fact, he escorted me from the courtroom after I had been acquitted by the jury. Some writers claim we were married right off, but that is not so. After the trial I went to my sister's place. Dick would visit all the time; in three weeks we were married. I tell you I love that boy, and if it wasn't for that widow with whom he had been stopping, I wouldn't be what I am today. I never swore or drank until last summer, when he left me and went to her home. There's nothing I would not do for Dick. Why, I've given him money time and again; and there's another thing. I never told a secret of him in my life.

"Officers of this city have time and again offered me money, as high as a thousand dollars, if I would tell them Dick's whereabouts, but every time I refused, and on occasions when he was concealed in my room. Marry again? Not I, as long as Dick Liddil lives, why, I couldn't love another man."

"How long has Dick been with the James gang?"

"He joined them just after the Glendale robbery [October 7, 1879]. Dick never told me of his exploits. He knew that was not my style of robbing. He was never connected with any robbery other than those at Glendale and Blue Cut. After the first we left the vicinity and lived for a time at Fort Scott, Kansas, and Carthage, Missouri. Then I wanted to go on a farm. Neither of us know how to do anything except work on a farm. Dick made preparations to rent, but he got wind of the fact that officers were after him. For a week or so he laid around in the woods, and then left, and kept out of reach of the officers.

"A few months before the Winston robbery, about a year ago, Dick talked to me and said he wanted to leave the gang and settle down. Then he spoke of telling the crowd. Afterward he joined Jesse, however, and took part in the Winston raid. Clarence Hite was in that. He never told me so, but I know it. Clarence visited my sister's house just after it occurred."

"What about the accounts in some papers stating that Liddil killed Wood Hite, the cousin of Jesse James?"

"That is false throughout. Bob Ford killed Hite and he told me so himself. He had a dread fear of Jesse after that on account of Hite was Jess's favorite cousin. I think Jesse would have killed Bob without any questions had they met and had Jesse known of this, which he never did find out, as you well know.

"Dick told me that the killing of Hite occurred at the breakfast table at the widow Bolton's place, after Wood Hite accused Liddil of dipping into the robbery receipts before they were divided. There was some shooting over it and Bob Ford shot and killed Hite. I think that Dick Liddil also got shot in the hip or in the leg. Now, Bob Ford told me the shooting occurred in the morning in an upstairs bedroom where

Bob and Charley Ford and Dick Liddil were asleep. Wood stormed up the steps, awoke the men, and then the shooting began. I'd rather be apt to believe Ford—I guess he and Dick were about the same when it came to being truthful—but Ford's story sounds more true. Why would they drag the body upstairs from the kitchen and let it stay there all day and bury it at night? Charley further claimed that when the shooting began he jumped out of the window, slipped on the snow on the roof and fell to the ground, injuring his leg. If Wood Hite had been killed in the kitchen it would have been an easy task to simply carry out the body then and there to bury it in the brush.

"Insofar as the dead man being Jesse James I cannot say right now since I have not seen the body yet. You know, he was killed in St. Joe yesterday."

After Mattie Collins had seen the remains of the dead man, she readily agreed it was that of Jesse James.

15 • • •

Dick Liddil's Confession

Shortly after Martha Bolton's visit with Governor Crittenden, Dick Liddil returned to Missouri. On January 21, 1882, he surrendered to Police Commissioner Craig. Soon afterward he accompanied Sheriff Timberlake to Kentucky in order to assist in the arrest of Clarence Hite, wanted in connection with several Missouri robberies. The boy was brought back to Missouri, tried and convicted for his complicity in these robberies, and sentenced to twenty-five years in the state prison at Jefferson City, Missouri, where he died after a short while from consumption.

On the 22nd of February, when Governor Crittenden was supposed to have come to Kansas City for the purpose of attending the Craig Rifles Ball and to celebrate Washington's birthday, was the time of his first interview with Dick Liddil.

Liddil and Ford met Governor Crittenden at the St. James Hotel at one o'clock on the morning of February 22nd, when a bargain was reached, not for the arrest, but for the death of Jesse James at the hands of Ford, and for other important activities on the part of Dick Liddil, one being his full confession, which follows, and which, I believe, appears in full for the first time.

The governor at first did not mention Liddil in the amnesty agreement, to which Ford balked, stating that the conditions include a complete pardon for Dick Liddil as well as for the Fords. Liddil visited Jefferson City several times, but Ford communicated with the authorities solely by telegraph. Governor Crittenden had finally agreed to Ford's terms concerning Liddil, although he never admitted that the

174

bargain with Ford was that he should kill Jesse James, or that he was to receive any reward for his part in the conspiracy.

The verbatim confession of Dick Liddil follows. I feel that the reader will find much interest in this document; it appears to be told in a truthful and straightforward manner.

"My name is James Andrew Liddil; I was born on September 15, 1852, in Jackson County, Missouri. My father's name is James M. Liddil, and he lives in Vernon County, Missouri. I have a half-brother about nine years old, who lives with my father. I have a sister, Alice Liddil, about twenty years old, who now lives at Independence, Missouri, with my uncle, Jack Liddil. I have another sister, Jennie, who is married to a man by the name of Baker, who lives in Vernon County, about five miles from Nevada.

"I have known Jesse James since the year '72 or '73. I met him at Bob Hudspeth's, who lives about ten miles west of Independence, Missouri. I was working there at the time. Jesse came with Ben Morrow, whose father lived about a mile and a half from the Hudspeth place. I think Ben Morrow was making his home at the Hudspeth's at the time. Within a few days of this time I met Frank James, the half-brother of Jesse, at Hudspeth's place. [There has never been any real proof brought forth to support his statement of the brothers, although rumor had it that Jesse was actually the son of a Dr. Woods of Kansas City.]

"They were both outlaws at this time and were on the dodge, though they did not appear to be apprehensive. I lived at Bob Hudspeth's for nine years, beginning 1871 or 1872. During the first four or five years I saw Jesse and Frank James at the Hudspeth home many times. He entertained them as friends, not through fear. During those four or five years I have seen them often at Silas Hudspeth's, Bob's brother. He also entertained them as friends. They never told me nor did I hear them tell anyone that they were in any robberies to this date. Both Hudspeths knew all the time, as I did myself and people generally, that they were dodging the officers. I never knew them to stay longer than one or two nights at any time during these years. During these times they were in the habit of stopping at Bob, Silas, or Rufus Hudspeth's, Jim Cummins's, Press Webb's, Jim Webb's, Tom Smith's, at Independence, Don Crisp's at the same place, Dan Reed's, Bud Burns's, Dick Talley's, old man Ralston's, and other places in Jackson County. Clell Miller, Cole and John Younger, and Tom Mc-

Daniels used to frequent some of the above places. They were dodging the officers, too, at the time.

"The first time I saw Jesse James after the Northfield bank robbery was at Ben Morrow's, in Jackson County. I met Ben and he told me that Jesse was supposed to be at his house that evening, and had said he wanted to see me. About 2 o'clock I went to Ben's, and I found Jesse in the yard getting some water from a barrel. We had a little chat and went out to where his horse was tied in the woods. He said he was broke and wanted to make a raise, and he wanted me to help him. I agreed. This was on Sunday. We separated and were to meet at Ben Morrow's next Wednesday evening. We met according to appointment, and he told me that he wanted to rob the C. & A. or the Missouri Pacific train. He said that he had two other men beside himself. He said that he had come up from General Jo Shelby's, in Lafayette County, where he had been since seeing me the preceding Sunday. We then went up to Jim Hulse's, getting there about 1 o'clock at night. We found Ed Miller there. Hulse entertained us as friends.

"We all three left the next night. I had no arms at that time. Jesse had a pair of .45 Colts, and Ed Miller had a breech-loading shotgun and a pair of Smith & Wesson .44's and an old-fashioned Navy cap-and-ball pistol. We then went from there to old Thomas Eddington's—not to the house, but hitched our horses out in the woods. Next morning I went up to the house to get some food for us. I told for whom I wanted it. After eating breakfast Ed Miller started over to Clay County for 'Father Grimes' [Wood Hite] and a man by the name of Smith, who lives about five or six miles from Kearney, and about three or four miles from Mrs. Samuel's. He was a single man, I learned. Ed Miller was gone two days, and returned with Grimes and Smith. The former he got at his aunt's, Mrs. Samuel. During this time Jesse was hiding at Ben Morrow's and I was at old man Eddington's. Upon Miller's return, I told him to go out in the brush, and I would go after Jesse, which I did. When Jesse and I returned Smith had run off and left. He was afraid he would be killed. He thought that Jesse was going to do it.

"After Smith left we disbanded, Jesse and Grimes going over to Mr. Ford's near Richmond, Ray County, and Miller going to see what had become of Smith. I stayed at Lamartine Hudspeth's. About three days after this Jesse and Grimes came back, and we three went back to Jim Hulse's. A little later after this Ed Miller came up there, also. He said Smith had gone home and acted crazy; lost his pistol, hat, and so on. The next morning I came up to Independence, took the train to Kansas City, and bought me a pair of Smith & Wesson pistols, .44 caliber, from Blitz, the pawnbroker in the *Times* Building. I went back to the train, mounted my horse at Independence, and rode down toward Dick Talley's, and met Jesse and Ed Miller on the road. We went off by the next creek in the woods, where we found Grimes and Bill Ryan. We talked the matter over, and determined there to rob the C. & A. train at Glendale. When we broke up that night, Miller and I went to Tucker Bassham's house. I don't know where the others went, but we were all to meet at the schoolhouse, several miles from Glendale. I did not know at that time who Bassham was, and we did not know his real name until after he was arrested. They called him 'Arkansas.' The next evening, about sundown, Ed Miller and I started for the schoolhouse, and Arkansas was to follow. The schoolhouse is about one mile from Bassham's house. We met at the schoolhouse and all went to Glendale together. We arrived there between 6 and 7 o'clock on October 8, 1879, and hitched our horses about thirty yards due south of the station. Bassham, Ryan, and myself captured Joe Moit's store, and fifteen or twenty men who were in it, and Jesse James, Wood Hite, and Ed Miller captured the depot. Jesse, who was the leader, then sent word to us to bring our prisoners over to the depot, which was done, and we put them all in the depot and guarded them. I think Jesse tore the telegraph apparatus to pieces.

"Bassham thought it was a sewing machine and wanted him to stop, since destroying it would do no good. A little east of the depot obstructions were placed upon the track to stop the train in case flagging failed. When the Eastbound train came in sight he made the operator signal the train to stop. The train stopped. The plan was that I was to capture the engineer and fireman; Bill Ryan was to uncouple the express car from the train, so that we could, after backing the train, run the engine forward again and leave the passenger coaches off to themselves. Bassham and Hite were to keep the passengers on the train, while Jesse James and Ed Miller robbed the express car. The cars had a patent coupling so that Ryan could not unfasten them, so he hailed Bassham and Hite to keep the passengers in. We carried out our respective parts without an exception, except the uncoupling. Fifteen or twenty shots were fired in all, most of them in the air, and a few of them at a man at the rear of the train with a lantern—Jesse said he fired three shots at this man. Ed Miller got a sledgehammer out of the engine and struck the door of the express car several times before the messenger would open it. They went in, and, I think, the messenger tried to get out and Jesse struck him with his pistol. After the car was robbed we were all standing on the depot platform together when someone fired a shot from the train, which went through the drawers and pants of Wood Hite on the outside, between the ankle and knee of his right leg. Jesse remarked, 'They are firing on us and we had better leave.' We then went to our horses, carrying the plunder in a common meal sack.

"We mounted and rode about six or seven miles to a little old log cabin, uninhabited, where we dismounted. Ed Miller carted the plunder. It was here, too, that Bob Ford fell from the rafters on us and nearly got himself killed. Here we divided the plunder equally, each getting $1,025.00. There was a good quantity of bonds, and these were destroyed. We left there all together and traced our steps several miles, when we began to break up, Ryan and Bassham going hom. We took Hite onto the Kansas City road, about halfway between Independence and the bridge over the Big Blue, and left him. He came to Kansas City, to Charley McBride's, I think, a relative. I did not know what Grimes's real name was until next spring, when I learned it was Robert Woodson Hite, and that he lived near Adairville, Kentucky, Adair County. Jesse, Ed, and myself rode down into the six-mile country after the robbery, and I left them in a thick woods, about three-fourths of a mile from Bob Hudspeth's place, and went on to Lamartine Hudspeth's. Lamartine lives about two miles from Bob. From Thursday to Saturday I carried them food. Saturday night, the time that the big raid was made, Jesse and Ed Miller left about 10 o'clock in the direction of Kansas City, and Jesse afterwards said that sometime during the next day [Sunday] they saw members of the raiding party returning to Kansas City.

"For two or three weeks after that I continued to stay in the six-mile area, and then left for Fort Scott, where I hauled coal for about four months. A few days after going toward Kansas City, Ed and Jesse left for the East, going through Kansas City. Ed went to George Hite's near Adairville, Kentucky, and Jesse went to Nashville, Tennessee, where his wife was then living. Frank James and his wife were also living there at that time. After leaving Fort Scott, I went to Carthage, Missouri, where I teamed it for two months, having two teams. Sam Strickland [black man] was with me nearly all of that time. From there I came to Jackson County, and stopping at McCraw's, where I learned that the officers had been looking for me ever since I left Jackson

County. I sent McCraw down to Carthage after Mattie Collins, Strickland, and my teams, and they drove them up. I dodged from one place to another, staying at Lamartine Hudspeth's especially. The same day that they returned from Carthage with the teams, Ed Lee, now deputy marshal under Murphy, and then constable of Osage Township, got after me at Lake City, and we had a little run of about two and a half miles. I was riding a horse from Bob Hudspeth's, which I had down to Lake City for the purpose of entering a race. I had ridden him two races before the chase began.

"I was unarmed at the time. Lee fired two shots at me, but I rode hard right for Hudspeth's, put the horse in the stable, struck out on foot, and next day went to Ben Morrow's, who knew I was dodging the officers, and bought a horse from him in a trade. I gave him one of my wagon horses and a set of harnesses for it, all valued at $125.00. I then rode to Jasper County, Missouri, where I stopped at the house of a man named Johnny Rohr, a German, for whom I worked by the month. I stayed there about a month. While at Fort Scott and Carthage I went by my right name, but at Rohr's I went by the name of James Anderson. I came back by horseback to Jackson County, and went to the home of Widow Broughton, who lived near the Hudspeth's. I stayed there one day and from there went to Mrs. Samuel's, near Kearney, in Clay County. I went to see Ed Miller, since John Samuel had come over and told me he was there. I crossed the river at Blue Mills. Upon arrival I made myself known to Mrs. Samuel. I had been there a few minutes when Jesse James came in. He had been there several days. While I was there I sold him one of my horses, a set of harness, and a wagon for $125.00 He never paid me, however, until he robbed the paymaster at Muscle Shoals, Alabama.

"We stayed about two days at Mrs. Samuel's, and then he and I went to Mrs. Bolton's, about one and a half miles east of Richmond. This is the same place where Sheriff Timberlake and Commissioner Craig made the raid in the early part of January 1882. We found there Charley Ford, Capline [Cap] Ford, Mrs. Bolton, and the children. They knew Jesse, but did not know me. We stayed there a day and a night, and left the place for Bill Ryan's in Jackson County, crossing the Missouri River at Blue Mills. We found Bill at home, and next night left, taking him with us. We crossed through the state to Cape Girardeau, where we crossed the Mississippi River, and went directly to young George Hite's in Logan County, Kentucky. He was living in the house of his father, George B. Hite, where Jeff Hite was afterwards arrested. We were on the road about three weeks, and I did not see any friends while on the route. We found Grimes there, and learned for the first timee here that his real name was Robert Woodson Hite. Jeff [Clarence] Hite was also there. We stayed there a couple of days, and leaving Bill Ryan there, Jesse and I went to Nashville. From Nashville we went to Jesse's home, which was about ten miles from Nashville on the pike, and a quarter of a mile from the Cumberland River. Jesse was going under the name of J. D. Howard, and he pretended to be a sporting man. His wife, son, and daughter were living there, as was Frank James, his wife, and their son. Frank was going by the name of J. W. Woodson. His little son, who was about three years old, was named Robert. Jesse's son was seven years old and called Tim, and his daughter, three years old, was named Mary. Frank's wife was called Fannie, and Jesse's wife was called Josie.

"Frank was engaged at the time in hauling saw logs. We all went up to Nashville very frequently, and made no attempt at concealment, apprehending no special danger. After remaining there about two weeks, Jesse and myself went back to Hites, where we had left Bill Ryan. Young George Hite knew that we were dodging the officers, and he entertained us as friends, and not because we was intimidated. During the day we kept hid in the woods, and at night we slept in the house. Old man George B. Hite brought food to us in the woods more often than anyone else. Clarence and Wood Hite brought it when their father did not. Bill Ryan was going under the name of Thomas Hill. The last time we arrived in the night, and left the same night, taking Bill Ryan with us.

"We started out to rob the Mammoth Cave Stage. It rained so hard, however, that we gave up the idea, after getting within one mile and a half of the place, and we came back to Hite's again. We stayed in the woods at night, and next morning I left for Jesse's place near Nashville, leaving Bill Ryan and Jesse, who said they would knock around the country and see what they could rob. In about ten days Jesse came home and told me that he and Bill Ryan had robbed the Mammoth Cave Stages. This was, I think, in the latter part of August 1880, or September 7th [it was September 3rd]. The stages were robbed within an hour of each other. A lawyer by the name of R. H. Roundtree of Lebanon, Kentucky, lost a handsome gold watch. Jesse got the watch and the key to it. On the key was inscribed the name of J. Proctor Knott and Mr. Roundtree. Jesse has the watch yet. Miss Lizzie Roundtree lost a fine diamond ring, which Jesse James's wife has had made smaller for her finger, and she wears it now. Jesse got from her another plain gold ring, which he gave to Millie Hite, a sister of Clarence Hite. Bill Ryan got one silver watch and a small gold chain. Jesse got another silver watch, which he gave me. This watch I traded with Frank James for a gold watch and chain, I giving a good horse to boot. This gold watch and chain I gave to Mattie Collins. One of the stage robberies Jesse and Ryan got about thirty dollars in cash, which they divided equally. Bill Ryan afterward pawned the watch he got with Dick Talley for a saddle. One of these silver watches, I learned, belonged to W. Welch of Plattsburg, Missouri, and the other I don't know to whom.

"When Jesse came home after this robbery he left Bill Ryan at Hite's again. After remaining at home about a week Jesse left for Hite's again in order to get Ryan, so we three might go up into Kentucky and rob a store about sixty miles from Adairville. Jesse went on horseback and I went on the train to Springfield and walked out to Hite's. The following night Clarence Hite and I went up to Adairville for the purpose of borrowing somebody's horse for an indefinite period of time. We found it hitched at Dr. Hendricks' hitching-post in front of his office. I held Clarence's horse while he got down and unhitched the animal. It belonged to young Simmons, who, I afterwards learned, was visiting the doctor's daughter. The mare was a jet black one with four white feet, and a fine one.

"We went back to Hite's, and the same night Jesse, Ryan, and I started for the store. On Tuesday morning, September 15, 1880, I left Jesse and Ryan in the woods and went into John Devoy's store to reconnoitre. I can't recall the name of the town, but it was some railroad station where they were mining coal. I came back in a short time and reported, and we then went down together. I was to guard the door and not let anyone out, and Jesse and Ryan were to rob the safe. We carried out the program but got only $4.25, and a gold watch and chain. This watch I pawned with a friend in Jackson County, and can get it at any time. Ryan got the change and I don't know what he did with it. This took place between 9 and 10 o'clock in the morning. We left and went toward the country in a beeline for Hite's getting there the following night. We told old man Hite, Wood Hite, and Clarence Hite where we had been and what we had done, but none of them made any objections to our staying around there.

"The horse that we got at Adairville was put in a stall at a grazing ground close to Adairville for the purpose of letting the owner find him, which was done. In a day or two Clarence Hite took Bill Ryan to Nashville in a buggy, where he left by train for Jackson County, Missouri. We intended to follow soon. Jesse and I stayed at Hite's for a few days and then rode down to Jesse's brother, near Nashville. We remained there about two weeks, attending the Nashville races, and then went to Atlanta, Georgia, to attend the races. When this was over we came back to Nashville, and Jesse and I took the train for St. Louis, going from there to Richmond, Ray County. Before leaving Jesse took his family to Nashville, where they stopped at a boarding house. Just after Ryan left for Kentucky and Jesse and I were still at Hite's, we decided to go down and rob the Gallatin safe. On the way down we overtook two young men, attempted to rob them, and had a shooting scrape. One man saw me drawing the pistol and shot at Jesse, who was a little ahead of him. The other man started to draw his, and I shot him through the right leg. He then turned and galloped off. Jesse and the other man exchanged a few shots, and Jesse took to the woods. My horse had run about fifty yards when I turned and the young man and I were closing in. He fired his last shot and then turned and galloped off. Jesse fired two shots at him from the woods and four before running into the woods. I shot three times. We did not get any money that time. We went back to Hite's and thence to Nashville, as I have before stated.

"After Jesse and I reached Richmond we went to Mrs. Bolton's, and met Jim Cummins there. We remained there a day and a night, and then went to Clay County, to Mrs. Samuel's. We were preparing for another strike. We put up in the house, and locked the horses in the stable. We stayed there two days and nights, and I left and rode to Bob Hudspeth's, crossing the river at Missouri City. I stayed there all night and then went to Bill Ryan's to tell him not to go away, since Jesse and Jim Cummins would be there in a couple days. I found him at home and stayed with him until Jesse and Cummins came over. They rode over and crossed the river at Leavenworth bridge. We all then started for Nashville, Tennessee, on horseback, having given up the idea of making a raid. Reaching the Iron Mountain road, I took the train and the other boys led my horse. We got to Nashville about December 1, 1880. Before starting for Tennessee this time, Jim Cummins and I took a horse apiece from a man named Duvall, who lives five or six miles from Richmond. Charley Ford told us where the horses were. These are the horses that Jesse and Jim Cummins rode over to Bill Ryan's on. Then Jesse and Jim took horses from men near Independence. When we got to Nashville my horse was traded with Frank James for the gold watch, as I have stated. Jim Cummins sold his horse through a man who stayed at H. H. Hummer's livery stable. Bill Ryan sold his at the same place, and Jesse sold his at Nashville to someone. Cummins went by the name of Wilson. Just after getting back to Nashville Jesse rented a house in East Nashville [Edgefield] and took his family and Cummins and Ryan to live with him.

"I started out at Frank James's just before the Muscle Shoals robbery. Frank moved to Edgefield, near to where Jesse was living, and I went with him. During this time and for about three months Jesse, Jim Cummins, and Bill Ryan made frequent trips around the country up to Donny Pense's and other places. While living at Edgefield Jesse tried to get us to have Cummins killed, but I would not agree to it. Cummins left, and we, fearing that he would inform on us, scattered. I went to Hite's, Jesse's family moved over to Frank's house, and Jesse, Frank, and Bill Ryan left for Alabama, where they robbed the United States paymaster, Smith, at Muscle Shoals. They got about five thousand, two hundred dollars and a Smith & Wesson .48 caliber pistol. This robbery took place about ten days after we left Edgefield. I did not know anything about it until after Ryan's capture. After the robbery the three came straight back to Nashville. Clarence Hite drove me to Springfield and went down to Nashville on the train with me. I did not let him know where the other boys were, or where they lived.

"The next day Bill Ryan started to Kentucky on horseback, was captured seven miles from Nashville, on the White Creek Pike, was brought back to Missouri and tried for complicity in the Glendale robbery, and was sentenced to twenty-five years hard labor in the Missouri State Penitentiary. As soon as his capture was known to all, we all left Edgefield and went to Hite's. Jesse's wife and family started to Donny Pense's, in Nelson County, Kentucky, and Frank's wife and child came on to Kansas City, putting up at the St. James Hotel. If I am not mistaken they registered on March 30, 1881, and left the next morning. Jesse told me that Thomas M. Mimms, who worked for J. M. James & Sons, Kansas City, either took her out to her father's [Mr. Ralston] or had her taken out there. Jesse, Frank, and I left Old Man Hite's on horseback for Donny Pense's. Jesse and I took our horses from near Adairville; I don't know the owner's name. When within six or seven miles of Donny Pense's [Civil War guerrilla friend of the Jameses and sheriff of Nelson County], Jesse killed his horse, and then he and I rode the same horse to Pense's. We were there about three days after being on the road. We found Jesse's wife and children there. Frank and I left there the same night as our arrival, for Doc Haskins's, about four miles from the Pense place. The next day Frank left for Alex Sears's, who was about one mile from Pense's. The next night after our arrival at Pense's Jesse went to Bob Hall's, about one and a half miles from here. About this time Clarence Hite came up on the train and stopped at Pense's, and from there came over to Bob Hall's, and stayed there about three days, when he, Clarence, and Jesse's family came to Kansas City, and, I think, to Charley McBride's, No. 318 East Seventeenth Street. Jesse and I started for Nelson County about a week later, and then rode to Louisville, Jesse riding a tired horse, which he had stolen from a black man in Nashville, and had let at Donny Pense's. This horse was stolen a little while before Ryan's capture. I rode the horse, a mare, which I had gotten near Adairville. We left these horses at a livery stable near the center of the city, fronting east, I think, and told the proprietor to keep them until we called.

"We have never called yet, and they are still there. We came through Quincy to Kearney, Missouri, and walked out to Mrs. Samuel's. Frank stayed at a Mr. Sears's in Nelson County, Kentucky, until about one week after we left, and then came out by the same route we did [I believe this is Sayers, not Sears]. Johnny Shilling met him near Kearney, and brought him to his mother's, Mrs. Samuel. Frank then wrote to Wood Hite at Adairville, to come out and stop by Mrs. Samuel's, and we remained until Wood arrived. Before he arrived, however, I took a train to Kearney and came back to Kansas City and walked down to Lamartine Hudspeth's. I bought a horse of him for $150. I left with him for security the watch gotten from Devoy, the Kentucky storekeeper. He has it now. He knew I was dodging the officers. I started back north of the river on horseback, crossing the river at Lexington, stopping at Mrs. Bolton's, where I was to remain, according to agreement, until Jesse or Frank either saw me, or sent word what to do. After I was there four or five days Clarence Hite came down to see me by train, and told me that Frank wanted me to come up to the old woman's [Mrs. Samuel].

"I left that night on horseback for her house, and Clarence Hite left by train for the same place. When I arrived next morning, Jesse was absent. Frank and Wood were there, and Clarence did not arrive til late in the evening. The first thing that Frank wanted was for me to go up with him into Platte County and get horses for him and Wood. We went and were gone four or five days, but did not find any good horses, so we did not get any. When we got back Jesse had arrived. We all stayed in the house. Our horses, that is, Jesse's and mine, were kept in the stable. In three or four days Wood and I took the evening train at Kearney, went to Liberty, and there got two horses, saddled and bridled, hitched to a rack near the Arthur House. We rode them back to Mrs. Samuel's. She knew we had gone to Liberty after them."

NOTE: The trips to Chillicothe and Winston, together with the Winston robbery, are herein described much the same as they were described by Liddil when he was on the witness stand in the trial of Frank James. The confession states that the train robbery trip to Chillicothe having failed because of a heavy rain, which made muddy roads and plain tracks, he and Jesse rode back through Plattsburg and took a look at the bank with the view of robbing it, but as it would take a third man to do the trick, they concluded not to attempt it. Strangely enough, no statement of the second unsuccessful trip, in which Gallatin was the objective point, was mentioned in the confession, although it was described with great particularity at the trial. On the other hand, the confession does say the party made a trip to Cameron, to rob a train there, but since the baggage was piled against the end doors of the express car, they abandoned the scheme. Of this Mr. Liddil made no mention in his testimony. After giving the particulars of the Winston robbery, herein, which he stated netted the gang $136. each, and after describing the retreat and the return to Mrs. Samuel's home after the robbery, the story goes on.

"We stayed here three or four days. Charley Ford came up while we were there. We were planning another robbery and Charley was to join us. We bought a two-horse wagon from an old lady and some harness from Bill Nichols. We hitched Charley Ford's and my horse to the wagon and at six started for Kansas City. We started about dark and laid the next day in the woods, reaching the Kansas City bridge about 8 o'clock the next night. Clarence wore a dress and a bonnet belonging to Mrs. Samuel, while crossing the bridge, she having loaned it to him for that purpose. Charley Ford and Wood Hite walked over. The others rode in the wagon. After getting across they all got into the wagon. Charley Ford and Jesse stopped in Kansas City, and the remainder went down the Independence road to about a couple of miles beyond the bridge over the Blue, where Frank and Wood met us. Clarence and I drove the wagon to Mr. Crow's. We got there soon in the morning and stayed all night, and then got Mr. Crow's little boy to come up to Independence and take our horses back.

"While on the road to Independence I let the horse I got from Lamartine Hudspeth go back to him a mile north of Lake City. We all three then came to Hudspeth's and got my breech-loading shotgun, which he had been keeping for me. We all met at a point in Independence and sent the horses back by the boy, whose name was Andy. We had come by agreement to meet the other boys at the wagon-gate about one and one-fourth miles south of Independence on the C. & A. Road. When we arrived we found Jesse, Frank, Charley, and Wood Hite. We went up to examine the Missouri Pacific that night, and stayed in the woods about one mile from the T. & K. We prowled around there for several hours and finally concluded to rob the Missouri Pacific train, East bound. This was on Friday night. Frank and Jesse, unknown to us, went out about mid-dawn, ostensibly to hunt for railroad ties with which to block the track, and while about it they fixed a piece of iron to the rail and to ditch the train.

"This plan did not suit the balance of us, but since the train was almost due, not much was said. The train came along and ran right over the iron, passing clear. The next night we were to take the Chicago & Alton train at Glendale, but we were too tired and gave up the idea. The train came along, and it was guarded by men we could plainly see on the platform. We then came up near Independence and disbanded. Wood and I went to Mrs. Bolton's, crossing in a skiff near Lexington. The other four came back to Kansas City. We stayed down there about two weeks more, when Jesse sent us word by Charley Ford to meet him right away at the same place as our last meeting near Independence. Charley had been going backward and forward between Richmond and Kansas City. While staying at Mrs. Bolton's during this time, Charley and I robbed a stage, one that runs between Excelsior Springs and Vibbard. It was going toward the springs. There was a merchant in it named Gant and the driver. Charley made them stand and I made them deliver. We got about thirteen dollars from the merchant and seventeen dollars from the driver. Charley had on a mask, but I had none. This took place between sundown and dark. We went back to Mrs. Bolton's from there. About a week after this Charley and Bob Ford, Wood Hite, and myself robbed a stage going from the Short Line Depot to Lexington. It was down in Ray County. We all wore masks. It occurred about dark. A mover came along and found us hidden and wanted to know what it meant. We explained the situation to him by capturing him and taking twenty dollars of his hard-earned money. In about five minutes or so the stage came along. There were eight passengers on it, I think, two of them women. Bob and Wood made them stand, while Charley and I robbed them. We made the men get out, but did not molest the women. We got about two hundred dollars in money, one gold watch and chain, a nickel-plated watch and gold chain, one silver watch, no chain, and one pocket-knife. Wood Hite got one of the watches, the silver one, which he afterwards sold to me. I gave it to Bob Ford and he has it yet. Bob got the nickel-plated watch and chain. Wood Hite afterwards won it or bought it from him, and give it to Cap Ford, who has it yet. The gold watch and chain fell to my lot, and I gave it to Ida Bolton. She has it yet. Hite got the knife, has it yet.

"We went back to Mrs. Bolton's after the robbery. Charley went back on the train, and Wood and I went to the appointed place with Jesse. After being at the rendezvous we found Charley Ford and shortly afterward Frank, and we went down to one mile of old man Ralston's, where we met Jesse and Clarence. We then went down to the U. & A. road, half a mile south of Doc Reed's. We stayed there all night and day. The following night we went up to within two hundred or three hundred yards of Old Man Ralston's. There we met Frank, who had left us for the purpose of getting provisions. He had a basket full, which I suppose he got from his father-in-law, Ralston. From there we went to a spot near Glendale. We lay in the bush all the next day, and I went down to a section house and got some meat.

"That night we robbed the C. & A. train, Easternbound. It was the night of Wednesday, September 7, 1881; this was called the Blue Cut robbery. Our program was this: Wood Hite and Charley Ford were to stop the train by swinging a red lantern. This red light was an ordinary lantern with a red piece of clothing tied around it. We had piled rocks upon the track so as to obstruct it. After the train had stopped Charley and Wood were to capture the engineer and fireman, and then rob the express car. Jim and Clarence were on one side of the train, upon the bank, and Frank and myself upon the other side. Besides our pistols, we had a breech-loading shotgun, and Frank had a Winchester rifle; Jesse James had a breech-loading shotgun and Clarence had a Winchester rifle. The train came along in due time and the engineer saw the red lantern; soon the engineer and fireman were captured. The fireman was made to take his sledgehammer and attempt to break down the door of the express car. After he had struck several blows the express messenger opened the door.

"Charley and Wood went in, and Charley struck the messenger several times and made him open the safe, which they then robbed. Very little was found in the safe, and Jesse suggested robbing the passengers. Charley and Wood commenced at the front of the train, Wood carrying the bag and Charley making the passengers disgorge. Clarence stood at the door on the platform, and Jesse and myself were at one time in the rear car, but this was after the passengers had been robbed. Frank got on one of the forward coaches. Just after the train stopped a man started back down the tracks with a lantern. We fired a number of shots at him, but when told that he was going to flag down a freight train we stopped shooting at him. No one was in sight besides ourselves when he stopped the train. When the train started again we all were on the way to Independence. About a mile or so from the scene of the robbery we stopped in the woods and divided the loot. This consisted of a breast pin, a set of earrings, five watches—two with and three without chains—two rings, one gold pin, and one with a set in it, and some money. Everything in the jewelry line was piled up and sold to the highest bidder—except two rings—Jesse got one and I the other. The bid money was thrown in with the rest of the cash and all was distributed equally among us. The six of us got one hundred sixty dollars apiece. As near as I can remember Jesse also got one of the watches, a nickel-plated one. Wood Hite got a gold watch belonging to the messenger. Charley Ford got two, a gold one and a silver one. I don't know what disposition was made of them. Clarence got the silver one. Jesse said he threw his away, and I gave mine to Mrs. Bolton. After the division Wood and I started for the Blue Mills ferry, with the intention of going to Mrs. Bolton's. The other four started for Kansas City. Wood and I were running into officers near Blue Mills ferry, but we pushed out into the woods. There we separated. Wood went down the river to cross at Sibley, and went to Mrs. Bolton's, and I went to Ben Morrow's. I got there in the morning after staying all night near there in the brush. I told him about the robbery and that I was in it. I also told him that Frank, Jesse, Wood Hite, Clarence Hite, and a man named Johnson from Texas were also in on it.

"I did not wish to tell on Charley Ford, and that is the reason I gave him these lies. [There is no question but that Bob Ford and Jim Cummins also were there.] I took breakfast at Morrow's and stayed around there, hid in the woods and stable for two nights. Morrow knew where I was all the time and furnished me with the food that I got. He brought me a couple bottles of whiskey also. When I left, he told me where I could get a skiff to cross the river. I did not go there, however, but went to Sibley and crossed the river in a skiff, one that I got loose from the bank and used. After crossing I went to Mrs. Bolton's. After being there a couple of weeks, Charley Ford brought us word from Jesse that he wanted us to go to Kentucky and rob the Louisville and Nashville road. Wood and I then took the train to Richmond and sent word to Jesse that we would meet them near Old Man Hite's, near Adairville, Kentucky. We arrived at Hite's, and, being there some five days, Wood and I had a shooting scrape, and I came back to Mrs. Bolton's. I had been back only about three nights when Frank, Clarence, and Charley Ford came in. They stayed only a day and a night, then leaving for Kentucky, wanting me to go with them, but I declined to do so.

"I remained here two or three weeks and then Bob Ford and I crossed over to Jackson County at Missouri City. We went to McGraw's and stayed about a week. He was out with the threshing machine when we got there, and I did not see him but once while there. We then went back to Mrs. Bolton's, crossing the Missouri River in a skiff. We arrived here Saturday night, December 3, 1881. Next morning I came down to breakfast, and Wood Hite, who had come from Kentucky two or three days before, came down with Ford a few minutes later. When he came in he spoke to me, and I told him not to speak to me. since he had accused me of stealing one hundred dollars in the division of the Blue Cut robbery money. I told him he said he could prove it, and I now wanted him to prove it. One thing led to another and then the firing commenced. He shot me through the right leg, and I fired five times at him, and snapped the barrel. I drew my other revolver when he commenced falling.

"Bob Ford fired shots at Wood, but I didn't know this until afterwards when he exhibited an empty chamber in his revolver. The shot that killed Wood Hite was through the head. It struck him almost two inches above the right eye and came out a little above the left ear. Bob claimed that his shot was the fatal one. He lived fifteen or twenty minutes, but did not speak. [The Jesse James death wound was almost exactly as this one.] We carried him upstairs, and that night, December 4th, Cap Ford and Bob Ford dug a grave in the woods, about a mile from the house, and buried him. They did not use a coffin. My leg was too sore to allow me to help them. I did not have a physician dress my wound, nor did I give it any attention until I surrendered. On the night of Thursday, the 29th of December, Jesse and Charley Ford came down to Mrs. Bolton's, where I had been since being wounded, and tried to get me to go with them. They claimed to have come from Nebraska. I declined to go. I mistrusted that Jesse intended to kill me, and so left. Jesse and Charley Ford left the next night for the old lady's, I was told. This was the last time I saw either of them. After the raid on Mrs. Bolton's, early in January, 1882, I concluded to surrender. Negotiations to that effect were made, and on the night of January 21, 1882, by direction of Governor Thomas T. Crittenden, I surrendered to Sheriff James R. Timberlake, Clay County, Missouri. Dick is a nickname for me since I have been on the dodge.

"Since on the run I have stopped at Bob Hudspeth's, six times; Thomas Eddington, four or five times; Ben Morrow's, three times; McCraw's, five or six times; Andy Ryan's, four or five times; Tom Conway's, five times; Dick Talley's, two times; Lamartine Hudspeth's, a great many times; all of these parties knew I was dodging the officers. They never made any objections to entertaining me. They were friends of mine. Others of our gang who were on the dodge were at Jim Hulse's. When Jesse, Ryan, Cummins, and I started for Tennessee in November 1880, as we passed through Lafayette County Jim Cummins and I went and stopped at General Jo Shelby's, and had a talk with him. We told him that Jesse and Ryan would be along after a while, and would stay all night with him, but we had become separated. He said he had a good many hired men working for him, and that so many of us together might excite suspicion, and that we had better go on and stop at some other home, and Jesse and Ryan could stay when they came. We thereupon passed on, leaving word for Jesse that we would be back the next morning. I did not know General Shelby personally, but Jim Cummins did. We stayed all night at the house about a mile off, and the next morning came back to Shelby's, and Jesse and Ryan were in the house. We stayed about an hour, the general bringing out his jug of brandy and giving us a drink. We then left, the general inviting us to call again. We continued on into Tennessee, Ryan and Cummins stopping at a man's by the name of Benjamin Sallee, who was a friend or a relative of Jesse, and Jesse and I stopping about four miles from there. The gold watch that Charley Ford got out of the Blue Cut robbery, he left it for a while at Bill Hulse's, in Clay County. I saw it there March 1, 1882, but don't know if it is there now

or not. The men who are now under arrest for robbing the C. & A.
train at Blue Cut were not in the robbery at all. I never saw any one
of them but John Bugler, and I saw him at Hudspeth's about the 10th
of November 1880. I went there with Bill Ryan, but did not go into
the house. Bugler was called out to the fence."

Memorandum of robberies as outlined by Dick Liddil:

"The Russellville bank robbery occurred in Logan County, Ken-
tucky. It is said to have taken place March 20, 1868. Jesse James
told me that Frank James, George Shepherd, John Jarrette, Cole
Younger, and himself and someone else executed this robbery. The
Liberty Bank robbery was in Clay County, Missouri, on February 13,
1866. Ten men were engaged. Jesse told me that it was committed by
Frank James, George Shepherd, Archie Clements, John Jarrette, Payne
Jones, Dick Burns, and I learned from Bill Burns that Bub Pense
[Pence] was also there. Jesse said that he himself was not there. He
said he has been accused of killing Wimers [Wymore] on the day of
the robbery, but that it was done by George Shepherd.

"The Gallatin Bank robbery occurred at Gallatin, Daviess County,
Missouri, on December 16, 1869. Two men were engaged. Jesse told me
that he and Jim White committed this robbery, but did not say who
killed John W. Sheets, the cashier. [Jim White is now serving a sentence
in the Texas State Prison.] The Corydon Bank robbery occurred at
Corydon, Iowa, and Jesse said that he, Frank James, Clell Miller,
Cole Younger, and John Younger were in on it. Jesse told me that the
Kansas City Fair holdup was committed by him, Frank, Jim Cummins,
Ol Shepherd, and Arthur McCoy. The Gaines place stage robbery occurred in January 1874, and Jesse told me that he and Frank were in
on it, I don't know who else.

"At the Gads Hill train robbery Jesse told me that he and Frank
and Bill Greenwood were among those on this occasion. Regarding
the killing of Detective Whicher, Jesse told me that he, Frank, Tom
McDaniels, and Jim Cummins were at Mrs. Samuel's when Whicher
came there. They captured him and Jesse, McDaniels, and Frank rode
off with him. Frank and McDaniels shot him. With regard to the
murder of Farmer Askew, Jesse told me that he watched for Askew
and finally got the chance to kill him. I learned from another source
that Clell Miller was also along. Jesse told me that he, Frank, Tom
McDaniels, Bud McDaniels, and Jim Hines were in on the robbery,
the one at Muncie, Kansas.

"With regard to the Huntington, West Virginia, bank robbery,

Jesse told me that he, Frank, Tom McDaniels, Clell Miller, and Jack Kean pulled that robbery. [Tom McDaniels was shot and killed soon after by the Dillon boys; Jack Kean (Thomas Webb) was sentenced to prison, and Clell Miller died at Northfield in 1876. It was most diffi- cult to learn much of Webb after his imprisonment at Moundsville, West Virginia. Even the prison records held no information, even the officials stating he had died there. However, the Census Records show him to have been working in the wagon shop at the prison in 1880. There was no record at the prison of his release or of his pardon. This was a challenge. With the aid of good people in West Virginia the original pardon for Webb was found in the West Virginia State Uni- versity Library. Webb had served seven years of his prison term and was pardoned by Governor Jackson in 1883. It is believed he then returned to his home in Pike County, Illinois.] At the Otterville train robbery Jesse told me that he, Frank, Cole Younger, Tom McDaniels, and Clell Miller were there.

"About the Northfield bank robbery: No details were given me but Ed Miller told me that he, Jesse, and Frank James a short time after the robbery went to Mrs. Samuel's. They were both wounded. Jesse told me that he also was at General Shelby's in Lafayette County before he got well of the wound."—Signed   James A. Liddil.

The signature was attested to by Commissioner Craig of Kansas City and W. O. Heckett, Secretary of the Kansas City Board of Police Commissioners.

Jesse Edwards James, Jesse's son, age 19.

Jesse Edwards James, Jesse's son, as a young man.

Studio photo of Mary James, daughter of Jesse.

Jim Cummins.

Dick Liddil.

Grave of Jim Cummins.

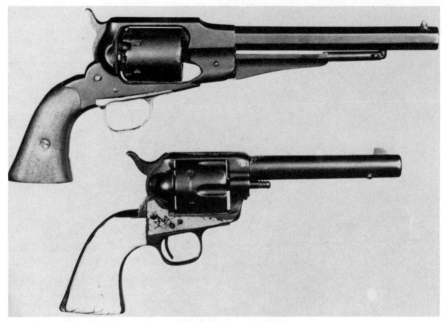

Jesse's Remington revolver and Belle Starr's pistol.

Smith & Wesson Schofield .45 Cal., which Jesse James favored.

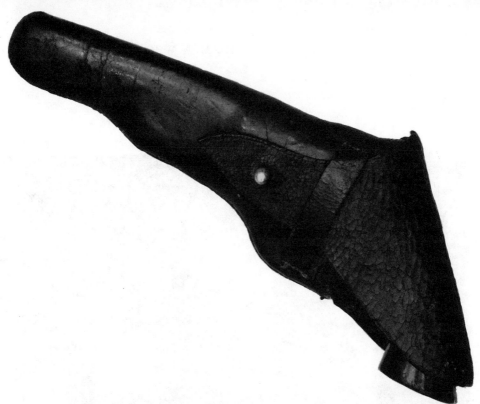

Smith & Wesson Model 2 Army—Hickok used this type of gun.

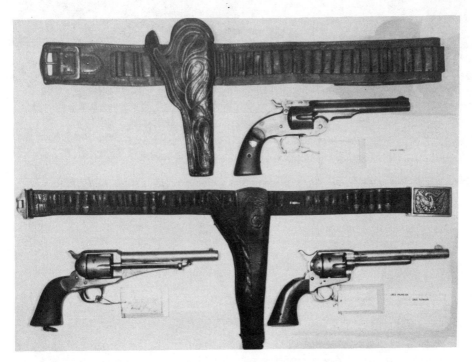

Top: Jesse James' .45 Smith & Wesson Schoffield, serial 366, given to the son of Governor Crittenden by Jesse's widow, for his kindness to the family. Left: Remington .44–.40 Frontier, Serial 15116; the gun which Frank James surrendered to Governor Crittenden. Right: Cole Younger's Colt Frontier model, also presented to the Missouri governor.

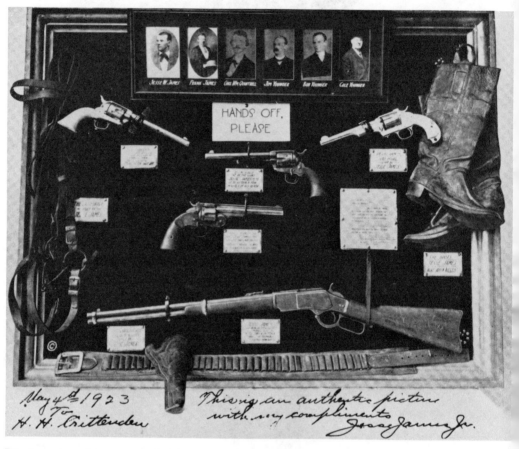

Display of outlaw guns and other possessions belonging to Frank and Jesse James and Cole Younger.

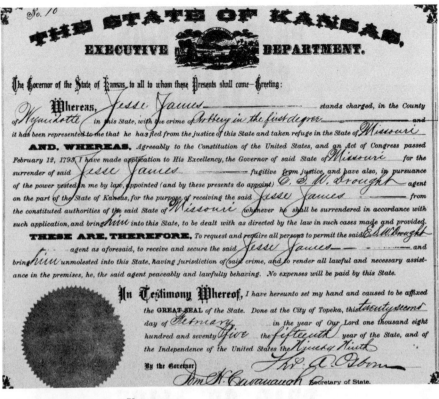

Jesse James warrant—Kansas.

Jesse James warrant—Missouri.

PROCLAMATION
$5,000⁰⁰

REWARD

FOR EACH of SEVEN ROBBERS of THE TRAIN at
WINSTON,MO.,JULY 15,1881, and THE MURDER of
CONDUCTER WESTFALL

$ 5,000.00

ADDITIONAL for ARREST or CAPTURE

DEAD OR ALIVE
OF JESSE OR FRANK JAMES

THIS NOTICE TAKES the PLACE of ALL PREVIOUS
REWARD NOTICES.
CONTACT SHERIFF, DAVIESS COUNTY, MISSOURI
IMMEDIATELY
T. T. CRITTENDEN, GOVERNOR
STATE OF MISSOURI
JULY 26, 1881

16 • • •

Jesse's Last Move

In June of 1881 Jesse James moved his family to Kansas City, where he rented a neat frame house on Woodland Avenue between 13th and 14th Streets.

So secret were the movements of the outlaw and his family that no one except the Mimms family even knew they were living in Kansas City. John W. Mimms had married Mary James, and they had twelve children of their own, six of whom reached maturity. Among these was Zerelda Amanda Mimms, who brought grief to her mother by her marriage to Jesse Woodson James, her double first cousin. In 1857 John W. and Mary Mimms sold their land in Logan County, Kentucky, and moved to Harlem, Missouri, a busy waterfront town just across the river from Kansas City.

John W. and Mary Mimms were living in Kansas City in 1860, moving back to Harlem in 1865. It was during that stay in Harlem that Jesse James was brought to the Mimms home and nursed by the family for a serious gunshot wound he had received while riding to Lexington, Missouri, to surrender after the end of the Civil War. It was then that Zerelda fell in love with him. By 1867 John W. and Mary Mimms were back in Kansas City, operating a boarding house on Second and High Streets. John Mimms died in April 1869. Mary was living in Kansas City in 1872 on Sixth Street, between Walnut and Grand Avenue. She moved back to Harlem shortly thereafter, but in 1877 was living at 1005 Grand Avenue, Kansas City, where she died on July 23rd of that year. She had been spared the agony of all the morbid reports carried in the papers after the death of Jesse James.

Never did she hear from Zee; Mary Mimms was buried in the Union Cemetery, Kansas City, Missouri.

It was in the house on Woodland Avenue that the James family occupied for about three months close to the scene of the dashing Kansas City Fair robbery of 1872, that the Winston robbery was planned. On the 13th of September Jesse, using the name of T. J. Jackson, rented a house on East Ninth Street, in the first block east of Woodland Avenue. After living there a month, the family moved to 1017 Troost Avenue.

It was while Jesse was living in Kansas City that Mrs. Frank James and her son, along with one of Jesse's children, to throw off suspicion, came to Kansas City and registered at the St. James Hotel. Frank went to 1017 Troost Avenue, where he stayed several days with his brother. It was at this time, too, that Jesse rode the train to visit his mother at Kearney, Missouri. He ran considerable risk in doing so, although he was careful to avoid any inquisitive persons. At that particular time when the conductor was taking in the tickets, he noted that a certain passenger had lost a finger joint. He was going through the train a second time when he stopped at the man's seat.

"Say, are you Jesse James?" he laughed. "I know that he's minus part of a finger and I see you are too."

"What! You compare me with that brigand?" Jesse retorted indignantly, being as prudent as he always was.

"Of course not, I was just joshing," said the conductor.

One can well imagine his surprise when he saw the death photo of Jesse James in the St. Joseph papers a few months later.

During the latter part of October of 1881 Jesse paid his mother a farewell visit at the Samuel farm. There he met Charley Ford, who stated he was fleeing from officers, and asked to be protected. His appeal to the outlaw was not made in vain.

"Well, Charley, it seems I can return the favor. The Fords protected me a number of times," replied Jesse.

Jesse explained that he was taking his family to St. Joseph, Missouri, and there Charley Ford could be sheltered under his roof. It was just part of the plot to exterminate Jesse James; it gave one of the Fords a full opportunity to spy on the outlaw.

On November 5, 1881, the James household effects were placed in a wagon and with his family, accompanied by Charley Ford, Jesse James started out for St. Joseph. En route, they again stopped at the home of his mother, where Robert Ford joined them, although he did not accompany them to St. Joseph, and probably did not know their destination at that time. They arrived there on November 8th, renting a house at the corner of Lafayette and 21st Streets, the family using the name of Thomas Howard—it was the last of his many aliases.

On the day before Christmas they moved to a neat frame cottage of seven rooms on Lafayette Street, near 13th, the address being 1318 Lafayette Street. The house was a one-story cottage, painted white, with green shutters, and romantically situated on the brow of a lofty hill east of the city, commanding a fine view of the principal portions of the city, the river, and the railroads, and adapted by nature for the perilous and desperate calling of Jesse James. The house had been formerly occupied by City Councilman Aylesbury, and he rented it to the Jameses for fourteen dollars a month.

Just east of the house was a deep, gulchlike ravine, and beyond a broad expanse of open country backed by a belt of timber. The house, except from the west side, could be seen for several miles. There was a large yard attached to the cottage, and a stable large enough to house two or three horses, several of which were found there on the morning of the murder. Charley and Bob Ford had been occupying one of the rooms in the rear of the dwelling, and were posing as the Johnson brothers, cousins of Jesse James. (However, they were not related as some sources claim to this date.)

St. Joseph had planned well for another Christmas Eve. Early in the evening Jesse could see the trees and ornaments in the various houses and watched the hustle and bustle of the last minute activities. It was like that everywhere—except at the James home at 1318 Lafayette—Jesse felt badly about it too, loving his two children as he did.

"Dammit!" muttered Jesse to himself. "The children can hang up their stockings, but what can I put in them?"

Zee noticed his frustration. The spirit of the season also had struck her. She was a good Christian woman and the Christmas season had always been an occasion at her home.

"Dave [she always called Jesse that], perhaps we can do something after all. I noticed a sign in town stating there was a party at the church. I am sure you can get some candy and popcorn there; maybe even a few toys."

"Yes, Mary [he usually called her that], it is worth a try."

Jesse donned his coat and walked briskly to the nearby Presbyterian church, where he quickly noted a variety of Christmas things, including several Santa Claus suits.

"I've got it! I'll dress up like Santa and thrill the children. I can get the suit back in an hour or so." So, muttering to himself, the noted outlaw stuffed some goodies into a small bag, together with the suit, and started for home.

It was no easy task to bypass his inquisitive children; even Zee looked a little perplexed when Jesse darted into one of the side bedrooms and locked the door. He later retreated to the same room, donned the suit, and, carrying the bag of candy and toys, slipped out into the night. Several minutes later a loud banging was heard on the front door and a hearty "Ho-ho-ho!" split the cold night air.

"Mother!" cried young Jesse [Tim, as they called him], "Who is at the door?"

As the door opened and "Santa" peered into the room, a look of awe and disbelief crossed the faces of the children, as well as that of Mrs. James.

"Tim and Mary, have you been good children?"

"Yes, Santa, ask Mom and Dad," and their anxious eyes darted about the room for a sign of their father.

After Jesse had distributed the toys and candy to his two children, his son rushed up to him and asked for more, at the same time digging into the bag that dangled at the side of "Santa Claus." Suddenly the mystified lad backed away—his searching tiny hands had come in contact with the butt of a Smith & Wesson .44.

"Shucks, you're not Santa, you're only my dad!" cried the boy.

It took a lot of persuading from both Jesse and Zee to convince the two disappointed children that Jesse had volunteered to help Old Saint Nick that night. After the children had been put to bed Jesse hurried back to the church and returned the Santa Claus suit, wondering with a smile which Santa had not worked that evening.

On March 12, 1882, Jesse and Charley rode into northern Kansas and southern Nebraska, having previously addressed a letter to one J. D. Calhoun at Lincoln, Nebraska, in reply to the man's ad regarding the sale of a farm in that area. The letter was dated March 2, 1882, and signed "Tho. Howard, No. 1318 Lafayette St., St. Joseph, Mo." The ad that Mr. Calhoun had placed in the Lincoln, Nebraska *Journal* gave a glowing account of the fine 160-acre farm he had for sale.

During their sojourn Jesse noted that the bank at Forest City, Kansas, a small village, would be an ideal place to stage a robbery. However, Charley begged him to abandon the idea, claiming he was ill and would not be of much use in the venture.

Before returning to St. Joseph, Jesse and Charley made several visits at their old haunts in Clay and Ray Counties, Missouri. There Charley met his brother Bob, telling him they would do Jesse in at the first chance. Jesse was glad to receive young Bob as a new recruit in a planned bank robbery at Platte City, Missouri.

Apparently Mrs. Samuel did not trust the Ford brothers; she probably knew a lot of their early crimes and their vengeful dispositions, especially Bob. She pulled Jesse aside the night before the three men left for St. Joseph.

"Jess, I don't trust those Fords. You'd best be on your guard all the time."

'Mother, don't worry. I know you mean well, but what does a graying mother know about recruits in this business?"

Mrs. Samuel just shook her head, patting her son on the shoulder with the stub of her right arm at the same time. It was the last time she saw him alive.

Jesse James and the Fords arrived in St. Joseph on March 23, 1882, riding directly from Kearney to their destination.

Jesse generally kept himself pretty close within doors during the daytime, only going out in the evening to buy the Kansas City papers and to look about the town. He avoided conversing too freely with the townspeople, although he did turn out to see the sights. On St. Patrick's Day he had ridden in the annual parade, riding a fine horse alongside those of the mayor and City Marshal Enos Craig. The family was under less restraint than when living at Kansas City, and some acquaintances were formed who remembered the Howards as a pleasant family.

Everyone seemed to like the two James children.

"No children could be brought up better than they were," was the usual reply when someone would ask the question.

"Mrs. Howard would take the children to Sunday school regularly, and she would read to them from their Sunday school papers and teach them how to pray. They were good children and I was very fond of them," one woman later said, tearfully.

The general impression of the neighbors regarding Mr. Thomas was that he was a retired businessman or a cattle buyer.

"He seemed familiar with the ways of the world," one merchant said. "He was always neatly dressed and clean."

The wife of a doctor who had treated Mrs. James now and then had this to say, "I am sure that, if he had been given the opportunity, he would have been a respectable and highly successful citizen."

17 • • •

Death of Jesse James

Bob and Charley Ford made frequent trips to their home in Ray County while living with Jesse James at St. Joseph, and had gone there the latter part of March to visit with their relatives.

Late on the night of April 1, 1882, Jesse rode up to the home of Elias (Capline) Ford and called Bob outside. He told him that he had work for him, and the two rode away together. The next day Elias Ford notified Sheriff Timberlake that Bob had gone to St. Joseph, no doubt in order to make final preparations for the Platte City robbery. The sheriff notified his posse to be ready at a moment's notice and kept an engine steamed up so they could race to St. Joseph.

After Jesse and Bob arrived at the suburbs of the city, Jesse seemed suspicious and would not allow Bob out of his sight for any length of time. Each morning he sent Bob downtown for the papers, telling him what certain time he must be back. These papers Jesse always read, the Kansas City and the St. Joseph papers, as well as the St. Joe local.

Sheriff Timberlake had warned Bob Ford to keep the papers from Jesse as much as possible, since some reporters were getting wind of Liddil's surrender, although news of it had not yet been published. When Jesse questioned Bob about Liddil, Bob said he knew nothing about Liddil that Jesse didn't know. On the morning of April 3rd Bob brought the papers in before breakfast. Jesse was seated in front of Bob, reading the *St. Louis Republican*. Bob finished scanning the *Kansas City Journal* and picked up the *Kansas City Times*. He almost dropped it as if it were a serpent, for the headlines, half a foot high, screamed out the news of Dick Liddil's surrender. Bob almost fainted at the suddenness of it. He made an effort to hide the paper under a

206

shawl on the chair. Jesse walked over to the chair, removed the shawl, tucked the paper under his arm, and went into the kitchen for breakfast. Ford knew that his game of deception was up. He moved around so that his revolver was close to his right hand.

Mrs. James poured out the coffee and then sat down at one end of the table. Charley Ford was at the other end, and the two children sat one on each side of their mother. Jesse spread the paper on the table in front of him, folding his arms and scanning the headlines.

"Hello, here! Surrender of Dick Liddil!" was all he said at first. Then he looked across the table at Bob, whose heart was in his throat and who thought he was about to die.

"Young man," Jesse went on, "I thought you told me you didn't know anything about Dick."

"I didn't."

"Well," said Jesse, "it's very strange. He surrendered three weeks ago, and you was right there in the neighborhood. It looks fishy to me."

Jesse glared at Bob until the young man could stand it no longer. He got up and walked back into the front room. Jesse followed him. Bob later said that he thought the shooting would begin at once, but Jesse spoke placatingly. Many people wondered why Jesse did not kill Ford then and there.

"Well, it's all right anyway, Bob."

Instantly the real purpose of Jesse's new attitude flashed upon Bob Ford. The outlaw was not going to kill him in front of his wife and children but would dispose of him that night on the ride to Platte City. Mrs. James was pregnant at the time, and apparently Jesse did not want to upset her. (She later had a miscarriage due to the stress of Jesse's murder.)

Jesse walked over to the bed and deliberately unbuckled his belt and threw it upon the bed. He also removed a pocket pistol, which he threw alongside his gunbelt containing one pistol. It was the first time in his life that Bob had seen Jesse not wearing his weapons. He realized that Jesse had removed them in order to quiet any suspicions. There was no doubt that Jesse wanted to impress upon Ford that he had forgotten the incident of the headlines, for he picked up a feather duster from the table and said, "Golly, that picture is awful dusty."

Ford later stated that there wasn't a speck of dust on that picture that he could see, and he also stated Zee was such a good housekeeper that she would never have permitted it to begin with. Jesse then climbed up on a chair beneath the picture and began to dust the frame.

Bob thought, "It is now or never. There he stands, unarmed. If I don't get him now, he'll get me tonight."

Bob pulled his revolver and leveled it as he sat. Jesse heard the hammer click as the gun was cocked and turned just as Bob pulled the trigger. The bullet struck the outlaw in the forehead and lodged behind the right ear. Jesse James, the world's greatest outlaw, fell like a giant oak, dead. Ford did not go near the body. Later he stated he fired only once, for he knew the heavy .44 slug had done its lethal work.

Charley Ford ran into the room, and right behind him was Mrs. James, who began to mourn while she bitterly upbraided Ford.

"It was an accident!" cried Bob Ford.

"Yes, an accident on purpose. You traitor, Bob Ford, traitor, traitor!" cried Mrs. James, as she tried in vain to wipe away the blood from the wound in Jesse's head.

Zee James was a neat and rather prepossessing person who had obviously been well reared among good and holy influences. She was slender, fair of face, light hair, blue eyes, and had a high forehead. She was wearing a neat-fitting calico. When she stood face to face with Ford's awful deed, she took the matter in a cool manner, other than for the first outburst. Perhaps she had lived in expectation of this tragedy for a long time. The two children were brought into the room, and they grieved as though they knew how the loss of a father's love and protection would change their lives.

Ford ran from the house, leaped over the plank fence, called to a passerby, asking him to notify the police that he had just killed Jesse James. In a little while the officials came, and the Fords surrendered. They sent telegrams to Governor Crittenden, Sheriff Timberlake, Commissioner Craig, and several others, before Marshal Enos Craig of St. Joseph put them in jail. The wires simply read: "I have got my man," and it was signed Bob Ford. Several read differently but in essence all were the same.

At 10 o'clock on the morning of the murder, Assistant Coroner James W. Heddens was notified, and he instructed Undertaker Sidenfaden to remove Jesse's remains to his establishment. As the body lay in a remote room of the building, reporters compared photographs of Jesse James with the dead man's features and searched for identifying scars.

Jesse James was about five feet eight or nine inches tall, of a firm and compact build, but rather on the slender side, wearing a size thirty-two belt. His hair was dark, not overly long, his eyes blue, well shaded with dark lashes, and the entire lower portion of his face was covered by a full growth of dark brown or sun-browned whiskers, which were carefully trimmed. His complexion was fair, and he was not sunburned at this time of the year in spite of his outdoor activities. He was neatly clad in a business suit of dark brown cashmere, which fit him neatly. He wore a shirt of spotless whiteness, with collar and cravat, and looked more like a substantial businessman than like the noted outlaw that he was.

Those who searched for scars found two large bullet wounds in the right side of the breast, within three inches of the nipple, a bullet wound in the leg, and the top of the middle finger of the left hand missing. Another identifying sign was a birthmark on the back of Jesse's right arm above the elbow, a dark brown spot in the shape of a potato. They also saw the results of Jesse's getting his left foot caught in the stirrup and dislocating an inside anklebone, which had never healed properly, but was pushed inward—was this ankle injured at the Gallatin bank robbery?

Through contact with relatives of Jesse James, I was informed that people who knew where to look also found another scar, this the result of the lancing of an abcess in Jesse's right groin, and which operation had been performed by Dr. Glen E. Bishop of St. Joseph, Missouri, who also saw the same scar on the body of the dead outlaw.

The reputable citizens of Missouri who identified the remains of Jesse James knew who he was; his ex-Quantrillian comrades knew who he was, yet in later years men came forward to say they were the real Jesse James. One important man to identify the body was Dr. George W. James, even though he has never been mentioned. Three brothers, George W. James, James H. James, and William James (no relation to Jesse) came from southern Illinois, later graduating from the Rush College in Chicago. All doctors, they settled in Missouri, Dr. George James establishing his medical practice at Claysville, about six miles from the James farm; Dr. William James settled at Lawson, about eight miles east and five miles north of the farm, and Dr. James H. James set up his practice at Elmira, five miles northeast of Lawson. Dr. George James on occasion was called to attend the James family, once taking care of a finger that Jesse had accidently shot the tip from. After Ford had killed Jesse James, Dr. George James was asked by Governor Crittenden to identify the body of Jesse. The doctor went to Lawson and took the Santa Fe train, about forty-five miles from St.

Joseph. On his return his brother Dr. William James met him at the train.

"Yes, it was Jesse, all right. The finger I tended was easy to identify."

I am indebted to James H. James, son of Dr. James H. James for this new information regarding the James story.

Bob Ford's talk with newspapermen before the inquest differs somewhat from his personal report to the governor, in which he stated he was alone in the room when Jesse was shot. Possibly he changed his story at the suggestion of the governor so that Charley Ford could share in the reward and full amnesty. This is what he said:

"So they say the dead man isn't Jesse James, do they? Then they are mistaken. I first met Jesse James three years ago, and I have made no mistake. He used to come over to the house when I was on my oldest brother's farm. Last November he moved here to St. Joe and went under the name of Thomas Howard. He rented a house on a hill, back of the Worlds Hotel, a quiet part of town and not thickly settled. My brother Charley and I had known nearly all of the gang, but have never worked with them otherwise.

"I was in collusion with the detectives, and was one of the party that went to Kentucky and arrested Clarence Hite, last February. Hite got twenty-five years in the penitentiary. Jesse never suspected that we were false to him, and since his gang was all broken up, he wanted new material and regarded us favorably.

"Today his wife and a boy of seven and a girl of three were in the kitchen. Jesse was in the front sitting room, where he slept. Never knew him to be so careless. He commenced brushing the dust off some pictures, but first took off his weapons and laid them on the bed. There was a Colt's revolver and a Smith & Wesson, each .45 caliber. He also had in the room a Winchester repeating rifle and a breech-loading shotgun.

"As he turned from the bed, we stepped between him and his guns and pulled on him. I was about eight feet from him when he heard my pistol cock. He turned his head like lightning. I fired. The bullet hit him over the left eye and came out or lodged near and behind the right ear. Charley had his finger on the trigger, but he saw that he was done for and did not shoot. Not one of us spoke a word. He fell dead at Charley's feet. We then got our hats, went to the telegraph office, and sent several wires."

The inquest began at 3 o'clock that afternoon in the Circuit Court room of the courthouse. Mrs. James arrived in the custody of Marshal Craig. The two Fords had been kept in separate rooms until the jury summoned them for testimony. They then entered the court. Since their arrest was merely a formality, and since they claimed to be afraid of attack by the public, they had asked permission to keep their guns even though they were in custody. Therefore, they were heavily armed when they appeared.

Bob Ford, the slayer of Jesse James, had reached the age of twenty years the January preceding the murder. He was rather slender of build, not over robust yet wiry, and capable of great endurance, as well as being shrewd and, no doubt, brave. His eyes were sunken and hazel color, large, restless, and piercing. His forehead was rather bold and high, and his hair was thick, short, and light brown color. He was five feet eight inches tall, and on the day of the murder he was wearing a nut-brown suit, with sack coat. His hands were long and slender, with tapering fingers. He appeared to have a skin problem, since there were a number of prominent pimples on his face. He seemed cool and collected throughout.

Charley Ford, Bob's brother, was larger, taller, and broader. His hair was dark, eyes dark brown, and he was dish-faced. His lower jaw protruded, and he had a decided bulldog look, and apparently he was more brutal than Bob, yet probably braver as well. Some people said Bob was the vicious one of the two. He was also cool, self-possessed, and moved upright, with a firm and solid tread. Charley lacked a few months of being twenty-five years old. He usually boasted a thin mustache and always wore some kind of a stickpin in his cravat, while Bob did not. On the morning of the killing Charley was wearing a gray coat and vest, cravat, and green-striped trousers.

Prior to the inquest an autopsy had been performed by Drs. George C. Catlett, Jacob Geiger, William Hoyt, and Assistant-Coroner James W. Heddens. The cap of the skull was removed to permit a thorough exposure of the brain, which was found to be above the average in size. The brain and skull were dreadfully shattered, large pieces of bone having been driven through the wound, which lacerated the entire cerebellum. The bullet that killed Jesse James remained in the Heddens family for many years, last being with Barret S. Heddens, Jr., of Kansas City, Missouri, until it disappeared. Assistant-Coroner James Heddens acted in this matter, since the coroner was in Jefferson City on business. Dr. Heddens established a fine practice in St. Joseph after struggling many years as a young doctor. His St. Joseph residence still stands next to the art gallery there. In 1922 he retired and moved to Pasadena, California, where he died in the early 1930s.

Charley Ford was the first witness to be called to the stand.

"My home is about two miles from Richmond, Missouri, where I have resided for the past three years. I left home on the 3rd day of November last at the request of Jesse James, who was then a resident of Kansas City. He removed to St. Joseph on the 5th, and I accompanied him. After moving to St. Joseph Jesse said he wanted to take a trip through Kansas to see how the banks were situated, and said he would get the men. He wanted to know if I knew anyone who would help us. I told him I thought I could get my brother to help us if I could go down and see him. We went to his mother's in Clay County and stayed until Friday night, and then to my brother's and stayed until Saturday, when we left for this city. On the way up Jesse said there was going to be a murder trial at Platte City and we could go over there, and if everything was all right we would rob the bank. He said when they were making the speeches everybody would be in the courthouse, and we would rob the bank. This morning we had come in from the barn, where we had been feeding and currying the horses, and Jesse complained of being warm. He pulled off his coat and threw it on the bed, and said he would take off his belt, since somebody might see it. Then he got up on a chair to brush off some pictures, and when he turned his back I gave my brother the wink to shoot Jesse; I intended to fire also, but Bob was a little quicker than I, and fired first. I had my finger on the trigger, and was just going to fire, but I saw his shot was a death-shot, and did not fire. He heard us cock our pistols and began to turn his head. The ball struck him in the head and he fell. We then went to the telegraph office and sent dispatches to Craig and Timberlake. After that we went to the marshal's office, where a policeman told us that the marshal had gone down in the direction of the house. We went down and gave ourselves up. We killed him because Governor Crittenden said he would like to have him captured, and that he would give ten thousand dollars reward to break up the band of outlaws.

"Jesse came to my house two years ago last summer. He was a sporting man and so was I. He gambled and drank a little, and so did I. I was acquainted with Miller, and Miller came in and introduced him as Mr. Jackson. He stayed until the next morning, when he left, and after that Miller told me it was Jesse James. I did not see him anymore for a long time. When I did see him I asked him where Miller was, and he said Miller was in bad health and he did not think he could live long. He was there two or three times last summer and once last fall, and asked me to go with him and rob banks and trains. I never robbed anything with him. My brother and I had made it up to kill him, but this is the first time we got a chance. I knew he was quicker than I, and I would not try when he had his arms on. He was so watchful no man could get the drop on him. I went to see my brother two weeks ago last Thursday night at my uncle's, Bill Ford. He had left Kansas City with the intention of making up a party and watching the house so that if Jesse came around they could get him. But the weather got bad and they gave it up, and I went to see my brother and told him what I wanted.

"We went to Nebraska together. We went first to Hiawatha, then to Pawnee City, next to Forest City, then to White Cloud, Kansas. He said he liked the bank at Forest City, and said he wanted to take that bank, but I told him I did not want to go into that, since I was sick. We then came up to Oregon. He said he wanted to look at that bank. We then returned here. He would go into the bank and get a bill changed, and while there would take a look to see whether they were caged up, what sort of a looking man it was, and whether they had a time lock on. We never traveled on the cars. Jesse said he preferred to travel on horseback because he couldn't stop at the small villages when on the cars. We spent the daytime in the house since coming here. He generally took the Kansas City papers and the *Police News*. At night we would walk uptown and get the papers. Jesse sometimes walked out east of town during the day. He had a good deal of money, some fifteen hundred dollars, but I don't know where he kept it. I had no expenses and used no money. My brother and I had planned the killing of Jesse. We were to get behind him if we could get him to lay his pistols off. This morning I gave my brother the wink. He had a Smith & Wesson and could get it out quicker than I could mine. I knew that it was nonsense to try to take him, for he said he would not surrender to a hundred men, and if three men should step out in front of him and shoot him he would kill them all before he fell. When shot he was about four feet from me. He fell on his face."

Robert Ford was then called to the stand. As he walked forward he was the center of all eyes in the room. It was hardly believable that this boyish-looking, slender young man could have killed Jesse James. His sunken eyes flitted around the courtroom as he took the stand. His evidence was given in a clear, loud voice, without a catch or a tremor.

"My name is Robert Ford and I am twenty-one years of age. My residence for the past three or four years has been in Ray County, Missouri, near the town of Richmond. In January last I had a conversation with Governor Crittenden, the result of which I became a detective to hunt down the James outlaws. My first meeting with Jesse James occurred about three years ago, when in company with Ed Miller he stopped at my house overnight and discussed the robbing of a railroad train; the members of his gang at that time were Dick Liddil, Wood Hite, Ed Miller, Clarence Hite, and Jim Cummins; I never met any of these except Ed Miller, Jim Cummins, and Wood Hite. Governor Crittenden asked me if I thought I could catch Jesse James, and I answered yes, and at this same interview I besought the governor to pardon Dick Liddil, and agreed to undertake the arrest of Jesse. The governor therefore agreed to pay ten thousand dollars apiece for the production of Jesse and Frank James, whether dead or alive. This interview occurred at the St. James Hotel in Kansas City.

"I have been with Jesse constantly since last Sunday night, but Charley has been watching for an opportunity to capture him since last November. I was with Jesse about ten days, when at his request I accompanied him to his mother's home and slept with him in the barn. We remained there for two days, then started on horseback for St. Joseph, stopping over night in a church, and before reaching the town we hid in a patch of timber until night, so as to make our entrance unobserved. That was one week ago last night. I rode a horse that had been stolen from a man named Robinson, of Clay County. Jesse and I had a talk yesterday about robbing the bank at Platte City, at which Charley and I both agreed to assist. Between eight and nine o'clock this morning while the three of us were in a room in Jesse's house Jesse pulled off his coat and also his pistols, two of which he constantly wore, and then got up onto a chair for the purpose of brushing off a picture. While Jesse was thus engaged Charley winked at me, so that I knew he meant for me to shoot; so, as quickly as possible, I drew my pistol and aiming at Jesse's head, which was not more than four feet from the muzzle of my weapon, I fired, and Jesse tumbled headlong from the chair on which he had been standing and fell on his face. Just before the killing Jesse and Charley had been currying the horses; I did not go out of the house because Jesse said it were better that I should not be seen about the house. I usually remained indoors all day, but at night I generally went down to the city to purchase papers. After the shooting I told Mrs. James it was accidental, but she would not believe me. I went directly from Jesse's house to the telegraph station and sent a dispatch to Governor Crittenden, informing him of what I had done. I have heard him frequently declare he would never be taken alive."

This closed the testimony on Monday, and court was adjourned to meet the next morning at 10 o'clock. Before that hour arrived, the courtroom where the coroner's inquest was being held was filled by people anxious to get a glimpse of Jesse's mother, Mrs. Samuel, and his widow, Zee. Prior to going to the courthouse, Mrs. Samuel and Zee James went to the Sidenfaden funeral parlor to view the remains. Mrs. Samuel almost swooned as she cried, "My poor boy! My dear son! My darling boy!"

When asked if the remains were those of her son, Mrs. Samuel replied, "Yes, it is Jesse, all right. Would to God it were not!"

There was considerable excitement all over St. Joseph, as well as in Kansas City, some seventy miles away. Not since the assassination of President James Garfield had the people been so concerned at the death of one man. Many persons in St. Joseph scoffed at the thought of its being Jesse James and declared it was a "put up" job to obtain the reward money. But it was Jesse, all right. An impressive list of identifiers made sure of that: Prosecuting Attorney William Wallace, Jackson County; Harrison Trow, James Wilkerson, J. Clay, Mattie Collins, Mr. Mimms, Mr. James, C. D. Axman, Lamartine Hudspeth (a longtime friend and ally of the Jameses and a close relative), Ben Morrow, who rode with Jesse during the war, and Sim Whitsett, also an exguerrilla, and Dr. James. Many times most of the last named men had given assistance to Jesse when he was on the run. They made no bones about it; in fact, they were rather proud of the fact that they had helped him. Members of the Stigers family of St. Joseph, close friends and advisers of the James family, also identified the remains as those of Jesse James, the outlaw.

After an intermission, Mrs. Samuel entered the courtroom, and then the inquest continued. Henry H. Craig, Kansas City Police Commissioner, was called to the stand, and he made this brief statement.

"I was not acquainted with Jesse James personally, but am positive the body of the dead man is the outlaw, since it corresponds with the description I have heard. I know Robert Ford, and for two months he has assisted Sheriff Timberlake and myself in the endeavor to capture

Jesse James. He was not employed regularly by us, but acted in good faith, and according to our instructions, and assisted in every way he could to aid us. Charley Ford I had never seen until I came to St. Joseph, but understand he and Robert had some understanding."

Sheriff Timberlake was next called and gave an interesting ilttle account.

"I was acquainted with Jesse James during his life and recognize the body as that of Jesse. I had known him since 1864, and saw him last time in 1870 and later. I chased him plenty, too, and he gave me rough times. I knew his face as well as anyone. He had the second joint of his third finger shot off, by which I also recognize him. Ford was acting under my instructions and said if he could see Charley Ford we could accomplish our end the sooner, and he acted squarely and to all agreements.

"There is a lot of misthinking about what the governor had to do with Jesse's demise. He has been misrepresented in this matter of the killing of Jesse James. He did not know where James was living, nor did I until after he was killed, or shortly before. Now let me tell you something else you did not know. Jesse James knew Bob Ford's mission, and he was only waiting for a chance to kill him. Bob knew that Jesse suspected him, and that it was a question between them who fell first. When I placed Bob Ford where Jesse picked him up, I said, 'Bob, Jesse knows that you have been with me as well as I do. He will kill you if he gets the chance.' He said to me, 'Yes, I know.' I then said, 'Capture him if you can when he first comes to meet you. If you can't do it, then wait for your chance. Don't allow yourself to be found alone with him.' At that time Charley Ford was a genuine friend and companion of Jesse. He never went into the scheme to take Jesse until Bob talked to him. I knew within three hours after the time that Jesse and Charley came along and took up Bob. I had no idea where they had gone. For ten days I suffered mental agony, expecting any hour to hear that Bob was dead, and when I at last did hear of the killing, and how it had been done, I knew in a minute that Jesse had taken off his revolvers in the presence of Bob to make him believe that he stood solid. He never dreamed that the drop would be taken upon him then. That very night, on the ride toward Platte City, which had been seemingly agreed upon, Jesse would have shot Bob Ford through the head."

Dick Liddil was next called to the witness stand.

"I have seen the body of the dead man and recognize it; I was with him a good deal last summer and know perfectly, I also recognize him from the wounds on the hand and on the right side."

Charles Alderman, livery stable operator in St. Joseph, had a few remarks to make.

"I am a trader. I was not acquainted with Jesse James in life. I have seen the body and recognize it as that of a man I traded horses with but did not know who he was; and last Saturday I got it back from Charles Ford, who had been at my place several times. He said he wanted a horse for his 'uncle,' who I now presume is Jesse James."

This statement led many people to believe that the Ford brothers were related to Jesse James, but Alderman had merely meant to show that when Charley Ford spoke of an uncle he had in mind Jesse James, who had sent him to get a horse. While living at St. Joseph with Jesse, both boys used the aliases of Charley and Bob Johnson, claiming to be nephews of Thomas Howard, 1318 Lafayette Street—this is how this false story got started.

Deputy Marshal Finley of St. Joseph, also made a statement.

"I was not acquainted with Jesse James. I went to the house where he was killed in answer to a telephone where a man was killed. I found him on his back, and from Mrs. James got the description of the two men who killed the man, and started a search for them. She said one of them was her nephew and the other a young man, both named Johnson, last man not related. As we were going out, we met the boys coming back. Bob said he was the man who killed the person in the house. 'He is the notorious Jesse James or I am mistaken, I can identify him.' He described the wounds on Jesse's body. He told us there were two watches and some diamonds in the house. We could not find them at first, but did find a necktie and a gold ring with the name of Jesse James on the inside. Afterward we found two watches in the trunk. There was some small change in an old pocketbook, which I gave to Mrs. James. On a one dollar gold piece as a scarf pin were the initials 'J.W.J.' Most of the property is now in the hands of the city marshal."

The name of Mrs. Zerelda Samuel, the mother of the dead outlaw, was called, and every man in the courtroom stretched his neck to get a good look at her. With her head erect and with a proud air, Mrs. Samuel passed up the center aisle, accompanied by Mrs. Turner, a friend, as well as by the widow and children of Jesse James.

Acting-coroner James W. Heddens asked Mrs. Samuel if the body was that of her son, Jesse James.

"Yes, it is Jesse, all right. I live in Clay County, and am the mother of Jesse James. I have seen the body since my arrival and have recognized it as that of my son, Jesse; the lady at my side is my daughter-in-law and the children are hers. He was a kind husband and son."

Here she broke down and moaned several times, "Oh, my poor boy!"

Bob Ford was again called to the stand for some reason. But the spectators liked the idea and listened intently to all the questions and answers. The questions were asked by the coroner.

"Did the governor tell you anything about a reward?"

"He said that ten thousand dollars had been offered for Jesse or Frank, dead or alive. I then entered into arrangements with Timberlake and Graig. I afterwards told Charley of the conversation I had with the officers and told him I would like for him to go along. He said if I was willing to go, all right. We started that night, and went up to Mrs. Samuel's and put the horses up.

"John Samuel [Jesse's half-brother] was wounded in a brawl, and they were expecting him to die. There were some friends of the family there whom Jesse did not wish to see, so we stayed in the barn all night until they left, and that was pretty near daylight, and we stayed in the house all next day, and that night we started away. That was on Thursday night; Friday night we stayed at his brother-in-law's place. We left Mrs. Samuel's place and went about three miles into the woods for fear the officers would surprise us at her house. We started from the woods and came up to another of his brother-in-law's and got supper there and started from there to here."

"This was last week?"

"Yes. We came at once to St. Joseph and then talked over the matter again, and how we could kill him."

"What have you been doing since you came here?"

"My brother and I go downtown sometimes at night and get the papers."

"What did you tell Jesse you were with him for?"

"I told him I was going in with him."

"Had you any plans made to rob any bank?"

"He had spoken of several but had made no particular selection."

"Well, now will you give us the particulars of the killing and what time it occurred?"

"After breakfast, between 8 and 9 o'clock this Monday, he, my brother and myself were in the room. He pulled off his pistols and got up on a chair to dust off some pictures and I drew my pistol and shot him."

"How close were you to him?"

"About six feet away."

"How close was the hand to him that held the pistol?"

"About four feet I should think."

"Did he say anything?"

"He started to turn his head but didn't say a word."

"How often has Charley been at home since he first went to Jesse's house to live?"

"Once during Christmas."

"Has he not been home since then?"

"No, sir, he came to my uncle's."

"How often has he been to your uncle's?"

"I saw him twice; once when he was there. I was in Kansas City."

"Was Jesse unarmed when you killed him?"

"Yes, sir."

"Do you remember ever hearing any of the Samuel family calling him by name?"

"They always called him 'Dave'; that was his nickname. They never called him anything but Dave."

"Did you ever hear anyone call him by name?"

"Yes, I heard his mother speak of him and call him Dave and he called her mother."

"Do you know of anyone that can identify him?"

"Yes, sir, Sheriff Timberlake can when he comes; he was with him during the war. There are others, too, who fought with him and can do so."

The coroner's jury returned the following verdict after less than an hour's deliberation.

State of Missouri)
                   SS
County of Buchanan)

An inquisition taken at St. Joseph, in the County of Buchanan, on the third day of April, 1822, before me, James W. Heddens, M.D., coroner of the county aforesaid, upon their view of the body of Jesse W. James, then and there lying dead, S. H. Sommers, W. H. Chouning, J. W. Moore, Thomas Norris, William Turner, W. H. George, good and lawful householders in the Township of Washington, who, being duly sworn and charged diligently to enquire and true presentment make, how and in what manner, and by whom the said Jesse W. James came to his death, upon their oaths do say:

That the body of the deceased is that of Jesse W. James and that he came to his death by a wound in the head, caused by a pistol shot fired intentionally by the hand of Robert Ford, in witness whereof as well the jurors aforesaid, have to this inquisition put their names at the place and the day aforesaid.

> James W. Heddens, Coroner
> S. H. Sommers, Foreman
> W. H. Chouning
> J. W. Moore
> Thos Norris
> Wm. Turner
> W. H. George

The inquest over, the Ford brothers were confined to the St. Joseph jail, charged in a warrant sworn out by Mrs. Jesse James for the murder of her husband, Jesse W. James.

The news created a sensation in Kansas City, even though the first reports were regarded as false. Even late on April 3rd many folks refused to believe that the legendary outlaw had been killed by a mere stripling of a boy. Police Commissioner Craig left for St. Joseph with an armed posse to protect the men who had slain the outlaw, as well as to guard the body of Jesse from morbid body-snatchers. At the police station it was learned that Bob Ford, a young man who had been hanging around the station for several weeks past, was the person who had committed the deed. From the police it was now for the first time learned that Ford was under the control of Craig and had been used as an instrument of the law.

There even was a dispute between the St. Joseph authorities and Sheriff Timberlake and Commissioner Craig regarding the disposition of the outlaw's remains. On April 5th Governor Crittenden sent a wire to O. M. Spencer, Prosecuting Attorney of Buchanan County at St. Joseph:

> Just informed your officers will not turn over the body of Jesse James to his wife nor deliver his arms to me. I hope you will have done both. Humanity suggests the one, and a preservation of such relics for the state the other. His jewelry should be held for the present. One paper says he had on my lost watch.

The governor placed little credit in the report that his fine watch stolen fifteen years earlier was found in the possession of Jesse James. There had been a newspaper hoax to the effect that the outlaw had told the governor he could have his watch back if he went after it and identified it. All this was imaginary.

Finally the body was turned over to the sheriff with the agreement that it should be buried in the front yard of the old James homestead at Kearney.

On the evening of April 5th, when the Eastbound train stopped at St. Joseph, the funeral cortege was in the charge of Marshal Craig. At 6 o'clock a carriage drove up to the station. Mrs. Samuel stepped out and, leaning on the arm of an officer, walked to the train. She insisted on inspecting the baggage car to see for herself that Jesse's body had been placed on board. Members of the mourning party were, besides Mrs. Samuels, Mrs. Zee James, the two James children, L. W. James (a cousin), and R. T. Mimms, brother of Jesse's widow.

At the depot a man tried to shoot Mrs. Samuel, but he was disarmed and thrown into the street. No official record has been kept of this attack nor of the assailant's name.

When the train reached Cameron, Missouri, at nine that evening, the special train that was to take the party to Kearney failed to arrive. Marshal Craig had the coffin removed into the caboose of a freight train, the weary party arriving in Kearney just before daylight.

The body of Jesse James was taken to the Kearney Hotel and again exposed to view, thus giving hundreds of persons an opportunity to identify the bandit whom they had once known. The body remained in state until after 2 o'clock, and had been viewed by over five hundred people, largely farmers of Clay County, who expressed no ill will toward the Fords. Around noon a collection was started for the benefit of Mrs. James and her two children, but less than ten dollars was collected.

At fifteen past two, April 6th, the casket, a metallic imitation rosewood, with a plate on which was engraved the name "Jesse James," was placed in an open spring wagon and driven toward Mt. Olivet Baptist Church, followed by a procession of twenty teams, carrying members, relatives, and acquaintances of the James family. In the second wagon rode Mrs. James and her two children, Mr. Mimms, and Mrs. Samuel; in the third wagon rode the pallbearers, Sheriff Timberlake, Deputy Sheriff Reed (long-time friend of Jesse), Charles Scott, J. B. Henderson, J. D. Ford (mayor of Liberty, Missouri and no relation to the Ford brothers), Benjamin Flanders, and James Vaughn (an ex-Quantrillian, who later wrote a book claiming he was Frank James). Rumor had it that the fine casket was paid for in the amount of $250 by the "guilty consciences" of Sheriff Timberlake and Commissioner Craig. In fact, the ledger sheet of the Sidenfaden funeral home shows the entry of this $250 that paid for the casket of Jesse James.

The church was reached before 3 o'clock, then the body was received by the pastor, Rev. J. M. P. Martin, of Kearney, who officiated at the services, assisted by Rev. D. H. Jones, of Lathrop, Missouri. The church in which the services were held was the Mt. Olivet Baptist Church, and was a building forty by sixty in dimensions, and was built in 1857. It stood about a quarter of a mile south of the railroad depot and three hundred yards from the tracks, on the end of a ridge that sloped toward the railroad. Just west of the church, and separated from it by a plank fence, was the cemetery, in which several members and relatives of the outlaw's family were buried, including little Archie Samuel, who was killed by the Pinkerton flare-bomb in 1875.

After the services, which were concluded at half-past 3 o'clock, the procession started toward the early home of the outlaw, four miles from town. It was hidden on the southern side by a gentle eminence and so could not be seen by the chance passerby. None but the relatives was allowed to watch the burial. The casket was taken into the house where John Samuel lay wounded, and there Frank James also viewed the last mortal remains of Jesse James. Later Frank stated he had not been there; neither statement has been challenged. John Samuel, on seeing the body, fell back in a paroxysm of grief. If anyone guessed that Frank was there, if he actually was, no mention was made of the suspicion.

At 5 o'clock the body was finally consigned to a very deep grave, dug opposite and near the kitchen, just inside the plank fence that separated the yard from the pasture and under a gigantic coffee-bean tree. After the casket had been lowered into the ground, Mrs. Samuel screamed that someone had cut off Jesse's right hand. So determined was she that the men had to lift the casket up and open it again, to assure her that she was mistaken. She calmed down somewhat after that. The coffee-bean tree has since been destroyed by a bolt of lightning, and Jesse's remains were reburied in the Kearney Cemetery in 1902, at the request of his dying wife. It now rests between the graves of Dr. Samuel, Jesse's step-father, and Mrs. Zerelda Samuel, his mother.

Mrs. Zee James returned to St. Joseph after the funeral and on April 8th offered her household effects (and one pistol) to be sold at auction. A large crowd of relic hunters paid $250 for worthless furniture, five dollars for a rickerty husk-bottom chair on which Jesse had been standing at the moment of the fatal shot, and an old valise brought twenty-four dollars. A small revolver sold for twenty-five dollars; somebody paid fifteen dollars for the little pup that Jesse had carried on his saddle between Kearney and St. Joseph as a present for his son. Souvenir collectors even ripped off pieces of the house and planks from the fence, and they considered themselves richer by such vandalism. At the end of the day it was discovered that two cartridge belts had been stolen from the house. Today these items would be worth considerable money.

In later years, Jesse's widow presented the governor's son, T. T. Crittenden, Jr., with the gun that Jesse had placed on the bed a minute before his death. It is a Smith & Wesson, Schofield Model, .45 caliber, Serial #366, year, 1873. On the right side is scratched the name "Laura," said to be the name of an early sweetheart of Jesse James. Today this revolver is in the possession of William O. Sweet, Attleboro, Massachusetts.

The death of Jesse James shook the State of Missouri from one end to the other. Heavy politics entered into the matter when Republicans made every effort to use the assassination of Jesse James to embarrass the Democrats. Well the Republicans knew that Governor Crittenden's association with the affair had not endeared him to the thousands of ex-Confederate Democrats. They introduced resolutions commending the governor for his actions, resolutions that, if acted upon by the Democrats, would rebuke their governor or endorse the murder of the outlaw Jesse James. Getting nowhere, the Republicans renewed old charges that the Democratic administration was allied with other notorious bandits of Missouri. Although other bands of robbers had been eliminated in the state, the governor's actions in granting full pardon to the notorious Ford brothers, Charley and Bob, and the one-sided trial of Frank James at Gallatin, Missouri, for the murder and robbery at Winston, gave the Republicans an opportunity to declare in 1884 that the old-line ex-Confederate and ex-guerrilla Democrats were still protecting members of the James band.

Corinth, Mississippi bank building.

Captain Hy. Craig, Police Commissioner, Kansas City, Missouri.

Governor T. T. Crittenden, Missouri.

Chief Thomas Speers, Kansas City Police Department.

Marshal Enos Craig, St. Joe.

Allan Pinkerton, detective.

Kansas City, Missouri, early days.

Cornelius Murphy, Marshal of Jackson County, Missouri.

Kansas City Police Department, officers in front, time of Jesse James.

Rare photo showing Kansas City Star office. Carried news of James.

Home where Jesse James resided in Nashville.

Rare photo, front Hite home, uncle of Jesse James, Adairvlle, Kentucky.

Rear photo of Jesse's Nashville home.

Type of car coach held up by outlaws.

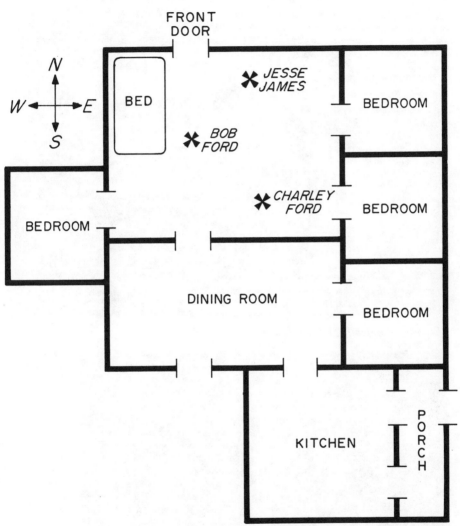

Diagram illustrating death of Jesse James.

Sketch of the death of Jesse James.

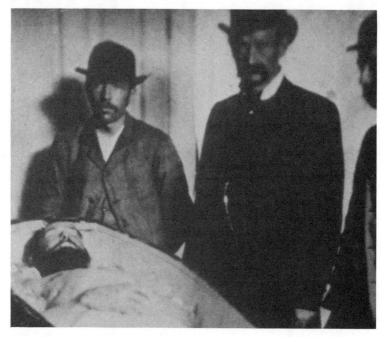

Jesse James in casket.

THE LETTER SHOWN HERE WAS WRITTEN BY A LITTLE GIRL IN COVINGTON, KENTUCKY ON APRIL 26th, 1882 TO MRS. JESSE JAMES.

DEAR MRS. JAMES,

DOUBTLESS YOU WILL BE SURPRISED TO RECEIVE A LETTER FROM A LITTLE GIRL, THIRTEEN YEARS OLD, BUT SYMPATHY FOR YOU AND YOUR FAMILY PROMPT ME TO WRITE. I HAVE ALWAYS TAKEN A GREAT INTEREST IN READING OF YOUR HUSBAND'S DARING EXPLOITS. THE WAY IN WHICH YOUR BRAVE HUSBAND MET HIS UNTIMELY DEATH WAS A VERY COWARDLY ACT. FROM WHAT I HAVE READ IN THE NEWSPAPERS, I KNOW THE WAR WAS THE CAUSE OF DRIVING YOUR HUSBAND TO DESPERATION AND I FEEL THAT IF THE GOVERNOR OF THE STATE OF MISSOURI HAD DEALT FAIRLY TOWARD HIM IT WOULD HAVE BEEN MUCH BETTER. I AM A LITTLE SOUTHERN GIRL MYSELF AND HAVE HEARD HOW BAD THE WAR WAS. I HOPE YOU WILL WRITE ON THE RECEIPT OF MY LETTER. I SEND MY SYMPATHY AND LOVE TO YOU.

Signed

LULIE P LLOYD
26 WEST 12 STREET
COVINGTON, KY

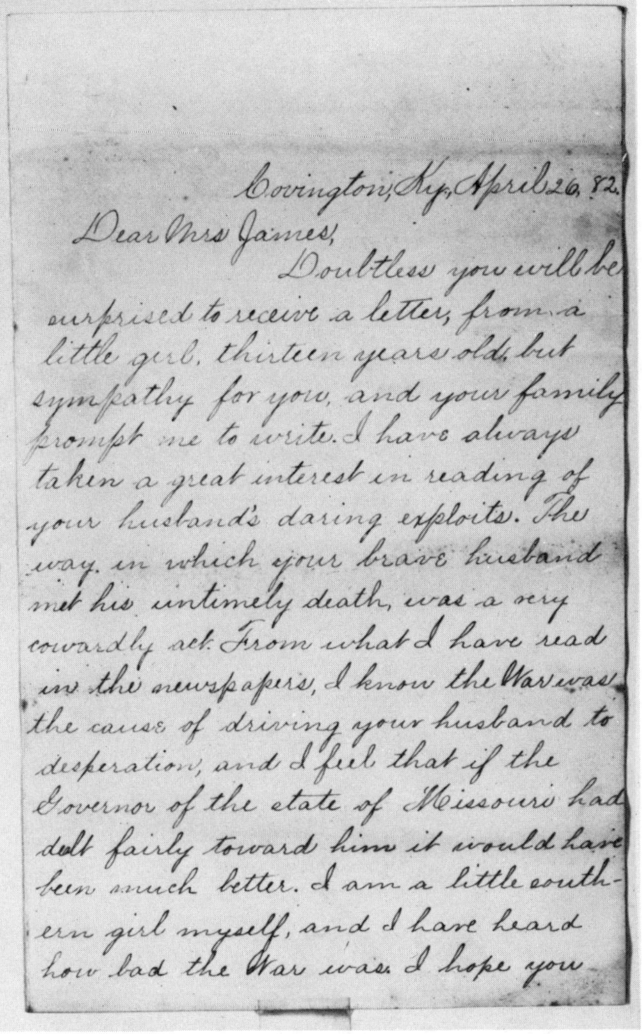
Covington, Ky, April 26. 82.

Dear Mrs James,

Doubtless you will be surprised to receive a letter, from a little girl, thirteen years old, but sympathy for you, and your family prompt me to write. I have always taken a great interest in reading of your husband's daring exploits. The way in which your brave husband met his untimely death, was a very cowardly act. From what I have read in the newspapers, I know the War was the cause of driving your husband to desperation, and I feel that if the Governor of the state of Missouri had delt fairly toward him it would have been much better. I am a little southern girl myself, and I have heard how bad the War was. I hope you

Letter of sympathy written by a thirteen-year-old girl to Mrs. Jesse James, 1882.

Graves of Jesse James and his mother.

WM. F. UHLMAN
PHOTOGRAPHIC SUPPLIES
The Stock House for the Professional

716 FRANCIS STREET
ST. JOSEPH, MO.

Mr. N. H. Rose,
  P.O. Box 463,
  San Antonio, Texas.

Sept. 14, 1927.

Dear Sir:
                    Replying to your letter of Sept.
12th, both the pictures of Jesse James, made
by Rudolph Uhlman and Alex Lozo, are genuine.
Both my Father and Mr. Lozo died about 25
years ago.   I was a youngster at the time
of the tragedy and helped to finish thousands
of these pictures at my Father's studio.

                    If the pictures you have of
Jesse James are with the eyes closed, they are
as they were originally taken of the corpse.
As I remember, the corpse was strapped to a
board in the undertaker's morgue and stood
upright, so that it could be photographed.
All the local photographers, my Father among
them, were privileged to take pictures of
the corpse and thousands of these pictures
were mailed all over the United States.   I
feel sure that the pictures that you have
of Jesse James are authentic.   At that time,
My Father sent a copy of this picture to a
celebrated artist in St. Louis and had it
reproduced with the eyes open.   This picture
was identically like the original, except the
eyes of the corpse were open to make it look
more lifelike.

                    Trusting this is the information
desired, I remain

                              Yours very truly,

                              Wm. F. Uhlman

Letter from William Uhlman to Noah Rose, 1927.

18 • • •

Fords Indicted and Case Dismissed

On April 17th the Ford brothers were indicted for the murder of Jesse James. Robert was charged with the murder in the first degree, Charley with aiding and abetting his brother in the killing. At noon the Fords were taken to the overcrowded courtroom. Major William Warner of Kansas City and Colonel John Doniphan and W. A. Reed of St. Joseph appeared as attorneys for the defense.

Robert Ford was the first arraigned. The indictment set forth that on the 3rd day of April, Charley and Robert Ford had willfully, feloniously, and with malice aforethought, killed Jesse W. James, and on this charge had been indicted for murder in the first degree.

After reading the charges, Prosecuting Attorney Spencer arose and asked of Bob, "What plea do you make?"

"Guilty!" replied Bob Ford, with a slight gesture of the hand and with a careless air, in a tone that could be distinctly heard all over the room.

When Charley Ford was asked the same question he at once gave the same reply.

Judge Sherman shifted to a more comfortable position. After a brief pause, during which time the only sound heard in the courtroom was the breathing of the assembled spectators and an occasional nervous movement, Judge Sherman arose to his feet, and with impressive dignity that approached solemnity, said, "In view of the circumstances there is only one thing I can do, and that is to pronounce sentence here

236

and now. Robert Ford, you have pleaded guilty before the court to the crime of murder in the first degree, and it becomes my duty to pass the sentence of death upon you. It is therefore the sentence of this court that you be taken to the Buchanan County jail and there safely kept until the 19th day of May 1882, at that time to be taken to some convenient place and hanged by the neck until you are dead, and may God have mercy on your soul!"

Robert then took his seat, and Charley Ford was commanded to stand up to take the same sentence. The prisoners never flinched at the sentence; but, on the contrary, took the news with an air that plainly indicated that they knew that it was only a farce, and their necks were as safe from the noose of the law as that of the judge who pronounced the sentence.

The prisoners were then taken immediately back to the city jail, accompanied by City Marshal Craig and his young son, who became most friendly with Bob Ford during his stay at the jail. In fact, so friendly did Bob feel toward the young man for his kindnesses in bringing candy and tobacco to the Fords, that he gave the boy the Smith & Wesson revolver that he had used to slay Jesse James, never realizing, of course, what value would be connected with the weapon in years to come. This same revolver was later sold by Corydon F. Craig, son of the marshal, in 1900 to E. Stanley Gary, of Baltimore, Maryland. Gary had this gun engraved with the following words: "Bob Ford Killed Jesse James With This Revolver at St. Joseph, Mo., 1882." This, naturally, puts to rest all the stories claiming that Jesse had been slain with a Colt. The pity of it is that this same Smith & Wesson, Model No. 3, .44 caliber, was stolen some years back while on display at a Missouri museum. Hopefully, one day someone will run across it and notify me.

Sergeant Ditsch and Officers Neugent and Nichols, of the Kansas City Police Department, together with Sheriff Timberlake and H. H. Craig, Police Commissioner of Kansas City, visited with the Fords in their cell on the same day they were sentenced to be hanged. The Fords made no bones about how they felt insofar as the governor effecting their release at an early date, accompanied by a full pardon.

"Damn, it would be a good joke on us if they really should hang us, wouldn't it?" laughed Bob Ford.

Insofar as Crittenden was concerned, it would have been better for him had he allowed the Ford brothers to hang. As it was, the Jesse James matter and the pardon of the Fords and Dick Liddil forever ruined the governor's further political ambitions. Many people agreed he would have done the state of Missouri a further service by disposing of the treacherous brothers.

At 2 o'clock that same day the authorities in St. Joseph received a telegram from Governor Crittenden granting full pardon to the Fords and ordered their immediate release from jail.

Bob Ford was then arrested by Sheriff Trigg of Ray County, who read a warrant charging him with the murder of Wood Hite. On May 13th he was indicted in Ray County on that charge. He was taken before Justice of the Peace James Demastice, where he waived examination and was released on two thousand dollars bail furnished by his father and Burnett Hughes. Later, on a change of venue, his trial was held at Plattsburg, county seat of Clinton County, Missouri.

On April 5, 1882, Governor Crittenden reminded the managers of the different railroads of the 1881 arrangement and demanded ten thousand dollars for the disposal of Jesse James. If it was paid, at least it did not reach the Fords. They had to accept any decision the governor made regarding it, since Charley was still an outlaw and his pardon meant more than money to him. Only about five hundred dollars found its way into the pockets of Bob and Charley Ford.

The money deals worked out by the governor meant nothing to the Fords; they now had to work for a living. They tried to reap a harvest from their vast publicity by touring the country with a play called *How I Killed Jesse James*, under the auspices of the showman George H. Bunnell. They were presented for one week at the corner of Broadway and Ninth Street in New York City beginning on Monday, September 18, 1882; then on September 25th opened at Bunnell's Museum at Court and Remsen Streets in Brooklyn, New York. In the East they were received fairly well, but in the Midwestern states and in the West they were practically booed off the boards. Several times they had to be spirited away through a back door to avoid an unfriendly crowd. One night while they were performing at the Theatre Comique in Kansas City, it was rumored that Frank James was going to kill them. Commissioner Craig and Sheriff Timberlake rushed police reserves to the scene, but nothing happened. However, Frank James actually was in the audience that night, but nobody recognized him. Perhaps he had used his old trick of cutting off his boot heels and wearing a flat hat to appear shorter. This trick had worked many times before in confusing witnesses in their descriptions of train robbers. Besides, Frank

James was too smart to be involved in such a stupid move; he already was thinking of surrendering.

About a year after the death of Jesse James, his son, Jesse Edwards James, and his grandmother, Mrs. Zerelda Samuel, were walking down Main Street in Kansas City, when suddenly they saw Charley Ford coming down the walk toward them. It was just a chance meeting, the first and last since the murder of Jesse.

Young Jesse saw Ford and recognized him at once, and the boy became very excited. Turning to his grandmother, he said, "Here comes the man who killed my father."

The sight of Charley Ford caused Mrs. Samuel to become weak and she sat down on a box in front of a shoe store. Ford saw her and went to walk by her, his head turned the other way. Waving the stump of her right arm, she called out to him, "You don't know me, Charley Ford?"

He stopped abruptly, as though he had been struck by a bolt of lightning.

"Yes, I know you. You are Mrs. Samuel."

"Yes, and you murdered my poor boy; you did it for the blood money. I ought to kill you right here."

Ford threw his hands in front of his face and lamented.

"Mrs. Samuel, don't say that. If you only knew what I have suffered, you wouldn't talk to me that way."

"And what have you made me and mine suffer?" she asked.

"Mrs. Samuel, I have been in the blackest hell of remorse ever since it was done. But I didn't kill him, Bob did, and I thought you knew that."

"Yes, and you knew Bob intended to do it when you brought him to my house. You ate bread under my roof with the blackest murder in your heart, and murder for money, too. There will come a day of terrible reckoning for you, Charley Ford."

"I did not know that Bob intended to kill Jesse until we got to St. Joseph, and then he told me that if I did not consent to it, he would kill me along with Jesse."

Ford repeated over and over again that he was suffering the worst agonies of remorse. The perspiration streamed down his face and there were tears in his eyes. He begged Mrs. Samuel to forgive him.

"If God can forgive you, I will."

Mrs. Samuel then inquired as to what he and Bob had done with the ten thousand dollars they received for killing her son.

"Mrs. Samuel, before God, we never got but a few hundred dollars of that reward."

Young Jesse James was watching Ford all the while, not saying a word. However, when they walked down the street a little ways he said to his grandmother, "If I ever grow to be a man I'm going to kill him."

"You'll never have the chance, my boy; God will never let an ornery cuss like that live until then."

Her words were prophetic.

On September 26, 1883, Charley and Bob Ford were at the Buckingham Theatre in Louisville, Kentucky, in their drama, portraying the deed as to the death of Jesse James.

The play, of course, was no better than could be expected, and it was a poorly constructed affair, the whole object being to show the Ford brothers, and it was expected that their personality would draw large crowds. The scene at the theater that night was a very unusual and strartling one, fully displaying the sympathy of the people there with regard to the deed. The house was packed to suffocation, and more than five hundred people were turned away. The aisles, galleries, and boxes were almost a solid mass of breathing humanity, and a more miscellaneous crowd was never before collected in that building.

When the curtain was run up on the first act and the two brothers walked onto the stage in their rough Western costume, there was a slight demonstration, but the house was soon restored to comparative silence. It was not until the last act, however, that the feeling of the audience was fully displayed. When "Jesse James" mounted the chair and began to rearrange the picture, there was a deadly silence in the theater, which was not broken until Bob Ford stepped forward, and, drawing his pistol, fired the "fatal" shot. The report had scarcely died away when two dozen men in the audience arose in their seats and hissed long and loud, crying "murderers" and "robbers" at them. The curtain was rung down a moment later, and the drama was over.

19 • • •

Trial of Bob Ford at Plattsburg

The morning train reaching Plattsburg, Missouri, on October 18, 1882, carried Bob Ford; his father, J. T. Ford; Martha Bolton, his sister; a large number of witnesses for and against Bob Ford; and his representing counsel, Colonel C. F. Garner. Long before the arrival of the train, hundreds of men, women, and children, some of whom had traveled a long distance, crowded the streets, and it appeared that all businesses in town had closed up. Bob Ford was also accompanied by a number of acquaintances from Richmond, Missouri, ready to give what moral support they could in his behalf.

Ford and his group of followers watched the reactions of the sight-seers as they walked downtown for an hour or two. Many of them could not believe that this young man had shot and killed the notorious outlaw, Jesse James; had been freed of that charge, and now was in town to stand trial for the murder of Wood Hite, Jesse's favorite cousin. At 11 o'clock Bob Ford entered the courthouse, and was met by the sheriff, who relieved him of his revolver. This court building was badly damaged by fire in 1895, but was rebuilt and added onto. On June 14, 1974, it was damaged by fire to such an extent that it was demolished and a new one built. Ford walked into the courtroom, which was filled to overflowing, and took a seat next to his counsel inside the bar before the bench.

Judge George W. Dunn had just reached the Ford case on the docket, and a moment later he called out, "State against Robert Ford."

241

Prosecuting Attorney James W. Garner of Ray County announced that, owing to the failure of some important witnesses upon behalf of the State to arrive, he desired the case passed over until the next morning, when he hoped that the State would be ready to proceed with the trial. Colonel C. F. Garner, on behalf of Bob Fard, said the defense was anxious to have the case tried and disposed of, but since some of their witnesses, too, were absent, he would enter no objections. The judge then ordered the case passed over until the following morning, and instructed the sheriff to summon a special venue of eighty jurors by that time.

A few minutes after that announcement the court took a recess, and hundreds of the curious crowded forward to get a better look at the notorious Robert, and he held an informal reception with the bar. The crowd refused to disperse as long as he remained, and an aisle was finally opened, through which he escaped to the sheriff's office, where his weapons were returned to him. Wherever he went during the day, a curious crowd followed him, and he was observed as though some high-ranking political figure was visiting Plattsburg. During the evening, a party of his admirers from Osboro took him around town and showed him the sights.

In the evening, during an interview, he said, "I passed through here with Jesse James and my brother Charley while on the way to St. Joseph just before the death of Jesse. Jesse and Clarence Hite were here just prior to the Winston train robbery, looking over the banks to rob them, but decided it was not a good layout. When the Kansas City papers quoted me after the Jesse matter, they lied. I did not say then or ever say that this country was not big enough for me and Frank James to live in. I am sure that Frank means me no harm. If he had wanted to injure me he would have done so long before he surrendered."

One person asked him if he had the assurance of Governor Crittenden that he would be pardoned in case of conviction there, and he replied that he did not have such a promise. Ford talked freely and answered all questions as best he could, with the exception of speaking about the Hite matter, for which he was to be tried. In order to stop the pestering along those lines, he finally stated, "Yes, I was in the house when the shooting occurred. I cannot discuss it any further than that."

Prosecuting Attorney Garner, of Ray County, and Attorney Joseph M. Lowe, of Clinton County, were to appear in the case for the benefit of the State of Missouri, while Colonels Garner and J. M. Riley were to represent the defendants. Colonel Riley was from Plattsburg, Missouri. Mrs. Samuel, Mrs. Jesse James, Police Commissioner Henry Craig and Chief of Police Tom Speers of Kansas City, Missouri, and Charley Ford, were expected to appear at the courthouse the day the trial began.

The morning train of the Wabash road brought more curious thrill-seekers into Plattsburg, all anxious to get a good look at the participants in the trial. With Speers, Craig, and a number of witnesses came Officer Geter of Kansas City. Since the people were looking for someone they wanted to make "Frank James," they picked Geter, since he fit the general description of Jesse's brother. People followed Geter around like he was a tin god, throwing barrages of questions at him. Soon tiring of all the unwanted attention, Officer Geter took off his long overcoat, displaying his police uniform, and he told the crowd who he was. Even then, it took the verification of Chief Speers to make some of them believe that Geter was not Frank James.

At 10:00 o'clock the case against Bob Ford was called, and the attorneys for the State announced themselves as ready to proceed with the trial. Colonel Garner, for the defendant, stated that some of his witnesses had not yet arrived, and they would have to consult as to the advisability of proceeding to trial without them, and the case would be passed over until the afternoon session. The courtroom was crowded in the morning, and when court was called to order after lunch, hundreds of the spectators were unable to obtain seats, and were unable to get into the courtroom. It was also noted that a large number of women were among the audience.

When the case was again called, Colonel Garner filed an affidavit for continuance; Bob being swore in at the desk, a look of disappointment filtered across the faces of those present. Colonel Garner then read the affidavit, which set forth, complete with legal trimmings, the absence of Dick Liddil and Sheriff James R. Timberlake of Clay County, who were important witnesses for the defendant, and whose attendance could not be assured for that term. According to what the affidavit implied, they were expected to prove, by Liddil, the following: "That Liddil and Wood Hite, both of whom were heavily armed with revolvers, suddenly became involved in a personal difficulty but that few words passed between them until both drew revolvers and commenced firing at each other, and continued until each had fired about five shots, the firing being rapid and continuous, occupying a few seconds of time; that Liddil received a flesh wound in the leg, and Wood Hite was fatally shot, dying instantly; that Hite brought on the fight, was the aggressor, made the attack, and was firing at Liddil when he was shot and killed by a bullet from the pistol fired by Liddil, and that Ford knew nothing of the difficulty until the firing commenced. Then the trouble occurred in the dining room, and was provoked by Hite in an effort to kill Liddil; that Liddil controlled and directed the disposition of the body." By Timberlake they expected to prove the following: "That early in January, 1882, Bob Ford procured the surrender of Liddil to Sheriff Timberlake, and he then communicated to him the killing of Wood Hite, and what he knew about it, and his reasons for not telling anyone of the killing; that Timberlake advised and enjoined upon them not to make public the killing of Hite, because it would prevent and defeat the efforts that were being made to capture Jesse James and others who were associated with him; that Timberlake was at that time sheriff of Clay County, and the surrender and conversation was with him as such sheriff."

The usual plea of learning of important evidence since their arrival was then set forth. Colonel Garner then spoke at some length in favor of a continuance, stating that his client was anxious to proceed to trial, and that it required the strongest argument he could use to get him to consent to a continuance.

Prosecuting Attorneys Garner and Lowe consulted for a moment, after which Garner stated that the prosecution would admit the matters set forth in the affidavit, but would reserve the privilege of impeaching the witnesses and rebutting the testimony, the same as if the witnesses were in attendance. This was quite a surprise to all in attendance, and it was agreed that the State had fired the first skirmish in facing the trial.

The special venue of eighty jurors was called, and a panel of forty selected. The prosecution concluded the challenge on the evening of October 19th, and it was thought that the defense would be ready with theirs in the morning.

The case against E. G. Robinson for killing his brother in De Kalb County was set for the following Monday, and an effort made to secure a special term for one Clay Cecil, since his attorney had been detained. At that time Charley Ford nor Mrs. Samuel, Mrs. Jesse James, or Mattie Collins had yet arrived in Plattsburg. Rumor was that Mattie Collins was ill.

The 20th of October still found great interest in the trial of Robert Ford for the murder of Wood Hite. Each session found the courtroom filled with the curious, and it was noted that the number of women attending had increased daily. On that morning Capline Ford, a brother of Bob, and Mattie Collins arrived in Plattsburg. Chief Tom Speers of Kansas City had returned to his home base, but was expected to return in time to present his evidence in the case. After some difficulty in selecting the jurors in the Bob Ford case, the following men were finally selected: Emaley Rose, Phillip Hefflinger, Harrison Groves, James B. Potter, A. J. Hill, Charles Daniels, Annanias Jackson, Jacob J. Hudson, J. P. Barnes, John B. Hill, Arthur Davidson, and M. W. Dorrer.

The indictment was read by Prosecuting Attorney Garner, after which, Colonel Garner, for the defense, stated that he reserved the privilege of making a statement of what his evidence was to be in advance. After the evidence for the State was in, he would make a statement if he so decided.

Mr. J. C. Morris, Constable of Richmond, was the first witness on the stand, and described the location of the house in which the killing occurred, which was occupied by the Fords, and known as the Harbison place. It was a mile northeast of Richmond, built on a hill, some two hundred yards from the road, with a wooded pasture between it and the road, a barn lot and wooded pasture on the east, an orchard on the south, and a field on the west. He stated that Bob had told him the previous night that Hite had come to their house a day or two after the Blue Cut train robbery, and was there several more times before his death. Morris was the officer who found the body of Hite buried in an old spring, a quarter of a mile east of the house in the wooded pasture, and assisted in digging up the body.

"I found the skull crushed on the right side," he said, "and a flesh wound in the muscle of his right arm. The thumb on the right hand was missing. The Ford boys were in business in Richmond up to September of last year, and Bob clerked for them for a while."

John Dawson, formerly city marshal of Richmond, corroborated Morris's testimony as to the conversation with Bob Ford the night prior to October 20th and also described the location of the home. He had seen several strangers at the house, whom Bob told him later were Jesse James, Dick Liddil, and Jim Cummins. He had accompanied the party that raided the Harbison place under command of Frank Tutt, and also the raid under Captain Craig of Kansas City. He also stated that Ford told him that Hite had been in the house several days before the killing.

"James Demasters, the justice of the peace for Richmond Township, was not present when the body was found," Dawson further stated, "but he arrived soon after, and discovered the place and condition of the body, which was somewhat decomposed. It was clad in a shirt, undershirt, underdrawers, and socks, and was wrapped in a filthy horse blanket. There was a fracture of the skull at the right temple and another on the left side of the head, commencing a little above the left ear, and extending back some distance; also a flesh wound in the right arm muscle."

It was also learned that Charles Sayers, a merchant at Richmond, visited St. Joseph the day after Jesse James had been killed, and in company with Joe Sanderson and J. E. Ball, called on Bob Ford at the jail. While there Bob Ford told them that he had killed Wood Hite; that Dick Liddil was in the corner of the room, and Hite came in at the door opposite and commenced firing. Mrs. Bolton and her children were in a third corner, and he was in the fourth, close to the head of the doorway. Since the room was filled with smoke, he was afraid his sister would be in danger, and he drew his revolver, shooting Hite, and killing him instantly. A rigid cross-examination failed to break down the testimony, and he said that Bob did not appear to be excited. Sanderson, also a Richmond merchant, testified that he had been in St. Joseph with Mr. Sayers, and corroborated his conversation with Ford at the jail.

Mrs. Martha (or Mattie) Bolton, a sister of Bob Ford, had this to say from the witness stand: "Hite first came to my house a year ago last June, but has visited us frequently since, and had been at my home several days before the killing. Bob had been away about a week, and returned accompanied by Dick Liddil, about daylight the morning of the killing. This occurred on December 5th, last, in the dining room. After the killing, the body was taken upstairs, where it remained until dark, when they took it out and buried it, but I don't know who did the burying. I don't know what became of his clothes or his revolvers, but some of the boys had worn his coat afterwards. I saw where they buried the body after it had been dug up. I gave my entire story to the coroner, but did not identify the body, since he was known to me as Doc Grimes."

During the cross examination, Mrs. Bolton said this: "Me and my family had eaten breakfast before Hite and Liddil were called down to eat theirs. I was standing in the southeast corner, Hite in the northeast, and Liddil between them, when the firing started, the latter being a few feet from me, and since my back was turned, I did not see who shot first. Bob Ford was standing in the north end of the house when the firing commenced, and I did not see him afterwards, since the room was filled with smoke. Hite and Bob entered the room by the east door, just before the shooting. I saw the body after Hite fell."

Several questions by the defense were objected to, and the objections sustained. The court then adjourned, to reconvene in the morning, with Mrs. Bolton again scheduled to take the stand.

Many observers, noting the many objections entered in the case thus far, stated that Ford's counsel showed a determined will to fight every step of the way.

October 21st proved to be the most exciting day of the trial up to that time, as agreed to by most observers. Some old-timers remarked that the scenes as were enacted that day had never been witnessed before in the courtroom of that county. At one time the excitement had reached such a pitch that the crowd, despite the efforts of Sheriff Algier and Judge Dunn to suppress it, cheered Prosecuting Attorney Lowe when denouncing a speech of Colonel C. F. Garner in which he indulged in some criticism of one of the witnesses.

The cross-examination of Mrs. Bolton, Bob's sister, was resumed on that morning also, and most of the time was used in this questioning. She stated there had been no conversation between Bob and either Hite or Liddil on the morning of the killing, and it was not more than a minute after they came when the shooting began. Hite had offered to shake hands with Dick Liddil, but the latter refused, and they both drew their guns.

"At that time Liddil was only a few feet from me," Mrs. Bolton said, "and Hite was facing Liddil only a few feet off, all being on the east side of the room. Bob was never absent from my home for more than a day at a time, until a week before the shooting, when he went to his uncle's in Clay County, and only returned on the morning of the shooting."

The day before objection had been raised to the question relating to what Bob had said after Hite fell, and while he was still alive, and it was again brought up, and debated to some length. The court finally said the evidence was admissible.

"Bob then proposed to take the body to Kansas City and deliver it to Chief Speers," Mrs. Bolton continued, "but Liddil objected, saying if they did Jesse would come and kill them both. Dick went into the north room immediately after this conversation and Bob went in soon afterwards."

On a redirect examination, Mrs. Bolton said: "The stove was in the center of the room, and one bullet passed through the pipe. Two of Hite's bullets struck the floor. Mr. Gibson, our hired hand knew nothing about the shooting, and left the place that morning. I saw Hite fire one shot and Liddil several, but did not see Bob shoot at all, though he said afterwards that he had fired one shot. Hite was still living when I left the room, and my children stated he was still upon being taken upstairs, and that he died sometime in the afternoon. I did not see the body after that, and don't know who buried it."

James S. Demasters was then placed on the witness stand, and he stated he examined the house the day after the body was found. He located the bullet marks in the opposite corners.

When the noon recess was taken, several prominent citizens informed Prosecuting Attorneys Garner and Lowe that while Mrs. Bolton was giving her testimony, she kept her eye on Bob, and answered the questions as he indicated through signs, and by nodding and shaking his head. This statement created much comment among those assembled, and upon court being reassembled, John Kemgere, one of Plattsburg's most prominent citizens, was put on the stand and testified as follows: "I was present during the examination of Mrs. Bolton this morning, and saw Bob Ford shake his head and prompt the witness. The effect on the witness was her answer from an affirmative to a negative. This was during the examination by Mr. Lowe."

The defense objected to the admission of the evidence, and J. W. Garner made an eloquent speech in favor of its admission, citing authorities and denouncing the course of the defendant. Colonel C. F. Garner responded in support of his objection, indulging in some criticism of the witness and intimating that the prosecution had placed Kemgere and others in the courtroom as spies and detectives in order to break down the testimony of its own witnesses, in case their evidence was to their advantage.

It was a difficult matter for the judge to keep the witness quiet during that inflammatory speech, and even then he interrupted several times. When Colonel Garner had concluded there was considerable confusion, but Colonel Lowe responded, stating that Coloner Garner's criticism could not affect Mr. Kemgere's standing in the community, and that Kemgere was the peer of any Garner who had ever set foot in that county. This was greeted with applause from the spectators, and when Mr. Lowe said he could produce dozens of the best citizens and ladies of the county to corroborate Mr. Kemgere's statements, he was again greeted with a roar of applause.

Colonel Garner stated that he had not witnessed such a scene as the one then taking place in any courtroom in the thirty-three years of his experience at the bar. Judge Dunn then reprimanded the attorneys in the case for engaging in such lengthy discussions regarding the most familiar points of the law of evidence, and he considered it far from being a compliment for them to do so, and he then reprimanded the defendant, but ruled out the testimony of Kemgere.

Captain Charles Ditsch, of the Kansas City Police Department, testified that Bob informed him of the killing of Hite in January, when Liddil surrendered, and said that he and his brother Capline buried Hite, but showed the grave in February, stating, "Here's our cemetery."

In cross-examination, he said the officers, when informed of Hite's death, advised Bob to keep it a secret for fear it might defeat the officers in their efforts to capture Jesse James and others of the gang. He said he was acting under the authority of Captain Craig, who received his authority from Governor Crittenden. The day Bob showed him the grave he examined the dining room of the house. He stated that Bob told him that Hite stood in the northeast corner and Liddil in the southwest. He then described the bullet holes, particularly over the window on the east side, stating that a bullet could not have passed through a man's head and then made that hole, unless he was stooping or the bullet deflected from the course. The parties had evidently shifted their positions while shooting.

J. M. Craig of Plattsburg, also testified: "I visited Bob in the St. Joseph jail the day after Jesse James had been killed, when one of the party asked Bob if Liddil killed Hite. Bob said Liddil had not; that he had killed Hite himself; that Liddil and Hite were shooting, and as he saw Liddil was not going to down Hite, he drew his own gun and fired and downed him himself."

John Vallandingham, Horace Brown, and George Essig, all of Plattsburg, and who were at St. Joseph, Missouri, with Mr. Craig, corroborated this testimony, the latter adding that they believed Bob said something about his sister and her children being in the room, and he wanted to keep them from injury.

Mrs. Martha Bolton was recalled to the stand, and she said her daughter, Ida, was in the yard at the time of the shooting, and she didn't know where her son, Tommy, was.

Court was then adjourned until Monday. Judge Dunn, Bob Ford, his father, and Mrs. Bolton, with a number of witnesses, went to Richmond that night to spend Sunday, and Police Commissioner Craig, Captain Ditsch, and Officer Geter went to Kansas City. People noted that Bob's face was all broken out with pimples or that he had the measles.

Silas Jones, an old-timer of Plattsburg, when asked what he thought of things and to describe Ford, he said this: "Robert Ford, in appearance, is an innocent, guileless sort of a chap. He does not impress you with the idea that he would be a formidable antagonist when confronted by an enemy on an equal footing with himself. He is evidently determined to make the best of circumstances and turn his individual account into questionable prominence. The impression prevails with me and others that Ford will be convicted, unless, however, the prosecution have more conclusive evidence that has been elicited up to this time, it is doubtful that a conviction can be secured. It remains to be seen as to whether anything can be brought out as to who fired the fatal shot."

On October 23rd it was announced that all evidence in the Bob Ford matter had been presented, and on the 24th would be argued before the jury. While the evidence had not been as interesting as first expected, and the excitement had worn off, there still was a goodly number of people in the courtroom to listen to the case on the 23rd.

At one time, when he cross-examined Orr Smith, Prosecuting Attorney J. W. Garner asked as to Charley Ford's character. Charley, who was seated just behind where the witness had sat in the audience, became very angry. The blood rushed to his face, his eyes fairly flashed fire, his hands clenched, and his lips moved as in expressions, accompanied by an ominous shaking of his head. Garner noted it and smiled, but paid no further attention to Charley.

The first witness that morning was Dr. W. Mosby, of Richmond, a practicing physician, who had been present at the coroner's inquest in the matter of Wood Hite's death, and who had examined the body, which was partly decayed. The head had been perforated by a ball that entered on the right side, nearly above the right eye, ranging backwards, Mosby told the prosecutor.

"I was unable to find a place of exit," he further stated, "and do not believe the bullet went through his head. On the left side of the head the connection of the bones was broken up entirely, the upper portion of the skull on that side being laid bare. I do not think these resulted from the bullet, but were inflicted by a blow. One bullet had also touched the surface of the right arm, but had not entered it."

Chief of Police Thomas N. Speers, of Kansas City, was next called as a witness: "Bob Ford came to my office to ascertain who comprised the raiding party under Captain Craig, shortly after the original raid in which he participated, disguised in an old uniform. I had been having the Ford place watched all the time to arrest men suspected of the Winston and Blue Cut robberies. I learned soon after the raid that Hite had been killed there, but did not allow it to be made public. The Jesse James gang then was composed of Jesse and Frank James, Dick Liddil, Clarence and Wood Hite, Jim Cummins, Charley and probably Bob Ford."

At that point the court refused to allow the prosecution to introduce Mr. Harbison, and the State rested its case.

The defense introduced Dr. James W. Smith, George J. Wesson, William M. Moss, A. K. Rayburn, and Ralph Esteb, all of Richmond, who testified that Bob clerked for his brothers in Richmond until the September previous to the killing, and stated they had never heard anything derogatory to his character during his stay there; and Esteb had visited the Harbison house, examined the room in which the killing had occurred, and made a diagram of the same. Four shots were embedded in the stairway partition, near the northeast corner of the room, and one passed through the door on the east side, near the same corner. Near the southwest corner two shots had struck the floor and had glanced off. One had entered the south wall, and one the west wall. The shots in the northeast corner had evidently been fired from the southwest, and those in the latter corner from the northeast. There was a bullet hole in the east side of the room, which had been fired from the northeast corner. He described the spring where the body of Hite had been buried as almost totally surrounded by thick brush.

Henry C. Mudder, when called to the stand, stated he had never heard anything against Bob Ford while he was in Richmond, and he described the location of the bullets in the room as did Ralph Esteb.

W. H. Byers, city marshal of Richmond, added his testimony as to Bob's good character while in that town. On cross-examination he stated Bob had told him that Hite and Liddil were at the house when Tutt raided it; that he offered to hide them under the porch, but since Hite was afraid of ruining a new suit he was wearing, they took to the brush.

Police Commissioner Henry Craig of Kansas City stated he had

advised Ford that the death of Hite be kept a secret; this was admitted
as evidence. He learned of the killing on January 24, 1882. The statements of Dick Liddil and Sheriff Timberlake as set forth in the affidavit
for continuance were then read as evidence.

Deputy Sheriff Wymer of Clay County stated that Bob Ford came
to Liberty in January and arranged for the surrender of Dick Liddil.
He then led Timberlake and two detectives to a belt of timber, some
eighteen miles from Liberty, where he left them, and half an hour later
returned with Liddil, who surrendered, and from that time Bob and
Liddil cooperated with the officers. They were instructed to keep the
Hite affair secret.

R. H. Jones, of the Kansas City Police Department, stated that
while marshal at Adairville, Kentucky, last year he arrested Wood
Hite, but that he escaped from his guards. The defense and the State
both closed their evidence, and were granted until morning to prepare
and present the instructions they wished to give to the jury. The case
was scheduled to be argued and submitted the following day.

On the evening of October 23rd, Sheriff Algier received a dispatch
from Richmond instructing him to arrest Charley Ford and hold him
to answer an indictment for train robbery. The sheriff went over to the
hotel where Charley and his father were staying, tapped him on the
shoulder, and told him he was under arrest.

"What the hell for?" cried Charley Ford.

"For highway robbery," replied the sheriff.

Charley submitted peacefully, allowing the sheriff to disarm him
and take possession of his pistols. The affair was kept as quiet as
possible, and most people knew nothing of it until after Charley had
been arrested. Both Charley and Bob were very indignant that the
arrest should have been timed for that particular moment.

"I was in Richmond all last summer," complained Charley, "if
they wanted to arrest me for something why didn't they do it then?
I was at the Harbison place the night of the robbery stated and knew
nothing of it until the morning after it had happened. Bob also was
with me most of that time. Chief Speers of Kansas City was most
indignant over my arrest also. He thinks as I do, that it was made at
this time to influence the case of my brother."

On October 24th Charley Ford was released on bond, charged
with robbing the stage buses near the depots at Lexington and Richmond, Missouri, in September of 1874. Judge Dunn, in chambers,
set the bond at five hundred dollars, which was immediately given by

Charley's father. The judge remarked later that he saw little or no evidence against Charley Ford.

Court was called to order at 10:00 o'clock on the morning of October 24th, and the judge read his instructions to the jury. Colonel J. M. Lowe, prosecuting attorney, then addressed the jury for an hour and a half, reviewing the testimony and making a complete chain of the evidence. He denied the assertion that the Missouri outlaws had surrendered to the State, as had been stated by witnesses for the defense, but on the contrary, in the lonely belt of timber, eighteen miles from Liberty, the State laid down its arms and ignominiously surrendered to the outlaws.

Colonel J. M. Riley used the remainder of the morning on behalf of the defendant, his speech being calm, impassionate, and argumentative. Noon recess was then called by the court.

After lunch, Colonel C. F. Garner spoke for two hours on behalf of the defendant, bringing all of his eloquence to bear on the jury, skillfully reviewing the testimony, and urging leniency on the part of the jury toward the mere boy he was defending, who, he said, was innocent as a lamb.

J. W. Garner, prosecuting attorney of Ray County, made the closing argument, which was declared by all to be one of the best efforts ever made in that courtroom.

At 5:00 o'clock that evening the case was submitted to the jury, who then retired to the jury room. The courtroom had been crowded all day with excited and interested citizens of the area. Bob Ford had remained preoccupied all during the day, and for the first time during his trial seemed anxious to escape attention for some privacy. Charley Ford, J. T. Ford, and Martha Bolton had been eager listeners all day long. The topic of conversation in Plattsburg that evening was centered around the trial and the possible outcome. Many people believed that the jury would render a guilty verdict, with recommendation to hang Bob Ford.

After some forty hours deliberation the jury, at 10:00 o'clock on the morning of October 26th, filed into their seats. Bob Ford was not present at the time, and it took about twenty minutes to locate him and to bring him to the courthouse. On arrival, Bob walked carelessly up to his counsel and sat down. The foreman passed the verdict to the clerk, who then read it from his desk: "We, the jury, find the defendant, Robert Ford, not guilty of charges as indicated in the indictment."

A large crowd had assembled to hear the verdict, and a look of relief was evident on most of the faces of those present. As for Ford, he did not seem to pay much attention to it. When his attorneys turned to congratulate him, he smiled, then turned and shook hands with the jurors, after which, he walked calmly from the courtroom.

Bob Ford had told some friends that in the event he was acquitted he would give them the inside story of the killing of Wood Hite. His attorney, however, made him promise that he would do nothing of the sort. Enough had been said, however, to indicate clearly that Ford had killed Wood Hite, and that his account of it, as given in his testimony, that Dick Liddil was not going to down Hite so he did it himself, was apparently correct.

Those discussing the trial and the events leading to the death of Hite agreed that the trouble had started in Adairville, Kentucky, where Hite's stepmother had been having affairs with a man named Hicks, or it was said to have been the case. Hite's stepmother sent a note to Hicks warning him that Wood Hite was suspicious and would kill him if he had the chance. However, Hite intercepted the message and killed the black man carrying it. Later, his stepmother swore out a warrant for Hite, accusing him of the black man's murder. Wood was arrested but managed to escape. Back at the home of Major George Hite, Wood's father, Liddil took up with Mrs. Hite and the trouble began. Wood and Liddil had a running fight with pistols about it, the matter resulting in no injuries, with both men departing for Missouri, later to meet at the Harbison place, where Bob Ford fired the fatal shot that killed Hite.

There was little doubt in the minds of all Missourians that Crittenden would pardon Ford had the verdict been a guilty one. It also appeared that Ford's attorneys and those of Frank James, who had surrendered, had come to an agreement that none of the James family would appear against Bob Ford; in turn, none of the Ford family would appear on behalf of the State against Frank James when his trial came to court.

Rumors had been spread around Plattsburg while the jury was out that some men were willing to "hang the jury" if the proper verdict was not given. The jury on the outset stood two for a verdict of murder in the second degree, and ten for acquittal. Under the instructions, the verdict was required to be for a murder in the first degree or second degree or an acquittal. Several members of the jury later asserted that if they could have returned a verdict of manslaughter they would have done so in a few minutes, but they did not think the evidence strong enough for a verdict of murder.

20 • • •

Death of Charley Ford

On May 6, 1884, the little town of Richmond, Missouri, was thrown into a state of excitement by the news that Charley Ford, brother of the man who had killed Jesse James, had committed suicide that morning.

The news of the shooting spread like wildfire and it was not long before a crowd of inquisitive people was racing toward the home of Charley's father, J. T. Ford, about a mile east of Richmond. There they found the body of the young man dressed in his trousers and shirt lying on the side of a bed. His hands were folded over his chest and a bullet hole in his left chest told the story of his death. The bullet had passed through his heart, and death must have been instantaneous. His face was placid, and there was a faint smile on his lips as if a feeling of pleasure and relief had come over him as life left his body.

The bedding was undisturbed and the room was in good order, indicating that he had died without a struggle. By Charley's side was a .45 calibre Colt's revolver, with which the deed was done. The weapon was held so close to his body that it burned part of his shirt.

The day before his death Charley Ford appeared happy and cheerful, giving no reason or sign that he intended to take his own life. About 8:00 o'clock he requested his mother to obtain some morphine for him, not telling her why he wanted the drug.

There were many speculations as to what caused Charley to commit suicide. Many said it was in remorse for his part in the slaying of Jesse James. Others claimed he was unable to endure any longer the pain that was caused by a disease gnawing at his system. Yet, there were still others who stated he feared the vengeance of Frank James, who would soon be at liberty after his acquittal at two trials—Gallatin,

Missouri and Huntsville, Alabama. His passing caused no regret; in fact, most people were pleased with the disappearance of Charley Ford from the haunts of Richmond. One man said, "This is the noblest act of his life."

The coroner summoned a jury to ascertain the cause of Ford's death, as is the legal custom. The evidence showed that Charley Ford was a habitual morphine eater, often consuming ten or twelve grains of the drug a day; that he was also seriously affected with a bladder disease, which at times was very painful, and that he also suffered greatly from indigestion.

Charley left no note explaining his action of self destruction. When the jury had heard all the evidence it brought in a quick verdict, "Charley Ford came to his death from a gunshot wound inflicted by his own hand." The witnesses who had been heard were: Capline Ford, a brother; Mattie Bolton, a sister; W. W. Mosby, Jr., and Perry Jacobs. Tom Jacobs, Charley's ten-year-old nephew, also was at the inquest, as was one Mr. Smith, later to become the father of Forrest Smith, former governor of the state of Missouri.

At the time of his death Charley Ford was under indictment in Clinton County for the alleged robbery of the passengers on the wagon-bus bringing passengers from the train to the depot at North Lexington, Missouri. However, due to his illness a forfeiture of his recognizance bond with leave to set aside had been taken.

The general impression was that Ford had died without a dime to his name, having spent what few hundred dollars he had collected for his part in the death of Jesse James, as well as having spent what money he may have earned while acting on the stage in the play called *How I Killed Jesse James*.

Robert Ford, who was in Kansas City at the time of his brother's death, was telegraphed to return home, and he arrived in Richmond the same night. Charley Ford was buried in the cemetery at Richmond, where, eight years later, brother Robert was to follow. Charley did not live with his parents at the time of his death, but was spending some time with them on a visit, hoping the country air and food would help his illness. But, he despaired and ended it all with a bullet.

The wire Capline Ford had sent to Bob Ford was simple:

Richmond, Mo. May 6

Robert Ford
    Charley shot and killed himself. Come home.
                Cap.

Somewhat shaken up by the news and himself fearing revenge at the hands of a James family member, Bob Ford hurried home to determine the truth of the matter. He later stated that the telegram was the first news he had received about his brother.

"Why do you think your brother killed himself?" was the question thrown at Bob Ford, right and left.

"The only cause I can think of is that he was depressed with his failing health. He was suffering from consumption, and frequently told me he never expected to get well. I know he came here last Thursday and wrote a letter to Captain Charles Ditsch in which he stated he was going to remain in Richmond until he got well. He also instructed the captain to forward all his mail to his parents' home. You know, the pain caused him to use a lot of morphine and I think this drug attributed to his death."

Charley Ford was still in his twenties at the time of his death, and by his connection with the James gang, and his participation in the death of Jesse James, had attained a note of notoriety in Missouri and elsewhere. At the time of his death Charley was also under indictment for alleged complicity in the holdup of the Chicago & Alton Eastbound passenger train at Blue Cut, when the train was stopped and the express car robbed of five hundred dollars and the passengers relieved of their money and valuables. Of course, his arrangement with Governor Crittenden would have squashed that matter, so this did not contribute to his suicide.

Soon after the assassination of Jesse James at St. Joseph, Missouri, Charley and his brother became engaged in a dramatic enterprise, organizing a company in Albany, New York, and traveling through the Eastern states giving exhibitions of how they had killed the noted outlaw. This venture was not successful, and they lost considerable money.

These financial losses, together with his rapidly declining health, caused Charley to become despondent, and at times he would talk in such a manner as to lead his friends to believe that his mind was failing. Both Bob and Charley had made Richmond their headquarters for months at a time, occupying a room in the courthouse, and people acquainted with Charley had ample opportunity to study his disposition. At times he would be bright and cheerful and in a short time become gloomy and despondent.

Charley Ford was not a handsome man but his appearance made it so that he was a man hard to forget. He was of medium height, weight about 120 pounds, and was light complexioned with light hair.

His face was drawn and emaciated, while the upper row of teeth projected, causing his upper lip to protrude. His voice was always pitched in a high, shrill key, and he spoke with a slight lisp.

Some citizens recalled the expression "The mills of the gods grind slowly, but they grind exceedingly small." And it was a fact that with only a few exceptions the careers of the members of the Younger-James gang ended in violence. The first member of the gang to perish was John Younger, who was killed in a fight with detectives at Monegaw Springs, Missouri, near Osceola, in 1874, shortly after the holdup of the train at Gads Hill. The Northfield fiasco in 1876 caused the deaths of Clell Miller, Bill Chadwell (using the alias of Bill Stiles), and Charlie Pitts (a Missouri lad whose real name was Sam Wells). Not only that, the Younger brothers, Cole, Jim, and Bob, were routed from the Minnesota swamps and captured, to be sentenced to life imprisonment at Stillwater. Bob Younger died while in prison, from consumption, as did his mother; Jim, after his release, committed suicide because the Parole Board refused him permission to marry his sweetheart, and Cole went back to Missouri, where he lived until 1916.

In 1879 the Chicago & Alton train was robbed at Glendale and a few months later Tucker Bassham was arrested for having participated in this robbery. He made a full confession and was sentenced to serve ten years in the Missouri State Penitentiary. When Bill Ryan was arrested in Tennessee after the robbery of the Muscle Shoals, Alabama, United States paymaster, Bassham was pardoned by the governor in order that he might testify against Ryan, since the authorities thought Ryan was a bigger fish than was Bassham. Later Tucker Bassham moved to Osage City, Kansas, where he lived out his life as a good citizen. Ryan was convicted at Independence, Missouri, for his complicity in several train robberies and was sent to the Missouri prison for twenty-five years. However, he was pardoned after serving a number of years, only to kill himself accidentally by riding his horse under a low-hanging tree branch and smashing his skull.

It was after the Blue Cut train robbery on September 7, 1881, that Wood Hite was killed by Bob Ford in a brawl at the widow Bolton's home, near Richmond. Clarence Hite, half-witted brother of Wood Hite, was arrested at his home in Kentucky for alleged participation in the Winston train robbery. He was tried at Gallatin, Missouri, found guilty, and sentenced to serve twenty-five years in prison. He died in March of 1883.

Two members of the James gang, Windy Bill Cummins and Ed Miller, apparently had been talking too much to suit Jesse James, so he set out to dispose of them. Ed Miller was tracked to southwest Missouri, where Jesse killed him. Before Cummins could be located, however, that fatal day of April 3, 1882, arrived, and Jesse James was no more.

Charley Ford and Dick Liddil were indicted for participation in the Blue Cut Train robbery but never were brought to trial. While others may have been members of the dreaded James gang, probably those of any importance to survive were: Frank James, acquitted of all indicted crimes, died a natural death at the old homestead in 1915; Cole Younger, who lived until 1916, dying at the home of a nephew in Lee's Summit, Missouri; Jim Cummins, who died at the Confederate Home at Higginsville, Missouri in 1927; Dick Liddil, who died in Cincinnati, Ohio, in 1893, and Tucker Bassham, before mentioned. Then, of course, there was George Shepherd, an earlier member of the gang. At the time of Jesse's death he was working as a night watchman at the Barker & Cotesworth Lumber Yard, Hickory and West 15th Streets, Kansas City.

21 ● ● ●

Bob Ford Saves a
Lawman's Life

Things had soured for Bob Ford in Missouri and elsewhere. It was 1885 and he was tired of being pointed to as the assassin of outlaw Jesse James. The suicide of his brother Charley had not helped matters much, either; no doubt some folks were looking for Bob to do the "Dutch Act" also.

Ford had returned to the Harbison place near Richmond, Missouri, where his sister Martha lived, in an effort to get some peace and quiet. But to no avail. He was pestered by the curious, condemned by the local friends of the James family. He had to leave Missouri, no question about it. Perhaps he could find peace in Kansas or even farther West. He recalled such places as Abilene, Wichita, Caldwell, and Medicine Lodge, in Kansas, due to his prior horse-stealing activities in that state. Bob had now taken on the role of a gambler; the little money he had made with brother Charley appearing on various stages and enacting their story *How I Killed Jesse James* had not amounted to much.

So, that hot midsummer day Bob Ford simply told his sister that he was heading for Kansas. He felt that he had to get away before he exploded. Besides, he was free as the proverbial bird, no longer wanted by the law, but a social outcast in most quarters.

"But, Bob," cautioned Martha, "you ought not go alone into Kansas the way things are with bandits, Indians, and heaven knows what else."

260

"Nothing here for me to stay," replied Bob, "besides, it might be one way for me to leave this vale of tears."

He did not realize how true those words were to be just seven years hence.

Ford did not bother with much gear. He saddled his horse, tied his bedroll and duster behind the saddle, buckled on his gunbelt, placed his Winchester repeater in the saddle scabbard, then leaped onto his mount and rode off in the direction of Kansas.

"From now on I'm going to take life easy and try to mind my own business," he shouted to his sister as he waved goodbye.

The sweeping prairie land lay quiet under the heat of a brassy sun as Bob Ford topped a grassy knoll, which afforded an arresting view in every direction. Shading his eyes with his hand, he looked out in the direction of Kansas. Nothing met his eye but the gentle undulation of the long and tough buffalo grass, dotted with large patches of scrub cedar and tall jackpines. He smiled as the pines bowed their heads to the pleasant breeze that had stirred up and that was adding a refreshing bite to the summer air.

"That's Kansas, all right," muttered Ford, "level, hot, and quiet."

Using his red bandana as a swab, Ford mopped the perspiration from his forehead and neck. It had been a long, hot ride from Missouri. His blue eyes moved slowly across the surrounding land. He liked what he saw and stood silently to enjoy the view. Ford leaned back in his saddle and muttered, "This place is so quiet one would think no danger lurked here at all."

As Ford rode forward he saw the yellowed skeleton of a man. He had been killed with an Indian lance and his friends had departed in too big of a hurry to bury the fallen man. It was a grim reminder of the unseen enemy who lurked on the rugged Kansas prairie ahead.

Now well off the main trail, Ford had traveled another five miles toward Wichita. Seeking to by-pass any hostile war parties, he had ridden through thickets, high brush, and across small creeks and streams. The waving buffalo grass now transformed into a land of boulders, sage, and chapparral. Ford was glad of the protection this offered him.

As horse and rider rounded a huge boulder the mare stopped shock still and pricked her ears. Her nostrils flared angrily and her body quivered. A faint whinny drifted from her mouth. Ford quickly leaned forward in the saddle and slipped his hand tightly over the mare's muzzle, whispering coaxing words all the while.

Ford knew no rattler had caused the alarm. He quickly dismounted and grabbed his saddle gun. The sage and thorn bushes were high in that area and offered good protection. He was certain neither he nor his horse had been seen by anyone.

Then came the answer. Ford could hear the loud rumble of many horses. He also knew the riders were not white men, for the echoing hoofbeats on the sandy ground told that these horses never were shod.

Bob used his rifle to push back a bit of the choke cherry brush. What he saw made an icy hand run down his spine. Just ahead of him, riding directly across his line of vision, came a war party of Shoshone Indian warriors, hideous in their ochre and vermilion paint, naked except for rough breech cloths and beaded and quilled moccasins. In their midst, bound tightly by his wrists and ankles to a raw-boned Indian pony, slumped a wounded white man, a blood-stained rag loosely tied about his head.

"My God!" gasped Ford. "I thought all the Indian troubles were over. Had I known this, I would have come by train."

He stiffened and clenched his rifle angrily. Even as he weighed the pitiful helplessness of the victim, one of the braves leaned over on his pony's side and grabbed the prisoner by his hair. Another dashed up and gave the man a cruel blow in the face. But the man's body was inert and his face visibly chalky beneath its mahogany tan, and he never felt the sting of the blow.

Even though seething with rage, Ford told himself that this was none of his business; he said he would mind his own affairs, and he felt he was too young to die yet. Even so, well he knew that if he took a snap shot at the column of warriors and managed to kill a few, he probably would be killed by the others and still not have rendered the white man any assistance. The Indians would be no easy game with their rifles and lances.

However, Ford decided to follow the party to see what might develop. As they passed he managed to get a look at the prisoner. He was a middle-aged man with gray hair and carefully molded features. He appeared to be about six feet tall and wore a buckskin jacket, chaps, and boots, attire that placed him in the category of a range rider. Yet there was something about him that spoke of the unusual. Double cartridge belts circled his large waist, meaning he was a man prepared for trouble. Cowboys usually only carried one belt gun, which gave them ample shooting power.

"Damn! He reminds me of Sheriff Timberlake," thought Ford.

"Wonder how old Jim's doing since all the hell he raised for me before I came in on the James deal."

One Indian held Ford's gaze for a moment. This brave had two pearl-handled Navy Colts protruding from his breech cloth. No doubt these were the prisoner's guns and had been taken by the Indian leader. From the way the warrior carried himself, this was obviously the case. Then the party disappeared from view, leaving only a cloud of fine dust and fading hoofbeats.

"By George, them ain't Shoshones, them's Osage, or I'll eat my hat," said Ford to himself.

Bob's first impulse was to follow the Indians. He replaced his Winchester in the saddle scabbard and bit his lower lip thoughtfully. He had no idea where the Indian camp was. The redmen were familiar with the terrain—he was not—and there was no sense of riding into a trap. He cast an anxious eye at the sky; not too many hours of daylight left, maybe six at the most. Ford decided his best plan was to follow at a safe distance and then execute his plans after day, if he had any.

"Yeah, reckon we'll tag along and see what we can do," Ford said aloud to his horse. "The old codger'd be dead now except they most likely want to torture the old guy or get some information from him that they want. Them bastards would not enjoy sticking a knife into a dead man." He smacked one fist into an open palm as he thought of the various ways an Indian could mutilate a human body.

Ford checked his weapons and ammunition and then eased his horse out of the thicket. The Indian pony tracks were easy to follow, for they left sharp prints in the sandy soil. The Indian party kept to the open ground on account of their scanty clothing, but even then they moved slowly as though they were actually riding through a growth of prickly pears. The war party obviously was not expecting anyone to follow. As he got nearer to them, Ford was able to pick up short bursts of guttural talk as it drifted back on the wind. He knew nothing of the Osage tongue, but surmised they were going to torture the old man. If so, the ceremony would occur when darkness fell, then the prisoner would feel the bite of the knife. By his motions, the Indian who appeared to be the leader, indicated that he would do the torturing.

Ford bit his lip in disgust as he built a mental picture of the man's body lying spread-eagle on the sand, with an oily figure standing over him, knife falling in a glittering arc, flickering in contrast with the hate-filled eyes of the redman. Then the sickening thud as the blade slammed down into human flesh and cut across the abdomen, making a melon-shaped slit that spewed blood and guts over the silvery glow of steel. The victim's last breath would be a cry of pain and anguish as he slipped into the great beyond as did others who had undergone such torture.

Bob Ford knew it was now up to him whether this gruesome vision of death would be just a vision or a reality. He had to get involved now, whether he liked it or not. It would be his guns and wit that would be the deciding factor. His past experience with Dutch Henry and Jesse James now would stand him in good stead. He was an accurate shot and was able to put a bullet where it did the most good. Maybe his actions here would make up for the matter of Jesse James—it was worth the try.

Waving their lances and jabbering in mad delight the Indians swung off to the right in a wide curve. Once again a brave heckled the prisoner. He grabbed the man's jacket and shook him like a dog would shake a rattler. The man's head rolled back and forth and his eyes flickered open.

From his hiding place Ford also noticed that and mused to himself, "Rescuing a man in his full senses would be a trifle easier than trying the same trick with a man who was unconscious. First, I've got to get me a passel of redskins."

The night air smelled good. The heavens were dotted with a bucket of winking stars, shooting little darts of light earthward, to make up for the absence of the contrasting paleness of the moon. Ford sighed a silent prayer, which was something new for him, as small clouds began to roll in from the east. He hoped for a moonless, somewhat cloudy night to put his plan into operation.

Inch by inch Ford slid silently toward the ruddy glow of a camp-fire that blossomed like a great red flower in a brush clearance. As he moved along the ground his head moved carefully from side to side, watching for a lurking enemy. Once he stopped short, thinking he had been discovered, but the noisemaker proved to be a harmless snake easing itself off a chokeberry bush.

Bob could now smell smoke—woodsmoke mingled with the more pungent aroma of buffalo chips. He figured he was about fifty yards from the camp, for now he could hear savage laughter and cries of drunken delight. The Indians were dancing around a fire at such a speed they must have been in some kind of trance; and they seemed to forget their prisoner who lay near the fire, bound hand and foot.

Faster and faster moved the braves, the warm glow of the fire etching the shadows of their greasy bodies into weird, grotesque shapes and projecting them across the clearing to a large rock, where it looked as if some kind of unearthly puppet show was taking place.

Ford worked on a definite plan. He knew an open onslaught against the dozen warriors would be suicide. He decided to use a plan that he had applied in other circumstances in the past. He removed fifteen cartridges from his looped belt and began extracting the lead from each of them. The sharp Bowie knife he always carried made short work of that task, and soon he had a little pile of gray gunpowder heaped next to his face. For a fuse he used a short piece of heavy twine he carried in his pocket. He then packed several small stones over the powder to give it more noise-power.

"This might give me enough time to rescue the old codger if I can distract those damned Indians long enough with this trick," thought Ford.

At that point the Indians ceased their dancing, coming to a shambling halt. The buck who assumed the role as leader gave the prisoner a vicious kick in the ribs. Ford knew it was time to act. Quickly he cupped his hands and struck a match. He applied the flame to one end of the string. Slowly the red glow inched its way to the gunpowder.

Bob edged his way around to the other side of the warriors, Winchester clenched and ready for action. His heart bounced with joy as he saw a number of shadows in the darkness—the Indian ponies. One part of his hunch had paid off, he kept his fingers crossed that the other would do likewise.

The old man was dragged to his feet, tottering about in his weakness. The leader cut the bonds and allowed the prisoner to rub his chafed wrists. The Indians looked on with sneers of disgust and hatred plainly written across their paint-daubed faces. Then the leader muttered something to his braves and four of them grabbed the old man and threw him to the ground in a spread-eagle form.

Ford inched in as close as he could, waiting for the explosion. It seemed an eternity as he waited for the flash.

Then it happened. A whoosh and a sheet of flame shot up from the ground to the rear of the redskins. It grabbed eagerly at the dry brush and weeds, spreading out like the fingers of a giant hand. The braves whirled and gasped in amazement. Shouting and pointing they grabbed their weapons and rushed toward the fire, which was now gaining a hold.

Ponies stomped and snorted as the flames grew larger and larger. A couple of braves came forward to quiet them before Ford had a chance to stampede the animals. The leader with the prisoner's pistols stood guard at the camp.

The two Indians sent to tend the horses passed right by Ford. With panther speed he leaped upon one of them, clamping one hand over the buck's mouth, and using his other to plunge the Bowie deep into the man's belly. He crashed to the ground. As the brave's companion started to utter a cry a finger of steel flashed through the air and buried itself deep in the man's throat, dropping him in his tracks.

Ford broke forward at a trot, keeping as close to the ground as he could. As he came at the chief, he saw the prisoner's eye twist in his direction and a gasp of surprise burst from his lips. The chief whirled and saw Ford. His hand flew to his breech cloth, clawing for one of the revolvers.

But Ford acted quicker. His Winchester spurted flame and hot lead, hitting the leader in the face, slamming him back into the fire, screams fading from his dying lips. As the buck dropped into the flames, the old man reached up and jerked his guns free.

"Use 'em if you can, mister!" cried Ford, levering a fresh cartridge into the chamber of his rifle. "I'm going to try and break us out with the ponies, got my own aways back."

His words were lost as the Winchester crashed out and bucked in his hands again and again, sending red fingers sun-fishing into the brush.

"Thanks, fella, whoever you are, I'll try and hold 'em back for you." The old man was thumbing back the hammer of one pistol and firing the other.

Ford nodded and ducked a swinging tomahawk and downed its owner with a snap shot. As the main body of warriors rushed forward, Ford levered the smoking carbine for all it was worth, sending a barrage of lead into their midst, killing, tripping, bowling them backwards. He never realized before how much he hated the treacherous redskins.

"Move back to the ponies, boy, grab us a couple. I'll hold 'em."

"I damned well believe you can!" Ford managed to grin, blood now trickling down his face from a slight wound in the forehead. "Fight like you've never fought before, old-timer."

Shaking blood and sweat from his eyes Ford stumbled and ran to where the ponies were milling about, frightened by the fire and gunshots. Falling over a rock, he cursed and jumped up again, grabbing a couple of manes and holding on tight. Ford held on grimly as the animals tried to go in the opposite direction. They dragged him a few yards but he was able to finally control them. Yanking the manes and tugging for all he was worth Bob Ford urged the horses back to the camp site.

"Thought they got ya, young feller, I'm about outta ammunition!" cried the old man.

All was quiet now except for the crackle of the fire. Several remaining braves had chosen to seek safety in flight. The others were dead or wounded. The old man stowed his empty guns and got up from the ground. He was able to force a smile as he stumbled toward Ford, who had to let one pony go to catch the falling man.

"Unconscious again! Hell, we gotta get out of this place," muttered Ford, swinging his gaze around the camp, taking in all with a quick glance. He knew the escaped braves would bring friends to run them down.

"If I can hoist the old gent up in front of me I can ride back to my own horse with him and then we can hightail it," Ford said to himself.

With care not to drop the old man, Bob slipped his arms underneath his body and lifted him off the ground and placed him across the pony's back. He was surprised that the man weighed as much as he did, because his body was in fine shape and his muscles were like knots of steel.

At last Ford was satisfied he could carry the wounded man in that awkward position. He grabbed the horse's mane in his hand, ready to leap upon its back, and as he did so something flashing in the firelight on the ground caught his eye. Curious, he bent down and picked it up.

It was a silver star and as Bob Ford flipped it over in his hands he read aloud, "Deputy Marshal, Abilene!"

Ford guessed that the badge had dropped from the man's pocket during the ordeal he underwent; yet, that did not prove that he was the owner of it. Hastily, he shoved the badge into his pocket for safekeeping, its bright reflection showing him in a brief glimpse his own face, bloody, haggard, and stubbly, his blue eyes bloodshot.

It was a grim business, holding onto the old-timer by his coat and steering the Indian bronc by means of his knees and a handful of mane. As the pony galloped farther and farther from the heat and the smoke, the roar of the flames died away and the air became pure and more breathable. Ford was thankful that his plan had worked, even though in later years he was unable to explain why he had gotten involved in the first place.

As he was riding Ford was thinking about making an escape from the area. He needed to look at the man's wounds and treat them as best he could. Suddenly he brought the pony to a halt. His sense of direction had thrown him off somewhat from where his own pony was tied. Ford put two fingers to his dry lips and whistled loud and clear. Shortly after, the whinny of a horse could be heard a short distance away. Soon Ford was mounted on his own sorrel, with the old man tied securely to the Indian pony.

It was dawn when Ford halted and made camp. He had ridden considerable distance from the fire and the threat of the flames and the danger of pursuit. Ford built a small fire and heated some water from his canteen in a small pot he carried with his sleeping gear. Gently he untied the blood-stained handkerchief and removed it from the man's head, disclosing a nasty wound.

"Reckon an arrow must have bounced along the side of his head," muttered Ford.

As he began to bathe the wound with warm water Ford noticed the man was coming to. The old man groaned and his eyes flickered open.

"Your're okay now, mister, so take it slow and easy."

"Sorry I don't recall all what happened."

"I guess not. I'm sorry, too, that I don't carry provisions and the like. I thought I'd be in Wichita or Abilene or some other Kansas town by now."

"Name's Jim McDonald, from Abilene," said the man, offering his hand.

Bob shook the hand, amazed at the strength therein.

"What's your handle, young man?" asked McDonald.

"Well," Bob Ford began, "you may have heard of me . . ." then he stopped, seemingly wondering if he should tell his name or not.

"Well, out with it, it can't be that bad."

"I'm Bob Ford, from Ray County, Missouri."

McDonald rubbed his chin, "Seems like I heard that name before, well, it don't matter nohow."

"Well, Jim, I knew you were from Abilene," grinned Ford.

"Yeah? How come?"

Ford tossed the badge on McDonald's stomach.

"Well, I'll be damned, a right smart fella."

"What I cannot figure out is why you are way out here," said Ford.

"Was on a mission for the marshal when the Osages jumped me. You know the rest."

Ford suggested they move on to the next town, which, according to McDonald, was Wichita, not too far a ride from where they were. Jim agreed, since they were without food or medicine, that they should reach town as quickly as possible.

Several hours later the riders were on the main trail leading into Wichita, one of the wildest towns on the frontier.

"When do you figure we'll hit town?" asked Bob.

"Waal, allowing nothing holds us up, I'd say we'll be a-ridin' down Douglas Avenue about sundown."

McDonald had been right. About six that evening the two men rode into Wichita. The strains of a familiar ballad of the day were carried over the cool night air by a violin that, judging by its howling and wailing tones, must have been one of the first ever created. And from one of the many saloons, gambling houses, and brothels situated in town, came raucous laughter and the squeals of delighted women who were making their way to the bedrooms always situated on the top floor. Now and then a gunshot punctuated the laughter and music, marking the end of a quarrel or the beginning of a fight.

"Well, this is the parting of the ways for us, Jim," said Ford. "I'm going to spend a few days here and then off to some other point. Seems I cannot stay long in one place for some reason or another."

McDonald grinned. "I understand, young fellow, and I'll be forever grateful for your saving my worthless hide."

That was the last time they saw each other. McDonald returned to Abilene in a few days with a story that most did not want to believe. Many questioned that the Ford was *the* Bob Ford, the assassin of Jesse James. Whenever McDonald was around the subject never was discussed. It is known that several days after Ford had been killed in Creede, Colorado, in 1892, an elderly gentleman, no longer a deputy marshal of Abilene, Kansas, wrote to the local papers telling what kind of a man he thought Bob Ford was.

22 • • •

Bob Ford in Colorado

Prior to moving into Colorado Bob Ford had gone to Las Vegas with Dick Liddil and opened a saloon there, thinking their notoriety would make them famous. Their saloon on Bridge Street in Old Town was a miserable failure. Liddil then took employment with J. W. Lynch, famous horse-racing magnate, and toured the circuits with him, caring for his animals. Dick died a natural death in Cincinnati, Ohio, and his body was brought back to Missouri by his family, where it was buried in Independence, Missouri.

Bob Ford next went to Walsenburg, Colorado, where he also opened a saloon. However, the customers failed to come into his place, and he soon abandoned the venture. Eventually he arrived at Pueblo, Colorado, and opened a fancy honkey-tonk in the section known as the Mesa. There was a clubhouse near the police station where he made friends among the barflies.

Edward O'Kelley, a member of the city police force in Pueblo, hated Bob Ford for his killing of Jesse James, and he was outspoken about it, especially when he was drunk, which was often. In 1889 Ford beat O'Kelley to the draw and could have killed him then and there, but too many of O'Kelley's whiskey-nose friends were around. Ford whacked O'Kelley over the head with his pistol and knocked him unconscious, then stooped over, picked up Ed's own gun, and left the saloon.

This incident was a partial springboard for Ed's later killing of Ford. Some have claimed that Bob Ford and O'Kelley shared a room (hardly likely) and quarreled over a diamond ring that Bob accused

270

Ed of stealing. Others took a more fantastic stand, stating that Bob's death was the result of a Missouri vendetta. Romanticists claimed that O'Kelley killed Ford in a quarrel over a girl, but O'Kelley never cared for any woman in his entire life. This was confirmed by his own brother, Dr. Frank O'Kelley, a Missourian from Patton, who fought long for Ed's release from prison. Dr. O'Kelley was a dear friend of mine.

In July of 1891 Ed got drunk while on duty and shot an unarmed black man named Ed Riley. The shooting occurred on what now is First Street. The authorities held Ed in jail until the man recovered, and if Ed hadn't been a member of the police force he would have been sent to prison then, but they wanted to hush it up. The official report read that O'Kelley was discharged from the Pueblo police department for being drunk on the job; nothing was ever mentioned of his shooting the black man.

It was my good fortune to have known Norval Jennings of New York City, many years prior to his death. Mr. Jennings was in Pueblo when Bob Ford was there; he also was a near-eyewitness to the shooting of Bob at Creede, Colorado, in 1892. He had many things to say about Ford. I would like to mention a few of these.

"Bob Ford spent many days in Pueblo, gambling and what not, and, although I did not meet him personally until I got to Creede, I saw him a half dozen times or more. I also witnessed some of the events that took place in his life while there.

"I was still working at the Phoenix Hotel in Pueblo during 1891, and often watched an elderly woman standing on Union Street, near the hotel entrance, selling artificial flowers to anyone who was interested in buying one. I often noticed that Bob Ford would never pass this woman without buying a flower. Sometimes he would tuck it in the lapel of his coat, or he would carry it into the hotel and give it to one of the waitresses.

"As a dishwasher there, it was easy for me to learn what was going on. I was still a teenager and looked the part, nobody paid much attention to me when they were talking. Sometimes I heard things that would have been dangerous, so I was quick to forget such conversations. The flower woman was known as 'Bokay Sallie' on account of the bouquets she sold as well as single flowers. Some people referred to her as 'Bad Luck Sallie.' I heard two men talking about it one evening.

" 'You know, Chuck, that flower lady is the jinx. I never paid any attention to her before last week. One evening I talked to her and the next night I almost got caught robbing a jewelry store. I'm staying clear of that one.'

" 'It was just a coincidence, Mack,' guessed the other man, with a laugh.

"Christmas Eve of that year, 1891, was a bitter cold one. I was busy in the kitchen as usual, washing dishes, and sometimes gathering them from the restaurant part of the hotel, or diner, as they called them in those days. I went to the alley door of the hotel to toss out some discarded vegetables and as I did so I saw two men struggling with the flower lady, trying to steal her purse.

"There wasn't much that I could do but stare in dismay. I was just turning to call for help when another man rushed at the two muggers, a heavy cane whacking down on the backs and heads of the two would-be robbers. The man appeared to be of slender build, light hair, not tall, not short, and wearing the clothing of the middle-class people of the day. Flowers were strewn all over the alley, and poor Sallie was crouching pitifully against the alley fence.

"Although he was a smaller man than those he attacked, the two bullies scurried away from the man with the cane, leaving their dazed victim wondering what was going on.

" 'Did they get your money, Sallie?' asked the man.

" 'No. Oh, it's you, Bob Ford. Oh, am I glad to see you. Those ruffians might have killed me.'

" 'Well, you were bad luck for them tonight, that's certain,' grinned Ford.

"The name Bob Ford stuck with me that evening and then I knew— he was the slayer of the noted Missouri outlaw Jesse James!

" 'C'mon, Sallie, let's go in and have a bite to eat. You look mighty hungry and cold.'

" 'I kain't go into such a fancy place as the Phoenix.'

" 'Why not? So long as you have money, you can go anywhere. I'll treat you to a Christmas dinner, how's that?'

"At first I thought the two were going to enter by the back door, but Ford said nothing to me; he simply took Sallie by the arm and they walked to the main entrance of the Phoenix, where all eyes were cast upon them. Without as much as a flicker of an eyelid they walked into the main dining room and ordered the best meal in the place.

"Occasionally I would peer through the kitchen door leading into the diner, where I could observe Sallie and Ford engaged in pleasant conversation. It seemed like poor Sallie thought she was Cinderella. I gave Ford the once over, good and plenty. He sure did not seem like the kind of a guy some people said he was. I could not help thinking how such a youthful fellow, almost ten years past, could have slain the mighty Jesse James. I guess Ford was around thirty when I first saw him in Pueblo. I tried to listen to some of their conversation but they were too far away. Anyhow, I could tell by their actions that none of it centered on Bob's past life.

"As the two were leaving I heard Ford say, 'Sallie, here's fifty dollars. Now you go and get a nice room and take it easy for a few days. Selling flowers is no snap.'

" 'Merry Christmas, Bob Ford, and God bless you for your kindness.'

"Funny thing, though, on the night of that Christmas Day, the Phoenix Hotel burned to the ground. I suppose that the owners wanted to blame Bad Luck Sallie for it. I never did hear any of their comments or if they ever knew she had had Christmas Eve dinner there with Bob Ford."

I kept in close contact with Mr. Jennings in hopes that further unpublished material concerning the life of Bob Ford might be revealed. Following is another account of an incident in Pueblo.

"One night in the Bucket of Blood Saloon in Pueblo I was present when Bob Ford walked into the place. No one paid too much attention to him, since many people did not know who he was, while, on the other hand, a number of low-dive cronies were aware of his identity. Ed O'Kelley did not put in an appearance that night, fortunately, for had he appeared the place would probably have turned into a shooting gallery, for a number of the drinkers there were friends of his and were half soused already.

"Of course, it was not a dull evening with all the gaming tables going full blast. I limited my own gambling to shooting craps and lost a few dollars, which I could ill afford to do. Yet, there seemed to be an ominous air of expectation hovering over the place. I could not put my finger on it, but something was in the air. When I saw a young, tossle-haired fellow, carrying a battered guitar, walk through the doorway, I immediately knew what was up. The low-divers were in a mood to harass Bob Ford.

"The guitar player, whose name I never did learn, strummed off a few nice and easy songs, seemingly anxious to hear for requests from his listeners, since that was the only way he could earn anything—the coins they tossed at his feet after each song had been sung.

"Suddenly a voice from the direction of the low-divers yelled out, 'We want to hear the Billy Gashade song!'

"Of course, the audience knew what that meant—it was 'The Ballad of Jesse James.'

"The young guitarist needed no second call—it was a prearranged deal to get on Ford's nerves. As soon as Ford had entered the saloon a runner went to notify the singer to appear at the proper moment.

"Ford fidgetted on his barstool but said nothing—he just waited.

"The mournful tune began, followed by:

> Poor Jesse had a wife to mourn for his life,
> Three children, they were brave
> But that dirty little coward that shot Mr. Howard
> Has laid poor Jesse in his grave.

(NOTE: Error in song as Jesse had only two children.)

"People began to look at each other. How long would this go on before there was some reaction from the young man at the bar. On went the song, the singer now thinking he had Ford in his pocket.

> It was Robert Ford, that dirty little coward,
> I wonder how he feels?
> For he ate of Jesse's bread and he slept in
>   Jesse's bed
> And laid poor Jesse in his grave.

"Now the audience found out what Ford intended to do. Everyone had expected him to flare into a temper tantrum, but Ford knew that half the battle was lost if he did not hold onto his temper. Would he walk over to the singer and whack him on the head with his pistol? Or would he simply turn tail and leave the saloon sheepishly?

"Ford gave a half turn on his barstool, pushed back the right side of his coat, exposing to view his .45 Colt. Great Scott! Surely he was not going to shoot the young man, I thought. People began to pale, me included, I thought perhaps the joke had been carried too far already.

"I saw Ford's right hand snake down to the pistol and before anyone knew what was happening the boom of its explosion filled the room. People peered through the cloud of black powder smoke, anxious to see what the bullet had hit. What they saw was the guitarist holding his right hand and yelling like an Apache Indian. There was some blood on the hand and people quickly concluded that Ford had shot the young man in the hand. But this was not the case. The blood was caused by the skin being pricked by the sharp ends of the guitar strings. Ford had cut the strings of the guitar with a .45 slug without it hitting any part of the player. From that time on no one ever tried to play this joke on Ford again, at least, not to my knowledge."

Creede, Colorado, 1892.

Saloon in Creede, showing Ford's old bar, 1896.

Randolph (Soapy) Smith.

Skagway, Alaska.

Rounding up some of Soapy Smith's gang, Skagway, Alaska.

Grave of Frank Reid, Skagway, Alaska.

Street in Creede, Dave's Place.

Ruins of Jimtown, Colorado, after fire.

Durango, Colorado, circa 1902.

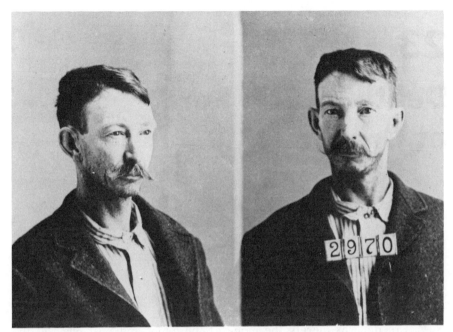

Ed O'Kelley, slayer of Bob Ford.

Funeral cortege, Creede, Colorado, death of Bob Ford.

23 • • •
Death of Bob Ford
at Creede

With the big rush for the mining camp of Creede, Colorado, O'Kelley
went with the crowd, and Bob Ford did also. Creede, named after
N. C. Creede, was merely the name of the depot and post office at the
end of the Denver & Rio Grande narrow gauge railroad, and was a
mile away from the section known as Jimtown and part of it known
as Victor. This area was only five blocks long with one street in a
gulch five hundred feet wide.

Another actor in the Ford-O'Kelley drama was Jefferson Randolph
(Soapy) Smith, and he also came to the Creede area with his gambling
and crooked gang. He earned this nickname because he would take
a piece of common brown soap the size of a French fried potato, wrap
a ten dollar bill around it, then wrap the same in a pink paper, before
dropping it into a Derby hat. You guessed it—there was never any
money in the packages taken from the hat, for Soapy was a sleight-of-
hand artist. The suckers fell hard for the trick, and it cost them a
dollar each to look at the package in the hat. Yes, Barnum was right!

Slippery Soapy Smith found that in Jimtown there was no interference in his vocation, for nobody knew where the county lines were
and therefore nobody had any jurisdiction. He took over the town,
appointing his brother-in-law, John Light, as marshal. Smith owned
and operated the Orleans Club on the east side of the canyon, and woe
betide any sucker who thought he had a chance to win anything in

Soapy's place. It was common knowledge that every game in the place was "fixed."

There was Faro Bank, Bird Cage, Roulette, Chuck-a-Luck, and Stud Poker, all as crooked as a dog's hind leg. Soapy was able to feed all his dealers and shills because he had a cook and a couple of helpers in the kitchen.

The other two gambling emporiums in Jimtown were Ford's Omaha Club and the Gunnison Club & Exchange. Smith wanted the other owners to accept his own methods, but they refused to go along with his crooked proposition. The Smith gang went to work on the Gunnison place first; each night they would go into the place as gamblers and start a row. Eventually there was the killing of Red McCune, one of the owners, who always tended bar. However, in the case of Bob Ford the Smith gang was afraid to start anything because they knew he was a dead shot and fast on the draw, not afraid of anything. Consequently, they confined their activities to sending him letters written in chicken blood. These warning letters told Ford that if he did not get out of town he would be given the same treatment that he gave Jesse James.

Of course, sooner or later this was bound to get on Ford's nerves. One night he got liquored up, leaped on his pony, and rode up and down the street. He stopped in front of the Central Theatre. There he made a speech to the crowd, telling them that there was a certain element in town writing him unsigned letters and threatening to bump him off. Ford said that if there was any man in town who cared to shoot it out with him, he would be happy to oblige. He would meet anyone interested on the mesa (west of the lower part of Jimtown). By that time the first electric lights had come to Amethyst Street; Ford pulled out his gun and shot out a light some fifty feet away, as a demonstration of his skill. After that Smith realized that Ford was a dangerous man to fool around with.

Norval Jennings told another interesting story pertaining to Ford.

"During the early spring of 1892 Ford was riding through a wooded section of the area around Creede. Passing through a belt of timber along a wide stream, he rode up to a camping place of a Mexican emigrant family. The plight of the campers indicated at once that they were a poor lot. Even their old plug horse seemed on its last legs, not able to pull the rickety wagon much farther. Not only that, the father of the family had died several days before and his body was still lying under a tree. The mother was ill, and three children, all under ten years of age, were crying pitifully and begging for food.

"Ford told the mother that he would return with a doctor and some supplies. He hurried back to Creede, called Doc Sommers, and they gathered up some goods and a wagon and a horse. These they took to the stranded family, prior to notifying the undertaker to make a small coffin for the dead husband. Ford and the doctor had rendered what help they could, then the undertaker arrived. Shortly after the father was buried in an unmarked grave, one of so many that dotted the trails West.

" 'Doc, why not take these people to the Wilson family up the creek aways? They got plenty room and they can stay there until they are able to travel again. This will help.' So saying, he handed Doc Sommers a one hundred dollar bill. It would indeed be impossible for anyone to have this bereaved woman and her children to say anything against Robert Ford, whom they did not even know, or probably ever learned who he was."

On Sunday night, April 17, 1892, Bob Ford and Joe Palmer went out and proceeded to shoot up the town. Buildings were perforated, window panes were broken, and the air cracked with pistol shots. Not an officer of the law appeared to quell the disturbance, however. One of them had a sudden attack of nausea and went home to bed. Another had forgotten his buttonhole bouquet and was ashamed to appear on the street without it. So with one excuse or another the lawmen kept out of the way and let the fun go on. It lasted from 9 o'clock in the evening until midnight, when the ammunition ran out and the jags got too heavy to carry, when it died out of its own volition.

The citizens of Creede, angry over the incident, decided to uphold the peace and dignity of the town. On Monday morning a number of them talked it over, deciding that the population was two too many at the time. A delegation of six-footers called upon Ford and Palmer, outlining what had taken place. Shortly after a hack drove up briskly to a door on Creede Avenue. Bob Ford and Joe Palmer came rushing out and piled into the hack, shut the door and pulled down the curtains. The order was given and the hack sped down the toll to Wason. A few minutes later an express wagon pulled up to the same door and sundry trunks, grips, and the possessions of the two departed men were piled therein and then emptied at the depot. The afternoon train took the things on board and then stopped at Wason to pick up two male passengers, who seemed anxious and worried about something and who took a long, last look at the bluffs of Willow Canyon as the train pulled away for Denver.

Palmer never returned to Creede, but Bob Ford wanted to do so. About a month after leaving that town he contacted Lute Johnson, owner of the Creede newspaper, begging his support to that end. Ford promised to be on his good behavior from then on. Ford realized that he had lost everything in Creede, but stated he wanted to start up another dancehall and saloon if permitted to do so. Through Jefferson's efforts Ford returned to Creede and opened up a dancehall in the Lincoln Exchange.

Soapy Smith was smart enough to get someone else to do his killing for him. Around his saloon Edward O'Kelley regularly looked for free drinks and odd jobs, and Smith picked him as a likely prospect, since he knew of O'Kelley's hatred for Ford. Smith reminded O'Kelley of the way he had shot the black man in Pueblo; then told him he had nothing to fear about killing Ford, since everything would be "fixed."

"You'll become world-known as the man who killed the man who killed Jesse James!" he promised.

There was another curious character in Jimtown who played a minor role in the drama. This man was an undersized French Canadian named Joe Duval. He was a booze hound and never did any kind of work, at least, not that anyone knew about. He came into town each morning on his little donkey and went from saloon to saloon to see if anyone would treat him. His attempt to speak English was so comical that it usually earned him a free drink.

At that time there was a big fire that emptied the Gulch of all its buildings. However, some of the wiser citizens had erected structures south of Jimtown on what was known as the School Land, and which is the site of the present town of Creede, Colorado. Shortly after the fire, Bob Ford secured a location on this land and had a floor put down. He erected a tent over the flooring, and this was to serve as a temporary saloon. His bartender, Joe McKee, on a visit to his mother in Kansas City, did not return in time for the opening, so Ford tended bar himself.

On the day of his death Ford was trying to perform one last act of kindness. Nellie Russell, a St. Joseph, Missouri, girl, reached Creede a few days prior to June 8th, and despairing of getting work, agreed to join Bob Ford's bevy of dance girls. Then she went off and got drunk, ending up by taking an overdose of morphine, the effects of which killed her. Ford drew up a subscription paper to raise money to give the girl a decent burial. He had written the paper on his bar, with Dot Evans Ford, his wife, ready to make the collections, when O'Kelley entered the tent.

The morning of June 8, 1892, was chilly and clear. Ford was alone at the bar, still writing the subscription paper, and cleaning up around the place. The Smith gang was aware of his being alone, and they encouraged Ed O'Kelley to saunter out into the street with a sawed-off shotgun under his coat. Seeing Joe Duval, Ed called him over and asked him to have a drink with him. They walked together to Ford's place, and O'Kelley shoved Duval through the tent opening ahead of him. When Bob turned his head to see who was coming, O'Kelley let him have it with both barrels, shooting him in the throat and almost taking his head off. Ford's collar button was later found embedded in a pole across the tent, and Soapy Smith carried it for the rest of his life as a good-luck charm. Ford died in the arms of his Jimtown mistress, Ella Mae Watterson.

The whole matter was prearranged and Marshal Light was right there, taking O'Kelley away at once, since some of the miners would have strung him up then and there. Although Soapy Smith had managed to be in Denver the day of the murder, he knew that O'Kelley had merely obeyed his instructions so he kept his promise to the extent of furnishing legal aid for O'Kelley.

Norval Jennings told me that he was working in the kitchen in Newman Vidal's log cabin restaurant near the Ford tent saloon the day Ford was killed. He was there when they brought the body of Ford from behind the bar. This same bar in 1937 was put into use by the Creede Elks Lodge. All but the one corner was refinished. Dozens of bullet holes can still be seen in the unfinished section of the Bob Ford tent saloon bar.

The trial of Ed O'Kelley and Joe Duval took place in Lake City, July 12, 1892, and O'Kelley was sentenced to life imprisonment at the Canon City Penitentiary, with ten days of each year in the dungeon. Joe Duval, the innocent bystander, so to speak, was given two years. Soapy Smith was quite a politician in Colorado, and soon the gears were working to get O'Kelley released. By 1902 he was a free man again, largely due to the efforts of his younger brother, Dr. Frank O'Kelley, and the political clout of Soapy Smith.

Bob Ford was buried up on the mesa south of the School Land. Norval Jennings reports that there was quite a large crowd at the funeral, with the procession winding its way up the side of the hill.

Ford's body was exhumed in August of 1892 and reburied at Richmond, Missouri, where his brother Charley also was buried.

After seeing to Bob's burial in Missouri, Dot Evans Ford returned to Creede the following month, where she became an entertainer at the Grand Theatre. She later remarried and moved to Durango, Colorado, with her husband, John Feeney. For a time she had also resided north of Aguilar, Las Animas County, Colorado. On June 15, 1902, Dot Evans Ford Feeney committed suicide by chloroform, ill health being given as the cause. She was about forty years old at the time. Her body was discovered by an adopted daughter, aged nine.

The citizens of Durango expressed regret at the passing of Mrs. Feeney, for she had been regarded as a member in good standing with the people. Her condition had been aggravated by the fact that she had lived almost in poverty, while her husband traveled the country with race track people. It was said that Mrs. Feeney abused her adopted children; yet, she must have had their welfare at heart, for she left them a two thousand dollar insurance policy.

What happened to the arch-conspirator Soapy Smith? He and his old crowd left Jimtown soon after the death of Ford and went to the Klondike because of the gold rush. At Skagway, it is said, Soapy and his crew netted over a million dollars in gold from their various types of robbery. In July of 1898 Frank Reid, an honest citizen tired of Soapy's crooked bunch, had vowed to run Smith out of town or die in the attempt. In July of that year the two men met on a wharf at Skagway. Soapy was armed with a .44-.40 Winchester rifle, Reid with a six-shooter. Smith was killed by a bullet through the heart, while Reid was wounded so seriously that he passed away twelve days later. Today Smith's grave is a tourist attraction at Skagway, visited by many; Reid's grave is seldom asked about.

One day I inquired of Norval Jennings how he had become acquainted with Bob Ford; this was his reply.

"Well, when the bottom dropped out of Jimtown after the fire and most of the restaurants had closed up I was out of work and broke. With no place to sleep and no way to get back to Kansas or to Pueblo, it was mighty rough. This was in March and the nights were very cold, sometimes as low as 20° below zero. I went from place to place to get warm by the big pot-bellied stoves they had in the saloons. On this particular night I walked into Ford's Omaha Club. There was not a soul in the place except Ford and his bartender. He came up, remarking how cold it was, and asking me what I was doing. I told him nothing; he then asked me where I was from and I told him from Minden Mines, Barton County, Missouri. He asked me if I was hungry and I told him I was. He told me I could help the bartender and could sleep and eat in the kitchen until I found something to do. That is what I did until the fire cleaned out Jimtown. This made business boom at Vidal's restaurant, and I got a job there until I was able to leave Jimtown. I went to Denver later in 1892 and worked at Torton's Restaurant on Arapaho Street, operated by Cavanagh-Vidal, the latter the same man whom I had worked for in Creede, or rather, Jimtown."

I asked Mr. Jennings if he thought Ford was a coward.

"All the books and newspapers never had a good word for Bob Ford, since they all jumped to the conclusion that Ford killed James in order to get the reward. So we will first take up the method by which Jesse James lived. He was, as everyone knows, a robber and sometimes a killer whenever resistance was offered. The story that he robbed the rich and gave to the poor is simply hogwash. He gave some money to hillbilly people in the fastness of the Ozarks to furnish him and his gang a hideout from time to time after they had made a big haul somewhere. There is no question in my mind that Ford killed James for self-preservation. I feel sure that Jesse would have killed Ford that very night of the day he, himself, was killed by the Fords. In every such drama there must be a hero and a villain. The people of Missouri chose to accept Jesse James as the hero and Ford as the villain, it is as simple as that. Jesse never would have been chosen the hero, of course, had it not been for his Civil War background, and having fought with Quantrill for the Confederacy, or, so they said. The lurid hack writers of the day, of course, added fuel to the matter of Jesse's death—fuel that will keep the fire burning forever."

I suggested to Mr. Jennings that Poker Alice Tubbs claimed she saw Ford killed.

"Poker Alice may have been there, but she was not there when I was, she was at Cripple Creek when Ford was slain. In a situation like this everyone wants to get into the act; all they do is cloud and confuse the issue so an honest historian gets sidetracked all the time. Ford's mistress I saw each morning when she came down for breakfast. She had very little to say at any time and put in most of her time upstairs in their apartment over the place. There was, however, a very popular high yellow gal that we all had known in Pueblo. She was tall and quite nice looking and everyone called her 'Topsy' and she seemed quite proud of the name. She was a hustler from Pueblo and wore boots and loved to shoot crap. She was in Ford's place one night and told me that she was going back to Pueblo, since the miners were getting too cheap; that all of them were dirty and most of them lousy. There was no running water in town. The only water of any kind was melted snow and the snow lay fifteen feet deep up against the walls of the canyon. So it was nothing to see people scratching or to see big graybacks walking across the green covering of the gambling tables.

"I never saw Ford armed when he was in his place, but he put on his shooting irons whenever he went out. Ford had no children and sold no meals in his place, other than coffee and doughnuts. The two fiddlers were paid nothing except what they could get from the dancers. When I went back there in 1941 and the people found out that I had been an eyewitness to all these things, the questions came fast and furious. It was hard for me to leave town, but I enjoyed the attention. I still maintain that if Bob Ford had been left alone he would have come out all right."

24 • • •

Finale--Death of Edward O'Kelley

The encounter that ended the life of Edward O'Kelley, the slayer of Bob Ford, occurred on the evening of January 13, 1904, in front of the McCord-Collins Building, on West First Street, Oklahoma City, Oklahoma.

Ed O'Kelley had been received with scorn and jeers wherever he had gone, a replay of what Bob Ford had gone through after the assassination of Jesse James. Ed returned to Patton, Missouri, around 1902, to attend the funeral of his mother, but even there he was no paragon of popularity, even with his own family. It is said that he brought presents for his family in an attempt to become endeared to them, but it did not work, so again he left Missouri a short time after the funeral. So, in 1904, Ed was wandering around the country, an outcast, his destiny about to be played out in Oklahoma City.

In a fierce fight that lasted about fifteen minutes police officer Joe Burnett shot and killed the man who killed Bob Ford, the man who killed Jesse James. It happened at 9 o'clock the evening of January 13th.

After the fight Burnett was taken to the office of Dr. Witten to have bandages placed on his ears, which had been badly chewed by his vicious assailant. He also suffered a slight flesh wound of the left hip, where a bullet had nicked off a piece of flesh about the size of a nickel.

Burnett first came upon O'Kelley on the south side of Front Street and just in front of the McCord-Collins Building.

290

"Hello, O'Kelley," said the policeman.

O'Kelley did not respond but immediately whirled on the officer with a gun in his right hand. He struck at Burnett, at the same time crying out, "You come with me. I'll arrest you for a change, you lousy son-of-a-bitch!"

As O'Kelley struck out Burnett grabbed his gun and held onto it with his left hand to the very end. O'Kelley shot the pistol empty, at the same time calling Burnett all the vile names he could think of.

"You'll not disarm me!" he cried. "I'll murder you!"

Burnett later stated that he probably would have been killed had not the brave baggageman from the railroad depot come forth and grabbed O'Kelley's hand, releasing the officer's weapon.

Burnett also stated that he fought with O'Kelley for about fifteen minutes and that his assailant chewed up both his ears. Also stated they were on the north side of the building near the second door west, and when the finish occurred they were around by the door on the east side of the house.

"I'd surely been killed if the baggageman from the Frisco Depot hadn't come and got my gun loose for me. Then I shot O'Kelley."

The fight was a terrific one, and was a death struggle from the onset. Things might have been different if O'Kelley's companion had not deserted him. This man fired one shot at the officer and then fled.

"Come back, you yellow-livered bastard!" cried O'Kelley. "We've got a chance to murder this fellow."

Investigation revealed that Burnett's left ear was powder-burned, and there were two bullet holes in the back of his overcoat and the left hip pocket was torn by a bullet. His gloves were burned and his clothing was on fire when friends reached his side after the fight. After O'Kelley had been shot Burnett fell exhausted to the sidewalk.

About a month before this incident Burnett had arrested O'Kelley as a suspicious character and the deceased had been greatly offended because of his arrest. O'Kelley made threats at the Lewis Hotel and was known to carry two guns with him all the time. He carried these pistols in his overcoat pockets and constantly kept his hands in his pockets while he was on the streets. The day before the shooting he had been on the streets without his overcoat and was arrested by Officer Bunker, but was later released and evidently went at once for his weapons. He told N. B. Pierrepont that the police had better not attempt to arrest him again.

O'Kelley's body was taken to the morgue at Street & Harper's

Furniture Store. He had a bullet wound in his left leg just about the knee. The bullet that killed him, however, entered his head just back of the left temple and had come out back of the right ear—a wound nearly like the one that killed Jesse James. O'Kelley was about six feet tall, had red hair and a stubby mustache, and in features and physique somewhat resembled that of Bob Fitzsimmons, the noted prizefighter.

A number of persons identified the dead man as the assassin of Bob Ford, among them being Otto Ewing of the Southern Club, who was once connected with Ford's saloon in Creede, Colorado, at the time of Ford's death. Ewing had spoken of this matter days before, telling the people of Ford's murder, that O'Kelley was a dangerous man to mess around with.

The tower man of the Choctaw line, who saw the fight, stated that a policeman stood across the street from where Burnett was fighting for his life, but he decided to run from the scene as did O'Kelley's cowardly companion. For a long time conversation in town dwelled upon the fight between Burnett and O'Kelley and on the flight of the cowardly police officer.

O'Kelley's companion was a heavy-set man, about thirty-five years old, with a heavy mustache and a week's growth of beard on his face. He was believed to have been Bob Jackson, the man who had held up a bawdy house on Second Street about a week prior to the fight. Lillian Johnson, the operator of the brothel, gave the police this information.

Jackson later jumped into a hack and ordered the driver to take him to the 700 block of West Reno. On First Street the hack passed two policemen, and Jackson poked a pistol against the cabby's back and told him he would kill him if he stopped the vehicle.

Shortly after the shooting occurred Police Officers Ballard and Couch found a man parading down First Street with a Winchester rifle and they took him to police headquarters. They found about fifty rounds of ammunition in his pockets. He told several conflicting stories, giving his name as Marvin E. Kerney, of Silver City, Iowa. In a memorandum book taken from his pocket the police found the following, "Guy Kerney, Silver City, Iowa. If I should be found dead please send me to Silver City."

Kerney told the police that his brother would be found on the street, carrying a double-barreled shotgun. He said they had come from Guthrie to hunt rabbits and quail, coming there on the invitation of a man named Smith, who resided near the brickyard on the Choctaw line west of Oklahoma City. He told the police they had a mother and three sisters living in Guthrie. The police decided to hold the man, however, believing him to be a member of a gang to which O'Kelley had belonged. Some of the men had been living at a place called The Tavern on West Main Street and were always heavily armed.

After Jackson's holdup of the bawdy house on West Second Street Detective Hogan called at the hotel and asked to be allowed to visit the rooms occupied by these three men. He was informed that the men had left; also, they had taken guns with them. The officers asked who had taken the guns and the clerk told him a man named Jerome Clemens.

Jerome Clemens was the man who was being tried in the court of Justice of the Peace Knight on a charge of vagrancy. The case was set before Justice Leach, but the prisoner asked for a change of venue.

O'Kelley, the man slain by Officer Burnett, had been under surveillance for some time, and, like several other characters of his ilk, had been a lounger at the notorious saloons on First Street, where so many thieves had been operating at the time.

B. E. Chapin, who was in the rear of the building at 225½ West Main Street, saw much of the fight and telephoned to police headquarters. He heard an officer call out to several men who were passing, "I am a policeman; come and help me."

He said one of the men replied, "We don't know whether you are the police or not," and then they ran away.

Edward O'Kelley was buried in the Oklahoma City potter's field, unmourned and without rites.

I personally contacted Dr. Frank O'Kelley of Patton, Missouri, and of the many items he related about his brother Ed, the following are of interest and fit in with this story.

"I was away in the West when Ed was killed and did not know anything about it until several years later. When I came home the folks did not have much to say to me or anyone else about it. They desired to avoid the unpleasant notoriety and didn't tell the neighbors much. All I knew was just rumors. I am not sure, but I think the man who killed him was named Burnett, and Ed probably was too drunk to know what he was doing. When you come down again we will take the old family skeleton out of the closet and look it over.

"Before he was killed Ed had become a hopeless wreck, both physically and mentally from his drinking and was *persona non grata* to his relatives, as well as his so-called friends. He stayed with Jesse's

son for a time in Kansas City and the young man tried to get Ed on
his feet. He was good to Ed and kept him up for quite a while. It was
hard for young Jesse James to keep from excessive drinking, too, for
the friends of his dad idolized him and they were all tough cookies
and hard drinkers, and tried to buy drinks for Jesse's son most of
the time.

"You probably will recall the Leeds, Missouri, train robbery near
Kansas City in which Jesse was said to have participated. Grandma
Samuel held up her right arm stump in court and swore that she was
sitting on the porch with little Jesse at the exact time of the robbery.
The judge looked at her and in effect told the young man after the
jury's first ballot had acquitted him, 'Well, Jesse, not guilty, but don't
do it again!' After the trial Jesse operated a pawn shop, which they
let him run to suit himself, and he got along fine. Of course, a lot of
this is hearsay, but one never knows.

"Ed was six feet tall, very slim, blue eyes, and red-headed. After
he went to the city he took on some weight. He was born in the Blue
Ridge Mountains in East Tennessee as were most of my family folks.
Ed was a natural born killer. Ford was his fourth man, and that is one
reason the court gave him a life sentence. We worked hard for his
release and did finally get him freed ten years later. Even so, Ed
followed the rule of the West—not to shoot a man in the back. When
he got ready to kill Ford, the victim was behind the bar looking the
other way. Ed called out, 'Hello, Bob!' And Bob, recognizing his voice
and realizing his time was up, wheeled around, but it was too late. Ed
let him have it with both barrels in his neck, just below the chin and
both literally and figuratively shot off Ford's damned head. Bob's
collar button was imbedded in a wooden pole in the tent. This Soapy
Smith retrieved and wore as a watch charm until he was killed in
Alaska.

"Ed killed Bob Ford because they had a fight in Pueblo in 1889.
Ford beat him to the draw, but instead of shooting him he hit Ed with
his gun and knocked him out. Ed's gun fell to the floor and Ford picked
it up and walked out. He also hated the way Ford had killed Jesse
James. Ed had been a policeman on the Pueblo force for several years,
but was suspended for drinking on the job. I was visiting him at the
time but he never said a word to me about it, and I did not find out
about it until a few weeks later. Ed's friend who told me also stated
that Ed would kill Ford for his insults.

"The story about a girl being involved is poppycock. Ed never married and never took up with any woman. He was associated with the Youngers but to what extent, I do not know. The story that Homer Croy wrote about Ed marrying into the Younger family is enough to make a horse laugh.

"When the trial of Ed came up money was spent from some source to hire lawyers against him, and some sob-sisters and church reformers made a ruckus about it all, calling Ed a killer of the worst sort. Most everybody in the West hated Ford, but in Creede were Carrie Nation, Billie Sunday, a bunch of Holy Rollers, and some Mormons, who created such a fuss that the jurors did what they did, I guess.

"The killing of Bob Ford had a tragic effect upon my life, too. Wherever I went, somewhere usually in the Southwest, I had to tell about it and compete with the romantic liars. I give you one horrible example of this. I was practicing medicine in Picher, Oklahoma, and one evening a man came in and introduced himself as Scout Younger. He was a fine fellow and was in Picher with a *Jesse James Show*, moving pictures and statues of the famous outlaws. It was about 1920 and Picher was a wild Western mining town, if there ever was one, and he had a good business. Later we became great friends and one day he said he wanted to put a statue of my brother with the others, if I did not mind. This was all right with me. Then he wanted a picture. I told him that I did not know of a photo of Ed [later one was found at the Canon City Prison, only one known], since he was touchy about that.

"He came back in a day or two and said he wanted one of my pictures and would have a statue made from that. They sent to Italy to have them made, he said. I gave him one that I had made in the Texas Panhandle, with a big Kaiser Wilhelm mustache. I told him so far as I knew my brother did not wear a mustache, never did at home. He told me that he would have the company take off the mustache, but he did not. I told him that if he ever brought the thing to Picher I would shoot his damned ass off. I think he was some courthouse relation to the outlaw Youngers, not sure what.

"Several years later my daughter was strolling down the avenue in Alton, Illinois, where she came upon a *Jesse James Show* with the bold, bad, and ugly outlaws standing out on the sidewalk. Right up in front was my statue. After recovering from the shock, she demanded of Scout Younger what he was doing using the statue of her father with all the train robbers. He said it was all a mistake and that he had sent the wrong picture to the sculptor. He said it cost three thousand dollars and looked so good he could not resist displaying it. He gave her a handful of tickets for the show and all was forgotten."

The pages of history have swallowed the characters of this book, leaving Jesse James a martyred hero, that same history depicting Bob Ford a low-livered coward, which he was not. Numerous books have been written about Jesse James through the years—this is the first one to deal with the life of Bob Ford.

Bibliography

Altrocchi, Julia Cooley, *Traces of Folklore and Furrow*, Caxton Print-
ers, Caldwell, Idaho, 1945.

Alvarez, N., *The James Boys in Missouri*, Ames Publishing Company,
1906.

Bancroft, Hubert Howe, *Outlaws*, Historical Publishers, San Fran-
cisco, 1887.

Benton, Jesse James, *Cow by the Tail*, Houghton, Mifflin Co., Boston,
1943.

Black, A. P., *End of the Long Horn Trail*, Selfridge Journal, Selfridge,
North Dakota.

Botin, B. A., *Treasury of American Folklore*, Crown Publishers, New
York, 1944.

Bradley, R. T., *Lives of Frank and Jesse James*, J. W. Marsh Co.,
St. Louis, Mo., 1882.

Breihan, Carl W., *Complete & Authentic Life of Jesse James*, Fred.
Fell, Inc., New York, 1953.

Breihan, Carl W., *The Day Jesse James Was Killed*, Fred. Fell, Inc.
New York, 1963.

Breihan, Carl W., *Escapades of Frank & Jesse James*, Fred. Fell, Inc.
New York, 1974.

Buel, James William, *The Border Outlaws*, Historical Publishing,
St. Louis, Mo., 1881.

Casey, Robert J., *The Texas Border*, Bobbs-Merrill Co., Indianapolis,
Indiana, 1950.

Clarke, Donald H., *Autobiography of Frank Tarbeaux*, Vanguard
Press, New York, N.Y., 1930.

Collier, William Ross-Westrate, Edwin Victor, *Dave Cook of the
Rockies*, Wilson Publishers, New York, 1936.

Collier, William Ross-Westrate, Edwin Victor, *The Reign of Soapy Smith*, Doubleday, Doran Co., New York, 1935.

Cooper, Courtney Ryley, *High Country, the Rockies*, Boston, Little, Brown & Co., Baston, Mass., 1926.

Crittenden, Henry Huston, *The Crittenden Memoirs*, G. P. Putnam's Sons, New York, 1936.

Croy, Homer, *Jesse James was My Neighbor*, Duell, Sloan, Pearce, New York, 1949.

Cummins, Jim, *The Story of Jim Cummins*, Reed Publishing Co., Denver, Colo., 1903.

Dacus, Joseph A., *Life and Adventures of Frank and Jesse James*, N.D. Thompson Publishing Co., St. Louis Mo., 1881.

Dale, Henry, *Adventures of the Younger Brothers*, Street & Smith, New York, 1890.

Dalton, Emmett, *When the Daltons Rode*, Doubleday, Doran & Co., Garden City, N.Y., 1931.

Dalton, Kit, *Under the Black Flag*, Lockhart Publishing Co., Memphis, Tenn., 1914.

Dibble, Roy Floyd, *Strenuous Americans*, Boni & Liveright Pub., New York, 1923.

Dobie, J. Frank, *Coronado's Children*, Southwest Press, Dallas, Texas, 1930.

Donald, Jay, *Outlaws of the Border*, Coburn & Newman Publishing Co., Chicago, 1882.

Doughitt, Katherine Christian, *Romance and Dim Trails*, William Tardy, Publishers, Dallas, Texas, 1938.

Edwards, Jennie, *Biography of John N. Edwards*, Jennie Edwards, Publisher, Kansas City, Mo., 1889.

Emrich, Duncan, *It's An Old Wild Custom*, Vanguard Press, New York, 1949.

Evans, Clyde, *Adventures of the Great Crime-Busters*, New Power Publications, New York, 1943.

Finger, Charles Joseph, *The Distant Prize*, Appleton-Century Co., New York, 1935.

Flynn, Robert DeShields, *The Poor Man in Politics*, Dance Brothers, Danville, Va., 1894.

Garwood, Darrell, *Crossroads of America*, W. W. Norton Co., New York, 1948.

Gish, Anthony, *American Bandits*, Haldeman-Julius Co., Girard, Kansas, 1938.

Gordon, Welche, *Jesse James and His Band of Outlaws*, Laird & Lee, Publishers, Chicago, Ills., 1890.

Haley, J. Evetts, *Jeff Milton, Good Man with a Gun*, University of Oklahoma Press, Norman, Okla., 1948.

Hall, Frank and Whitten, Lindsey, *Jesse James Rides Again*, LaHoma Publishing Co., Lawton, Okla., 1948.

Hendricks, George David, *The Bad Man of the West*, Naylor Co., San Antonio, Texas, 1941.

Hendron, J. W., *The Story of Billy the Kid*, Rydal Press, Santa Fe, New Mexico, 1948.

Hill, J. L., *End of the Cattle Trail*, George W. Moyle Pub. Co., Long Beach, Calif.

Holbrook, Stewart H., *The Story of American Railroads*, Crown Publishers, New York, 1947.

Holloway, Carroll C., *Texas Gun Lore*, Naylor Co., San Antonio, Texas, 1951.

Horan, James D., *Desperate Men*, G. P. Putnam's Sons, New York, 1949.

Horan, James D., *Desperate Women*, G. P. Putnam's Sons, New York, 1952.

Hough, Emerson, *The Story of the Outlaw*, Outing Publishing Co., New York, 1907.

Hubbard, Freeman, H., *Railroad Avenue*, McGraw-Hill, New York, 1945.

Hunter, J. Marvin and Noah H. Rose, *Album of Gunfighters*, Bandera, Texas, 1951.

Jackson, Mary E., *Life of Nellie Bailey*, R. E. Martin Publishers, Topeka, Kansas, 1885.

Jackson, Mary E., *Bank and Train Robbers*, Henneberry Co., Chicago, Ills., 1881.

James, Edgar, *James Boys: Deeds & Daring*, I. & M. Ottenheimer Co., Baltimore, Md., 1912.

James, Jesse Edwards, *Jesse James, My Father*, Jesse E. James, Publisher, Independence, Mo., 1899.

King, Frank M., *Mavericks*, Trail's End Publishing Co., Pasadena, Calif., 1947.

Love, Robertus, *Rise and Fall of Jesse James*, G. P. Putnam's Sons, New York, 1926.

Marshall, James, *Santa Fe Railroad*, Random House, New York, 1945.

Miller, George, Jr., *Trial of Frank James for Murder*, E. W. Stephens

Press, Columbus, Mo., 1898.

Mumey, Nolie, *Creede, Colorado*, Artcraft Press, Denver, Colo., 1949.

Nash, Jay Robert, *Bloodletters & Badmen*, M. Evans & Co., New York, 1973.

Otero, Miguel Antonio, *My Life on the Frontier*, Press of the Pioners, New York, 1935.

Parkhill, Forbes, *Wildest of the West*, Henry Holt & Co., New York, 1951.

Pinkerton, William A., *Train Robberies*, 1907 Jamestown, Va.

Raine, William McLeod, *Guns of the Frontier*, Houghton, Mifflin Co., Boston, 1940.

Rainey, George, *No Man's Land*, Cooperative Pub. Co., Guthrie, Okla., 1937.

Rascoe, Burton, *The Bandit Quen*, Random House, New York, 1941.

Ray, Charles E., *The James Boys & Bob Ford*, Regan Pub. Co., Chicago, Ills., 1893.

Russell, Jesse Lewis, *Behind These Ozark Hills*, Hobson Press, New York, 1947.

Shackelford, William Yancey, *Gunfighters of the Old West*, Haldemann-Julius, Girard, Kansas, 1943.

Sprague, Marshall, *Money Mountain*, Brown, Little, Brown Co., Boston, 1953.

Stanley, F., *Desperadoes of New Mexico*, World Press, Denver, Colo., 1953.

Stanley, F., *The Las Vegas Story*, World Press, Denver, Colo., 1951.

Sutton, Fred Ellsworth, *Hands Up*, Bobbs-Merrill Co., Indianapolis, Ind., 1927.

Targ, William, *The Great American West*, World Pub. Co., New York, 1946.

Thorndike, Thaddeus, *Lives and Exploits of the Jameses*, I. & M. Ottenheomer, Baltimore, 1909.

Trachtman, *The Gunfighters*, Time-Life Books, New York, 1974.

Triplett, Frank, *Life and Times of Jesse James*, N. D. Thompson Co., St. Louis, Mo., 1884.

Turner, Fitzhugh, *Dirty Little Coward of Fauquier County*, Warrentonn, Va., 1953.

Vestal, Stanley, *The Missouri*, Farrar & Rinehart, Inc., New York, 1945.

Warman, Cy., *Frontier Stories*, Charles Scribner's Sons, New York, 1898.

Willison, George Finlay, *Here They Dug for Gold*, Brentano's Publishers, New York, 1931.

Younger, Scout, *Facts of the Most Notorious Outlaws*, personal pamphlet.

Wayland, John W., *The Washingtons and Their Homes*, McClure, Staunton, Va., 1944.

MISCELLANEOUS

Census Records, 1850, Clark County, Missouri, 977.834x2 pe. L.D.S. Geneology Society, Salt Lake City, Utah.

Census Records, 1880, Census System, Missouri, 36600 pt. 1176, Ray and Clay Counties.

Census Records, 1850, 1860, 1870, 1880, Ray, Clay, and Clark Counties, Missouri.

Colorado Prospector, 1970.

Fauquier Democrat, various issues, Warrenton, Virginia.

Ford, Fred A., Blue Mills, Missouri.

Fauquier County, Virginia, Will Book 30, p. 267–271.

Godsell, *Skagway Terror*, Fury Magazine, October, 1957.

Gott, John R., Arlington, Virginia.

Gott, John K. and Betty Toone, Robert Ford, *Lost Virginian*.

History of Clay and Platte Counties, Missouri, St. Louis Historical Society, 1885.

Groome, H. C., Fauquier County, Virginia, Historical Notes, Warrenton, Virginia, 1914.

Jacobs, Vic D., Richmond, Missouri.

Kansas City Daily Journal, May 7, 1884, April 18, 1882.

Kansas City Journal, July 17, 1881, January 7, 1882, January 9, 1882, April 4, 1882.

Kansas City Times, February 22, 1881, July 17, 1881, January 21, 1891, April 4, 5, 6, 1882, August 3, 1948.

Missouri Republican, September 10, 1881.

North Star, Oklahoma City, Okla., June 23, 1955.

Oklahoman, Oklahoma City, Okla., January 14, 1904, January 19, 1904.

Paxton's Annals of Platte County.

Portrait & Biographical Record of Clay, Ray, Carroll, Linn, and Chariton Counties, Missouri, 1893.

Personal interviews and/or correspondence with those listed in the acknowledgments.

Pueblo Daily Chieftan, Pueblo, Colo., June 9, 1892.

Pullen, William E. and Joan M. Beamis, *Background of a Bandit*, Privately published, 1970.

Ray County Historical Society, Richmond, Mo.

Rocky Mountain News, Pueblo, Colorado, June 9, 1892.

St. Louis Republican, September 9, 1883, September 9, 1888.

St. Joseph Daily Gazette, April 3, 4, 5, 1882, April 21, 27, 1882, October 27, 1882.

St. Joseph, Missouri, Museum *Graphic*.

St. Joseph Western News, April 7, 1882.

Smith, Duane, Fort Lewis College, Durango, Colorado.

Steffa, Don, *Tales of Noted Frontier Characters*, Pacific Monthly, October, 1953.

Turner, Fitzhugh, *Fauquier Democrat*, October, 1953.